Algériennes

TO MY FRIEND RICHARD HIPPEAU

DELOUPY

Library of Congress Cataloging-in-Publication Data

Names: Meralli, Swann, author. | Deloupy, 1968- illustrator. | Hahnenberger, Ivanka, translator.
Title: Algériennes : the forgotten women of the Algerian Revolution / [text by] Swann Meralli and [illustrations by] Deloupy ; translated by Ivanka Hahnenberger.
Other titles: Algériennes. English | Graphic medicine.
Description: University Park : The Pennsylvania State University Press, [2020] | Series: Graphic medicine | English translation from the French of Algériennes: 1954-1962, originally published: Paris : Marabout, 2018. | Includes bibliographical references.
Summary: "A graphic novel depicting the stories of women who fought with the National Liberation Front in the Algerian War of Independence"—Provided by publisher.
Identifiers: LCCN 2019056972 | ISBN 9780271086231 (cloth)
Subjects: LCSH: Women—Algeria—Comic books, strips, etc. | Algeria—History—Revolution, 1954-1962—Comic books, strips, etc. | Algeria—History—Revolution, 1954-1962—Participation, Female—Comic books, strips, etc. | LCGFT: Graphic novels.
Classification: LCC PN6747.M47 A4413 2020 | DDC 741.5/944—dc23
LC record available at https://lccn.loc.gov/2019056972

Printed in Lithuania
Published by The Pennsylvania State University Press,
University Park, PA 16802-1003

Translated by Ivanka Hahnenberger

The Pennsylvania State University Press is a member of the Association of University Presses.

It is the policy of The Pennsylvania State University Press to use acid-free paper. Publications on uncoated stock satisfy the minimum requirements of American National Standard for Information Sciences—Permanence of Paper for Printed Library Material, ANSI Z39.48-1992.

SWANN MERALLI AND DELOUPY

Algériennes

THE FORGOTTEN WOMEN OF THE ALGERIAN REVOLUTION

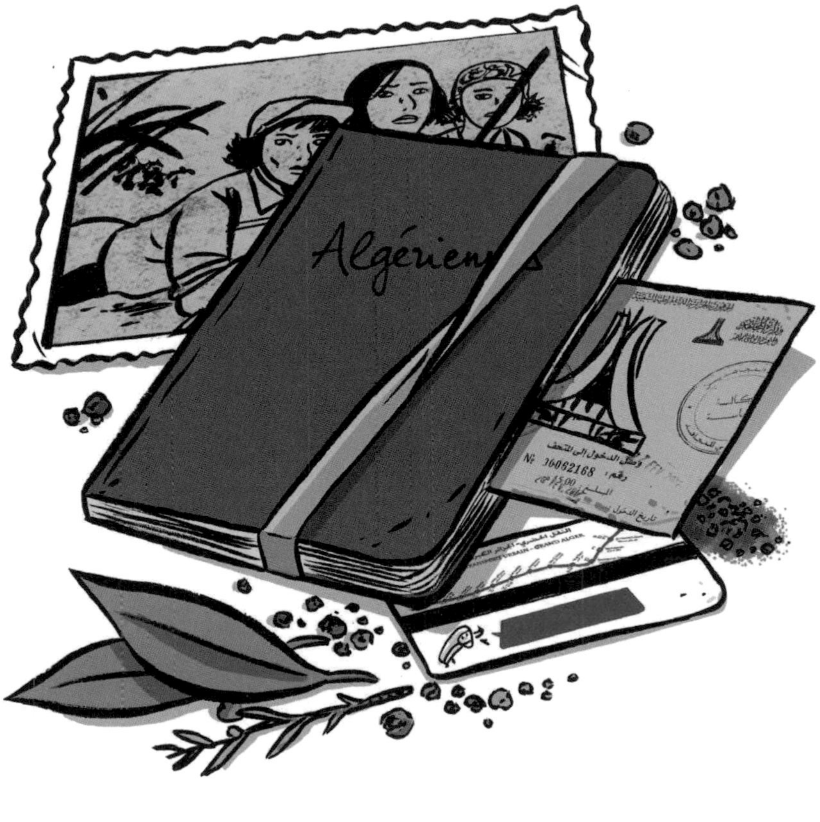
Algériennes

The Pennsylvania State University Press
University Park, Pennsylvania

The authors of this book have attempted to be as faithful to the historical record as possible. But, while inspired by real events, this book is a work of fiction. Names, characters, places, events, and incidents are the products of the authors' imagination or used in a fictitious manner. Any resemblance to actual persons, living or dead, is purely coincidental.

A Note on Terms and Context

FLN (p. 1) is the acronym for Front de Libération National, or National Liberation Front, the ruling party of the Algerian state and the principal nationalist movement during the Algerian war.

An **"enfant d'appelé"** (p. 3) is a child of those who were called up for military service to serve in the Algerian war—literally, a "child of one called up." The **maquis** (p. 12) were rural guerrilla bands of fighters. A **"harki"** (p. 14) was an Algerian Muslim who fought on the side of the French. **Mujahidates** (p. 30) were women soldiers in the Algerian national liberation movement. The **"paras"** (p. 36) were a paratroop unit of the French Special Forces.

"Bicot" (p. 34) was a derogatory term for Arabs. A **douar** (p. 57) is an Algerian village. **"Fellagha"** (p. 61) is a pejorative Arabic word referring to Algerian nationalists.

The **OAS** (the Organisation Armée Secrète, or Secret Army Organization) was an extremist French anti-independence organization. The newspaper headlines on page 99 refer to OAS commandos opening fire on soldiers and a "vigorous military response," and the graffiti reads, "The OAS is watching."

The handwritten war journal pictured on page 102 includes, in larger letters, "I think we behaved pretty badly toward the Muslims . . ." as well as words and phrases evoking memory, loss, death, and injustice.

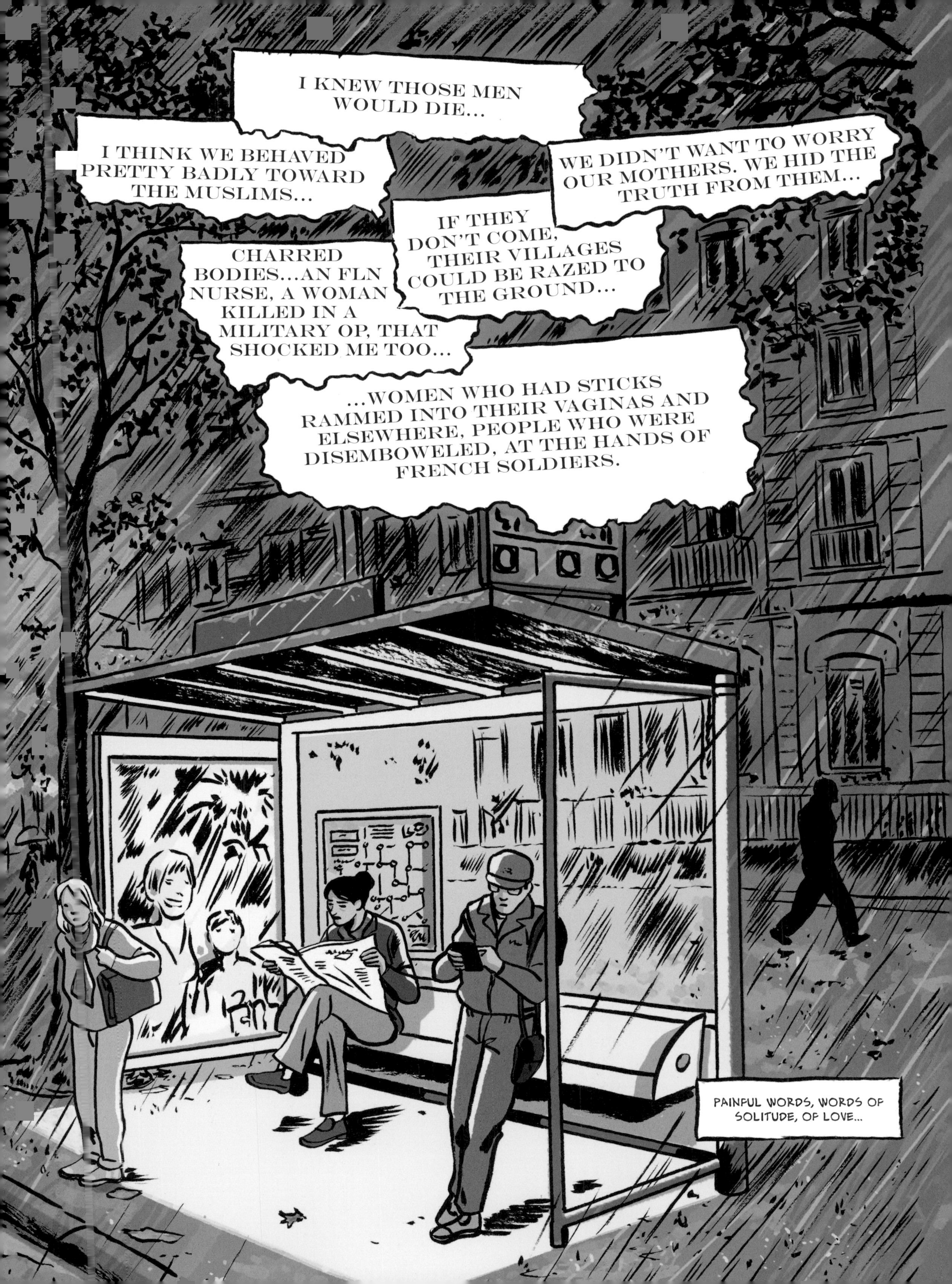

I KNEW THOSE MEN WOULD DIE...
I THINK WE BEHAVED PRETTY BADLY TOWARD THE MUSLIMS...
WE DIDN'T WANT TO WORRY OUR MOTHERS. WE HID THE TRUTH FROM THEM...
IF THEY DON'T COME, THEIR VILLAGES COULD BE RAZED TO THE GROUND...
CHARRED BODIES...AN FLN NURSE, A WOMAN KILLED IN A MILITARY OP, THAT SHOCKED ME TOO...
...WOMEN WHO HAD STICKS RAMMED INTO THEIR VAGINAS AND ELSEWHERE, PEOPLE WHO WERE DISEMBOWELED, AT THE HANDS OF FRENCH SOLDIERS.
PAINFUL WORDS, WORDS OF SOLITUDE, OF LOVE...

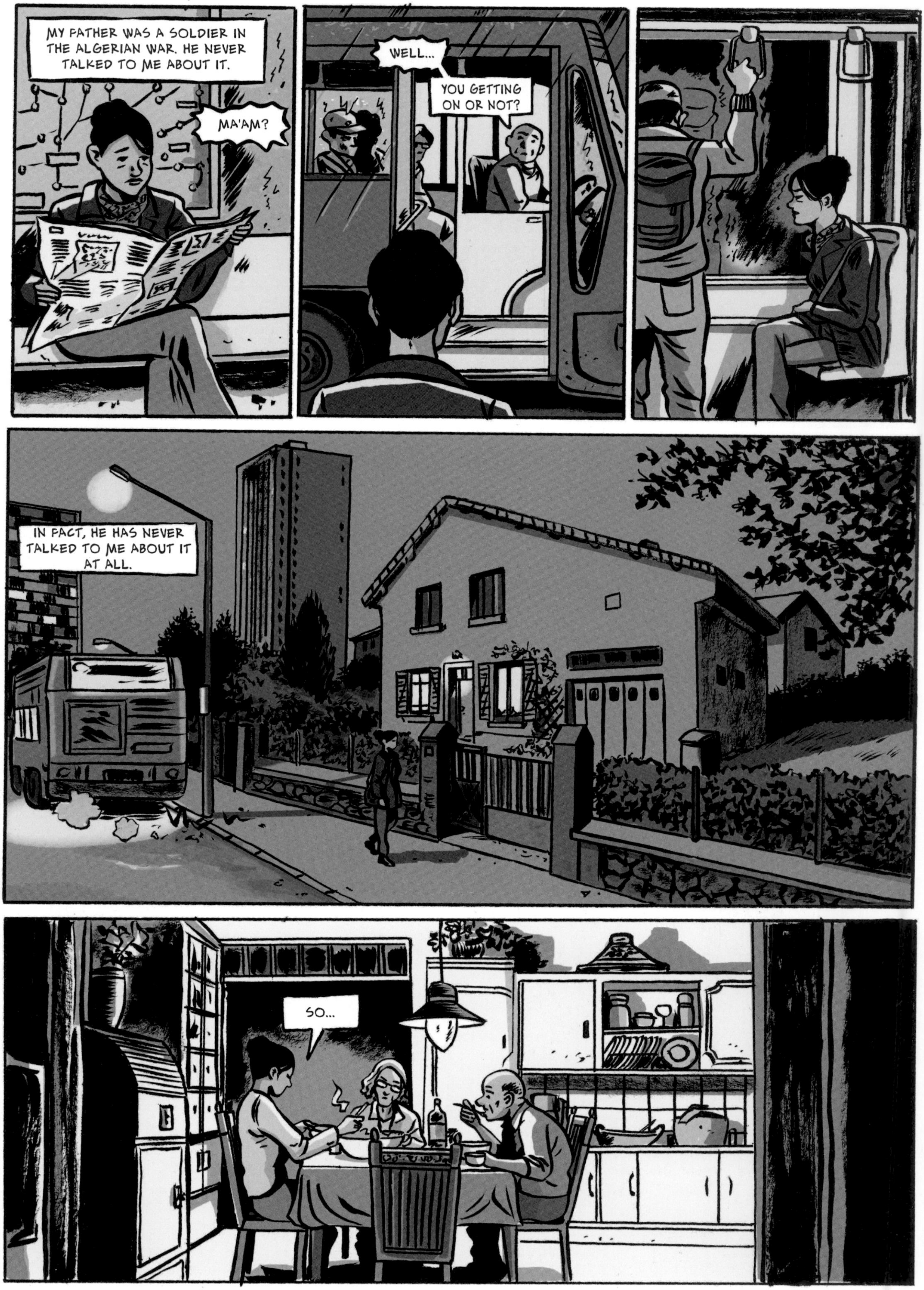
MY FATHER WAS A SOLDIER IN THE ALGERIAN WAR. HE NEVER TALKED TO ME ABOUT IT.
MA'AM?
WELL...
YOU GETTING ON OR NOT?
IN FACT, HE HAS NEVER TALKED TO ME ABOUT IT AT ALL.
SO...

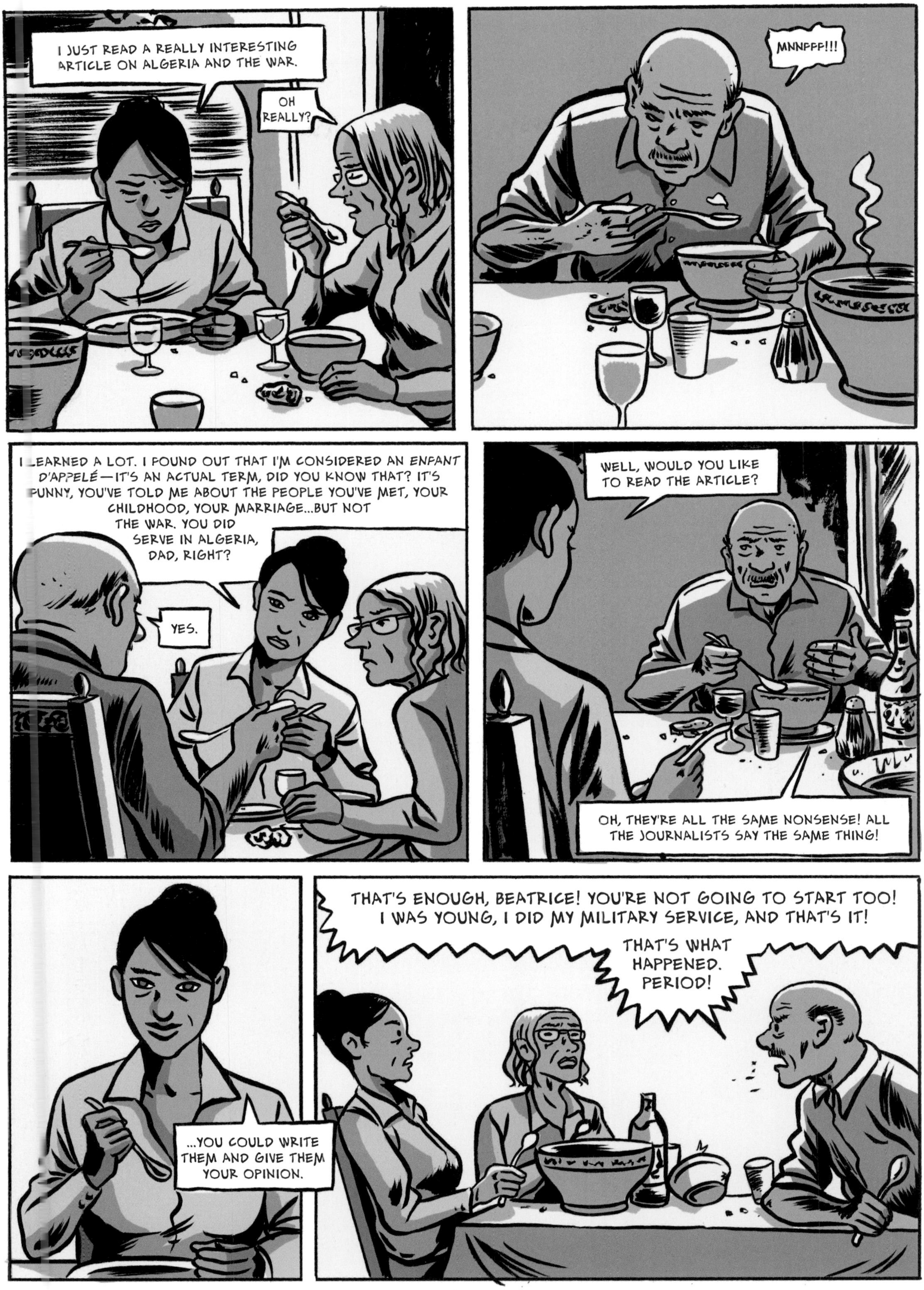
I JUST READ A REALLY INTERESTING ARTICLE ON ALGERIA AND THE WAR.
OH REALLY?
MNNFFF!!!
I LEARNED A LOT. I FOUND OUT THAT I'M CONSIDERED AN *ENFANT D'APPELÉ*—IT'S AN ACTUAL TERM, DID YOU KNOW THAT? IT'S FUNNY, YOU'VE TOLD ME ABOUT THE PEOPLE YOU'VE MET, YOUR CHILDHOOD, YOUR MARRIAGE...BUT NOT THE WAR. YOU DID SERVE IN ALGERIA, DAD, RIGHT?
YES.
WELL, WOULD YOU LIKE TO READ THE ARTICLE?
OH, THEY'RE ALL THE SAME NONSENSE! ALL THE JOURNALISTS SAY THE SAME THING!
...YOU COULD WRITE THEM AND GIVE THEM YOUR OPINION.
THAT'S ENOUGH, BEATRICE! YOU'RE NOT GOING TO START TOO! I WAS YOUNG, I DID MY MILITARY SERVICE, AND THAT'S IT!
THAT'S WHAT HAPPENED. PERIOD!

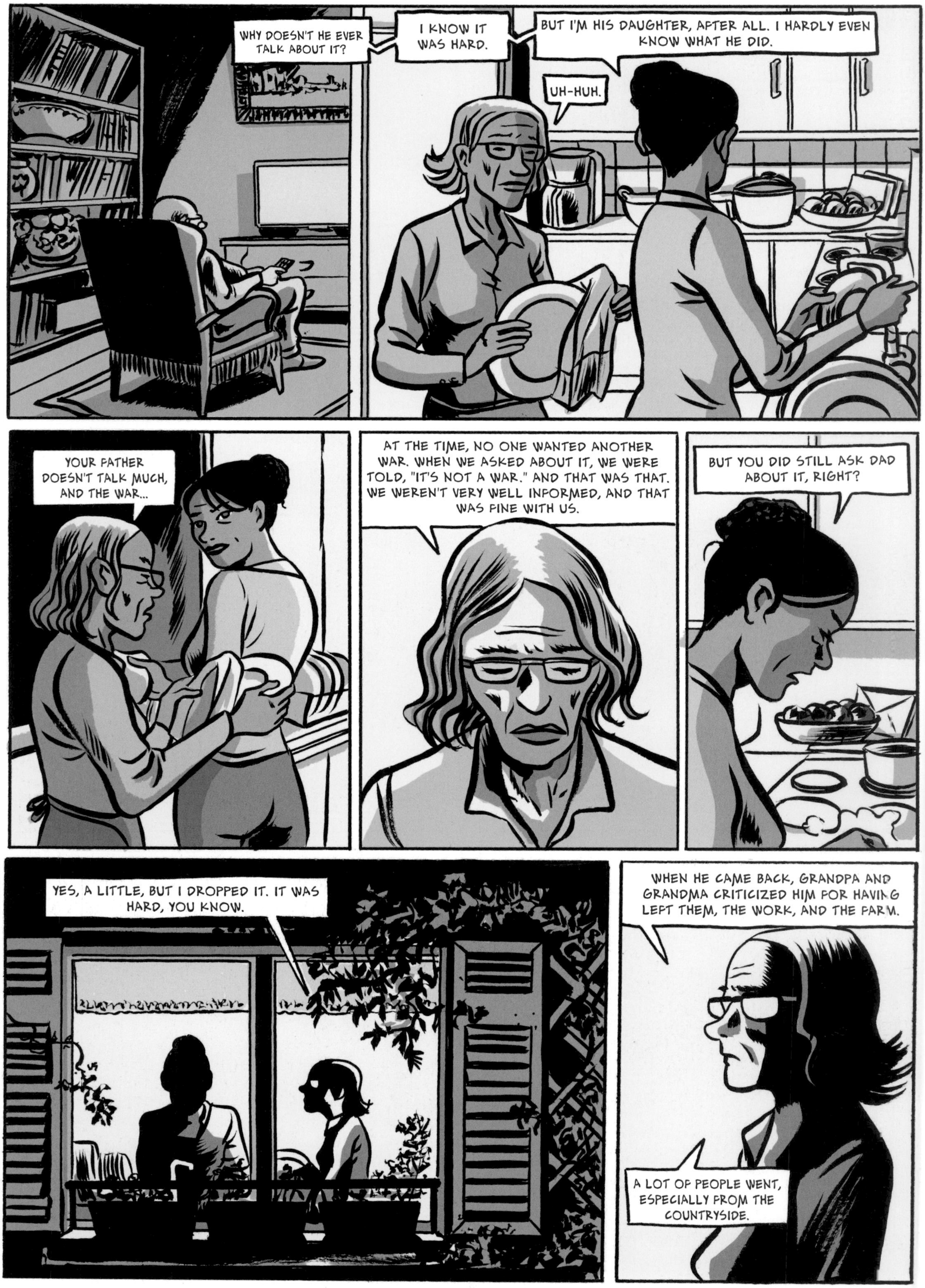
WHY DOESN'T HE EVER TALK ABOUT IT?
I KNOW IT WAS HARD.
BUT I'M HIS DAUGHTER, AFTER ALL. I HARDLY EVEN KNOW WHAT HE DID.
UH-HUH.
YOUR FATHER DOESN'T TALK MUCH, AND THE WAR...
AT THE TIME, NO ONE WANTED ANOTHER WAR. WHEN WE ASKED ABOUT IT, WE WERE TOLD, "IT'S NOT A WAR." AND THAT WAS THAT. WE WEREN'T VERY WELL INFORMED, AND THAT WAS FINE WITH US.
BUT YOU DID STILL ASK DAD ABOUT IT, RIGHT?
YES, A LITTLE, BUT I DROPPED IT. IT WAS HARD, YOU KNOW.
WHEN HE CAME BACK, GRANDPA AND GRANDMA CRITICIZED HIM FOR HAVING LEFT THEM, THE WORK, AND THE FARM.
A LOT OF PEOPLE WENT, ESPECIALLY FROM THE COUNTRYSIDE.

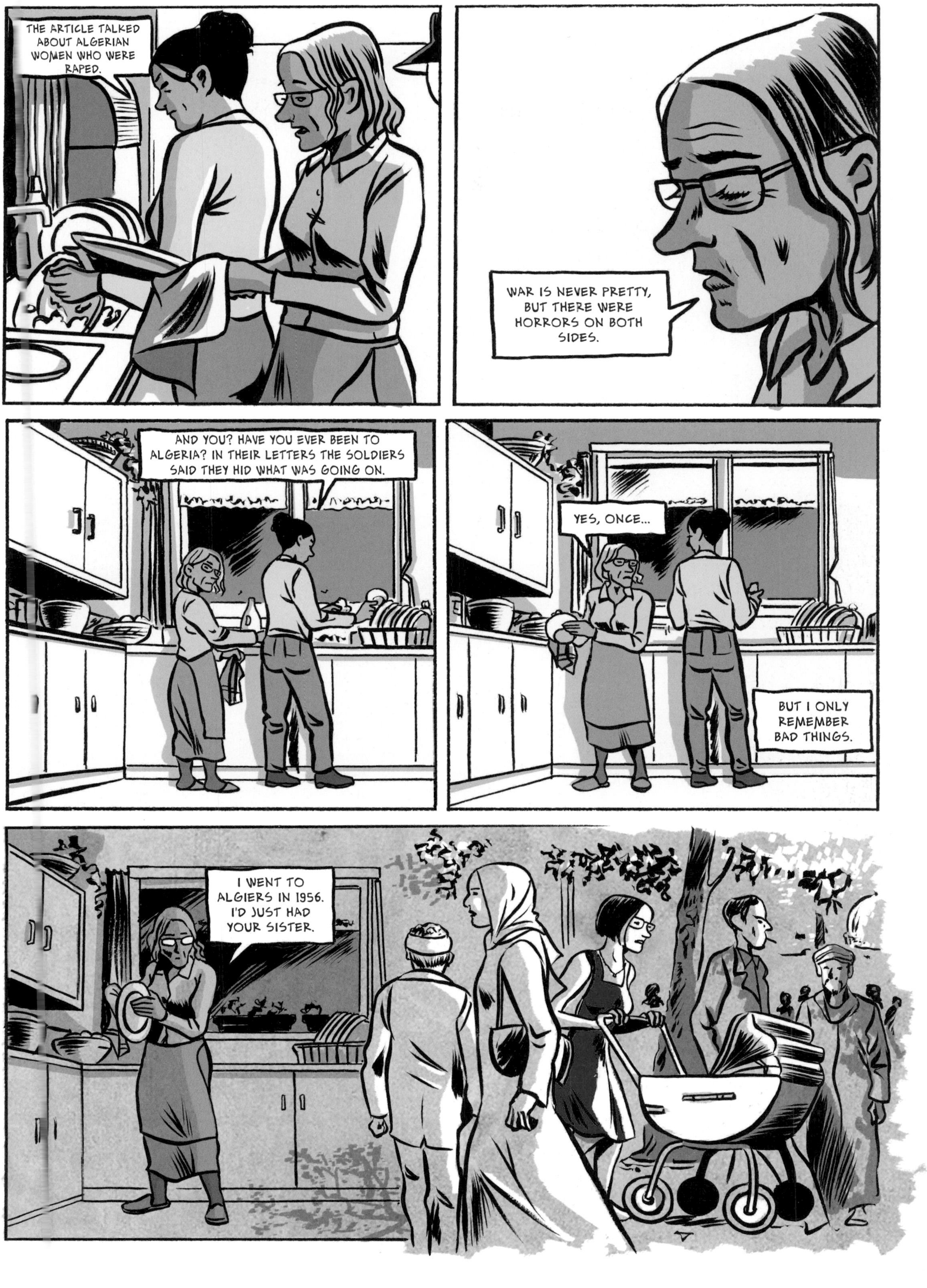
THE ARTICLE TALKED ABOUT ALGERIAN WOMEN WHO WERE RAPED.
WAR IS NEVER PRETTY, BUT THERE WERE HORRORS ON BOTH SIDES.
AND YOU? HAVE YOU EVER BEEN TO ALGERIA? IN THEIR LETTERS THE SOLDIERS SAID THEY HID WHAT WAS GOING ON.
YES, ONCE...
BUT I ONLY REMEMBER BAD THINGS.
I WENT TO ALGIERS IN 1956. I'D JUST HAD YOUR SISTER.

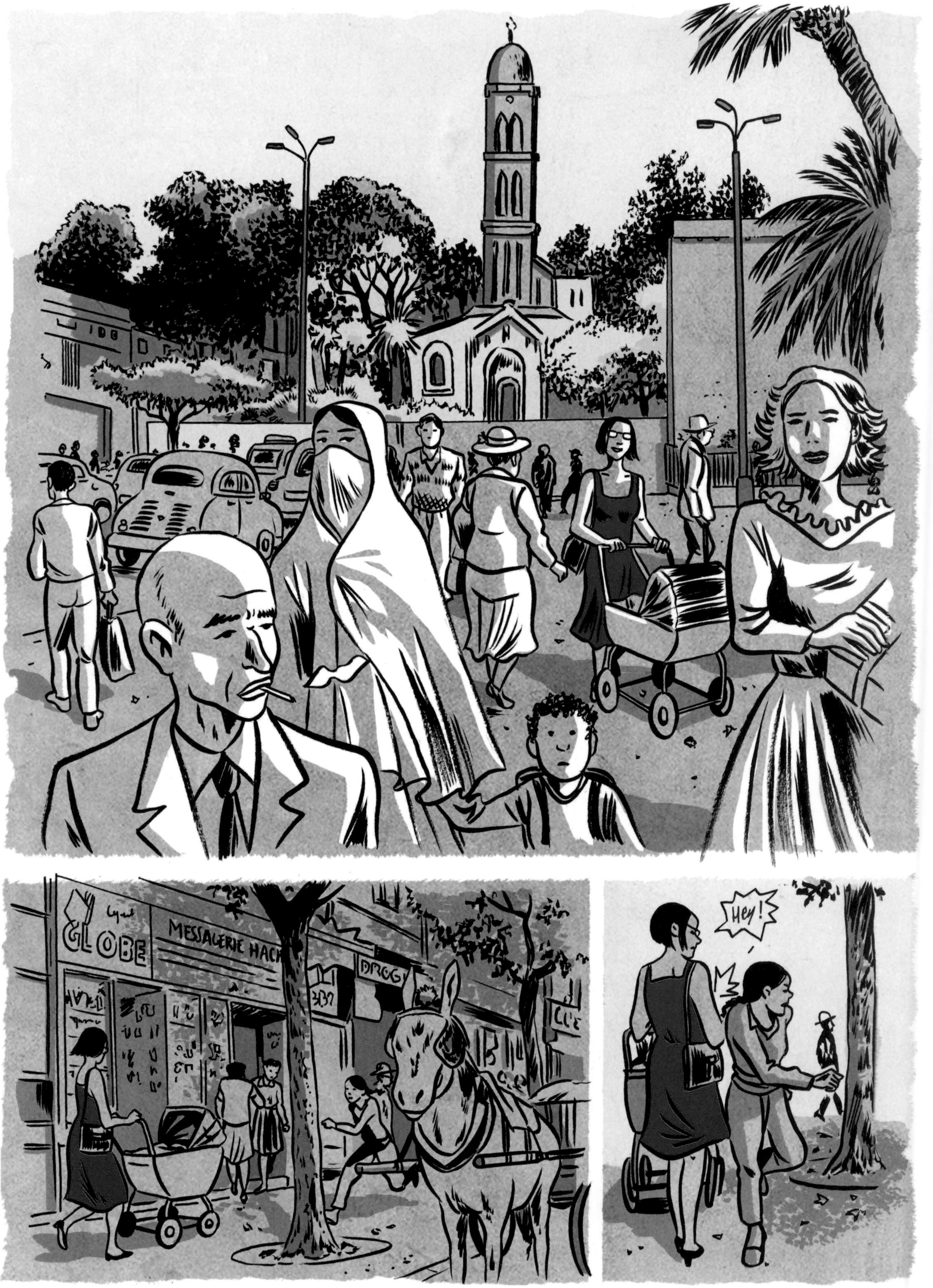
GLOBE
MESSAGERIE HACH
DROG
Hey!

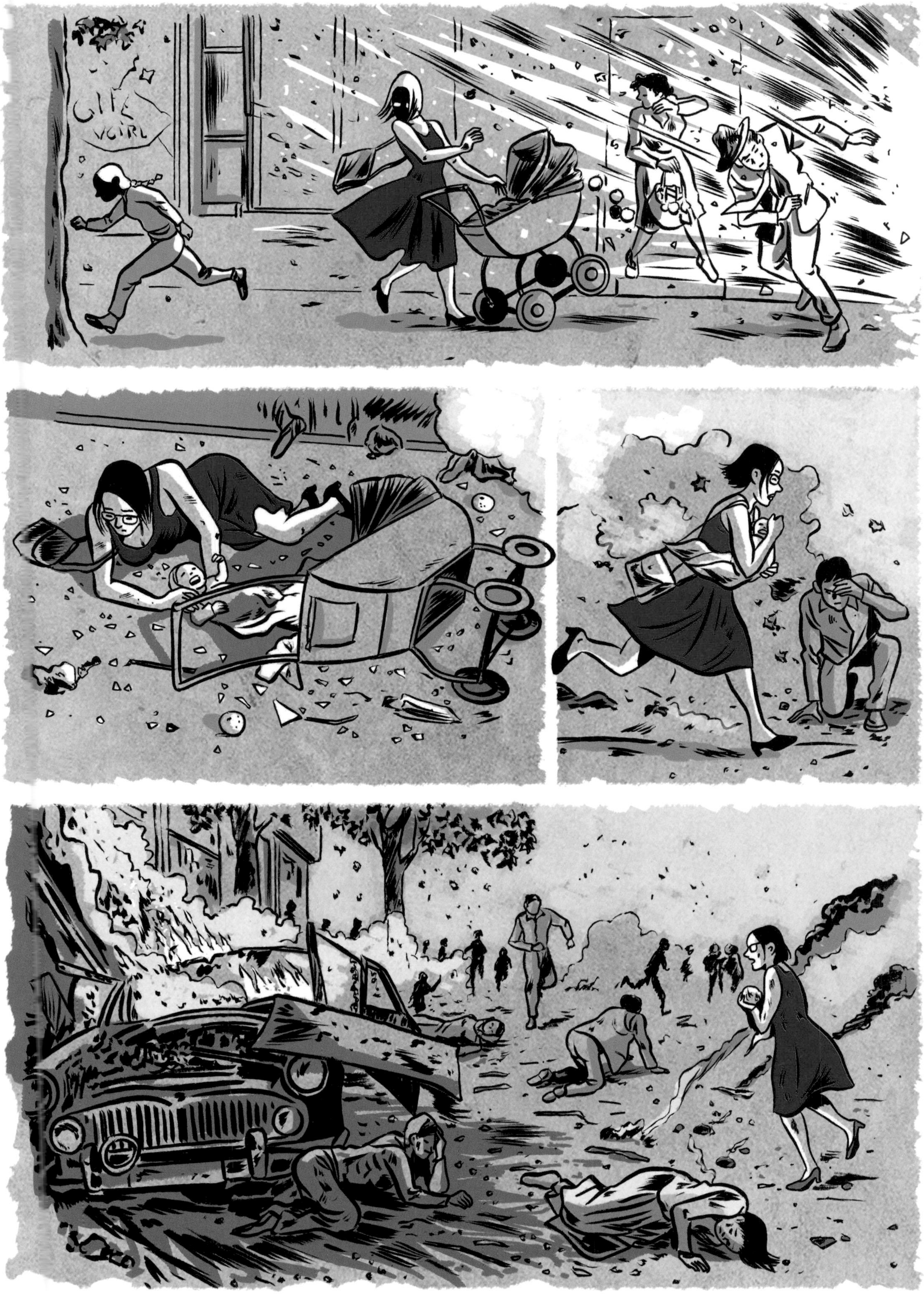

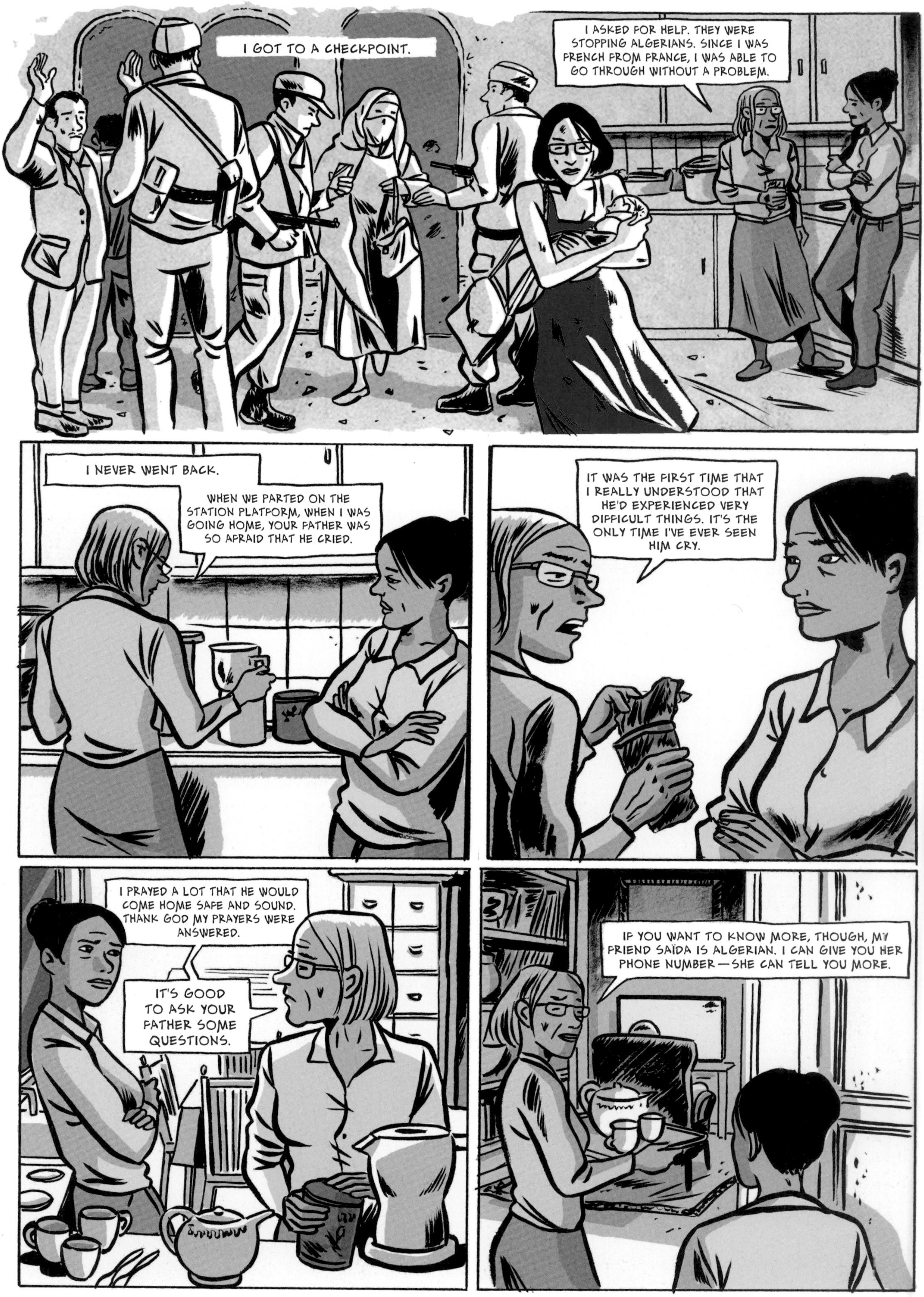
I GOT TO A CHECKPOINT.
I ASKED FOR HELP. THEY WERE STOPPING ALGERIANS. SINCE I WAS FRENCH FROM FRANCE, I WAS ABLE TO GO THROUGH WITHOUT A PROBLEM.
I NEVER WENT BACK.
WHEN WE PARTED ON THE STATION PLATFORM, WHEN I WAS GOING HOME, YOUR FATHER WAS SO AFRAID THAT HE CRIED.
IT WAS THE FIRST TIME THAT I REALLY UNDERSTOOD THAT HE'D EXPERIENCED VERY DIFFICULT THINGS. IT'S THE ONLY TIME I'VE EVER SEEN HIM CRY.
I PRAYED A LOT THAT HE WOULD COME HOME SAFE AND SOUND. THANK GOD MY PRAYERS WERE ANSWERED.
IT'S GOOD TO ASK YOUR FATHER SOME QUESTIONS.
IF YOU WANT TO KNOW MORE, THOUGH, MY FRIEND SAÏDA IS ALGERIAN. I CAN GIVE YOU HER PHONE NUMBER—SHE CAN TELL YOU MORE.

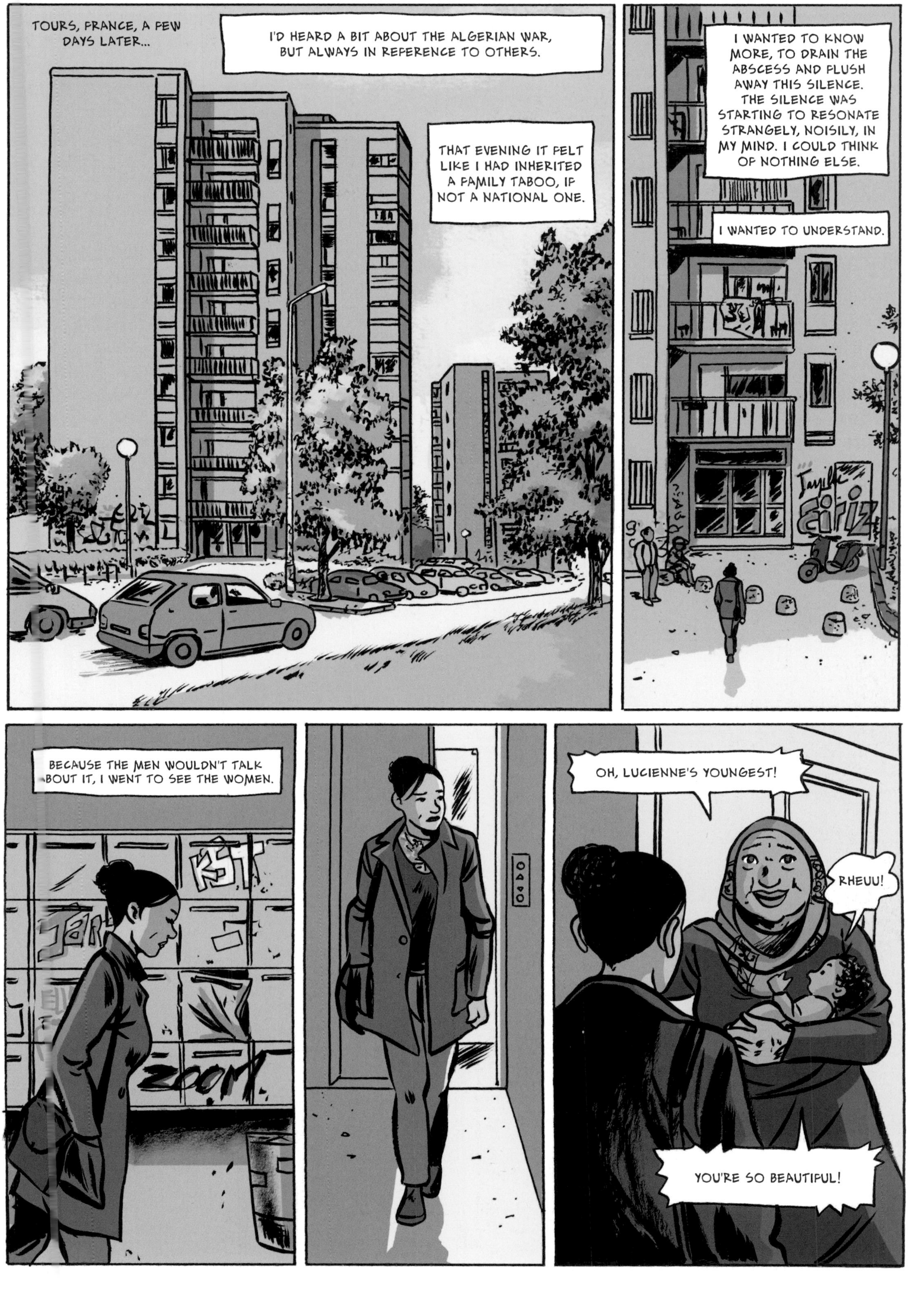
TOURS, FRANCE, A FEW DAYS LATER...
I'D HEARD A BIT ABOUT THE ALGERIAN WAR, BUT ALWAYS IN REFERENCE TO OTHERS.
THAT EVENING IT FELT LIKE I HAD INHERITED A FAMILY TABOO, IF NOT A NATIONAL ONE.
I WANTED TO KNOW MORE, TO DRAIN THE ABSCESS AND FLUSH AWAY THIS SILENCE. THE SILENCE WAS STARTING TO RESONATE STRANGELY, NOISILY, IN MY MIND. I COULD THINK OF NOTHING ELSE.
I WANTED TO UNDERSTAND.
BECAUSE THE MEN WOULDN'T TALK ABOUT IT, I WENT TO SEE THE WOMEN.
OH, LUCIENNE'S YOUNGEST!
RHEUU!
YOU'RE SO BEAUTIFUL!

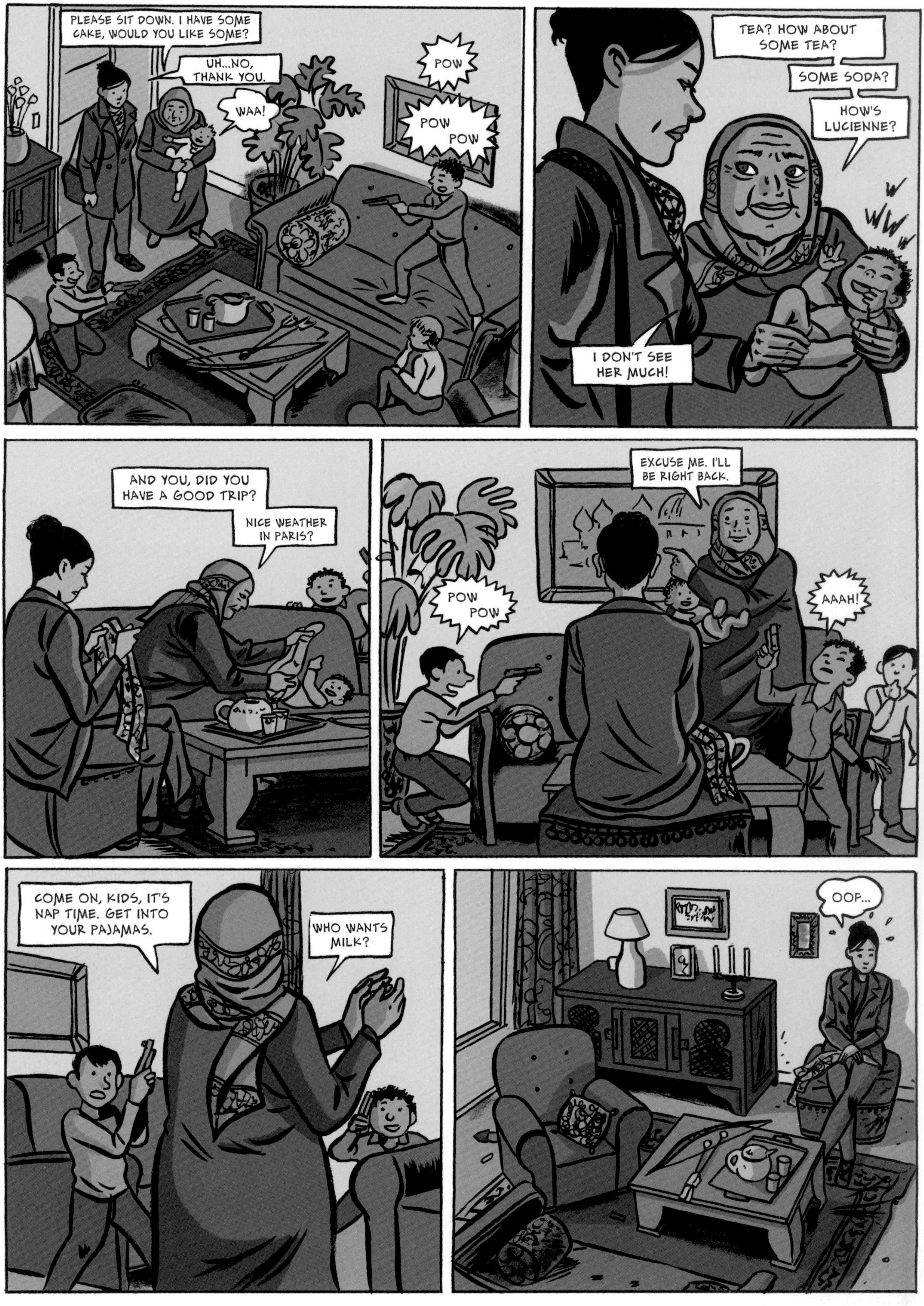

PLEASE SIT DOWN. I HAVE SOME CAKE, WOULD YOU LIKE SOME?
UH...NO, THANK YOU.
WAA!
POW
POW POW
TEA? HOW ABOUT SOME TEA?
SOME SODA?
HOW'S LUCIENNE?
I DON'T SEE HER MUCH!
AND YOU, DID YOU HAVE A GOOD TRIP?
NICE WEATHER IN PARIS?
EXCUSE ME. I'LL BE RIGHT BACK.
POW POW
AAAH!
COME ON, KIDS, IT'S NAP TIME. GET INTO YOUR PAJAMAS.
WHO WANTS MILK?
OOF...

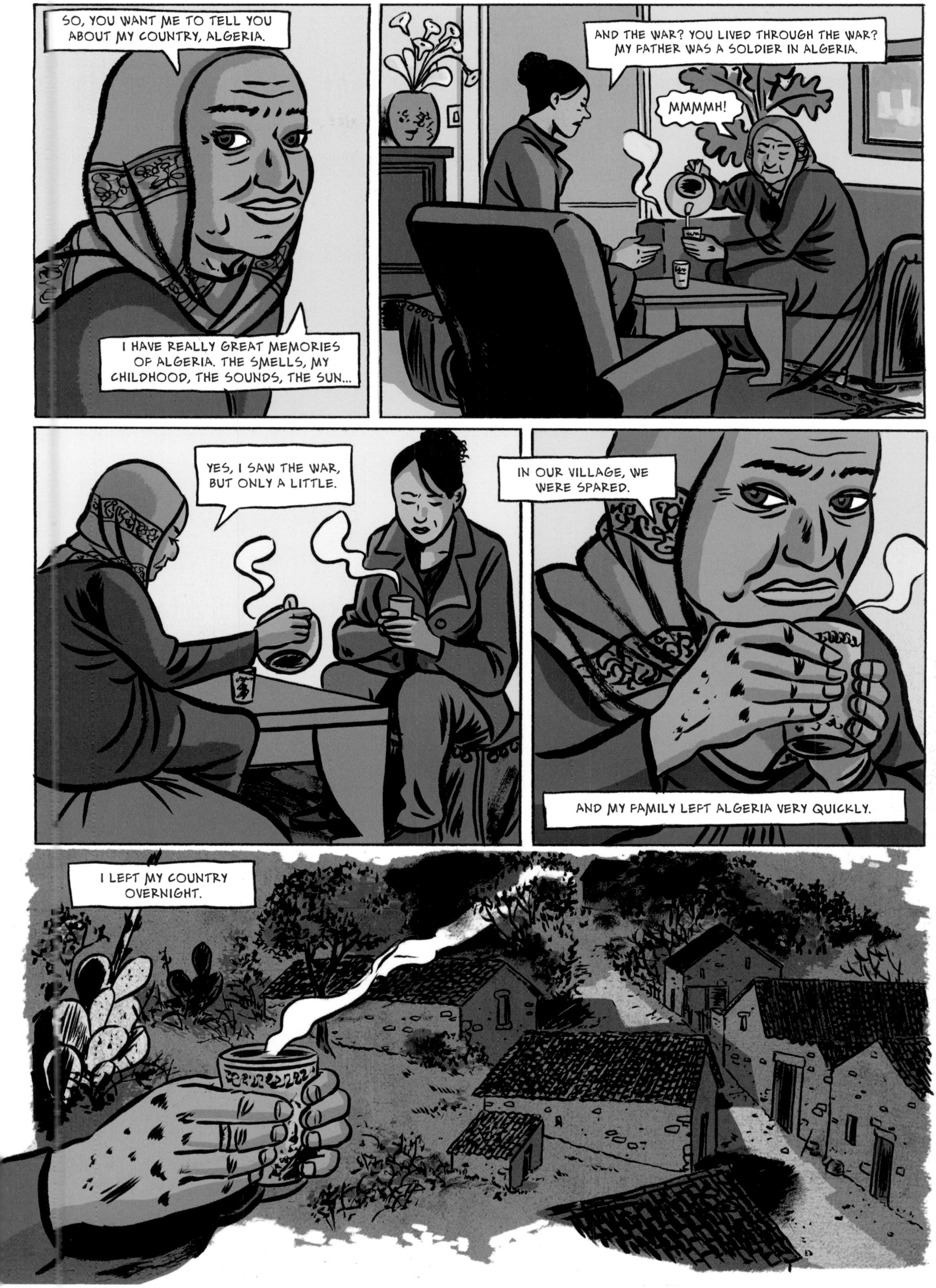
SO, YOU WANT ME TO TELL YOU ABOUT MY COUNTRY, ALGERIA.
I HAVE REALLY GREAT MEMORIES OF ALGERIA. THE SMELLS, MY CHILDHOOD, THE SOUNDS, THE SUN...
AND THE WAR? YOU LIVED THROUGH THE WAR? MY FATHER WAS A SOLDIER IN ALGERIA.
MMMMH!
YES, I SAW THE WAR, BUT ONLY A LITTLE.
IN OUR VILLAGE, WE WERE SPARED.
AND MY FAMILY LEFT ALGERIA VERY QUICKLY.
I LEFT MY COUNTRY OVERNIGHT.

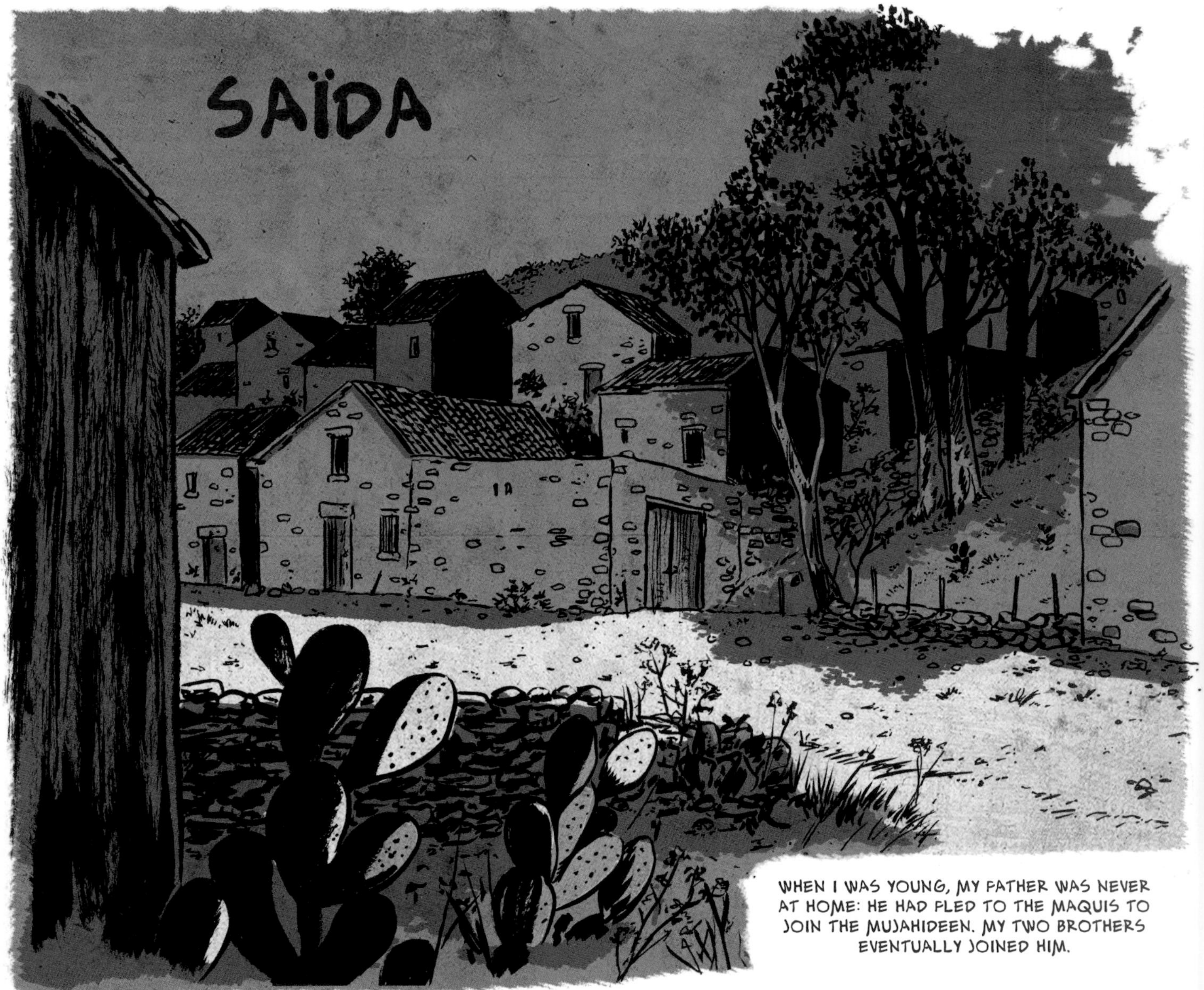
SAÏDA
WHEN I WAS YOUNG, MY FATHER WAS NEVER AT HOME: HE HAD FLED TO THE MAQUIS TO JOIN THE MUJAHIDEEN. MY TWO BROTHERS EVENTUALLY JOINED HIM.

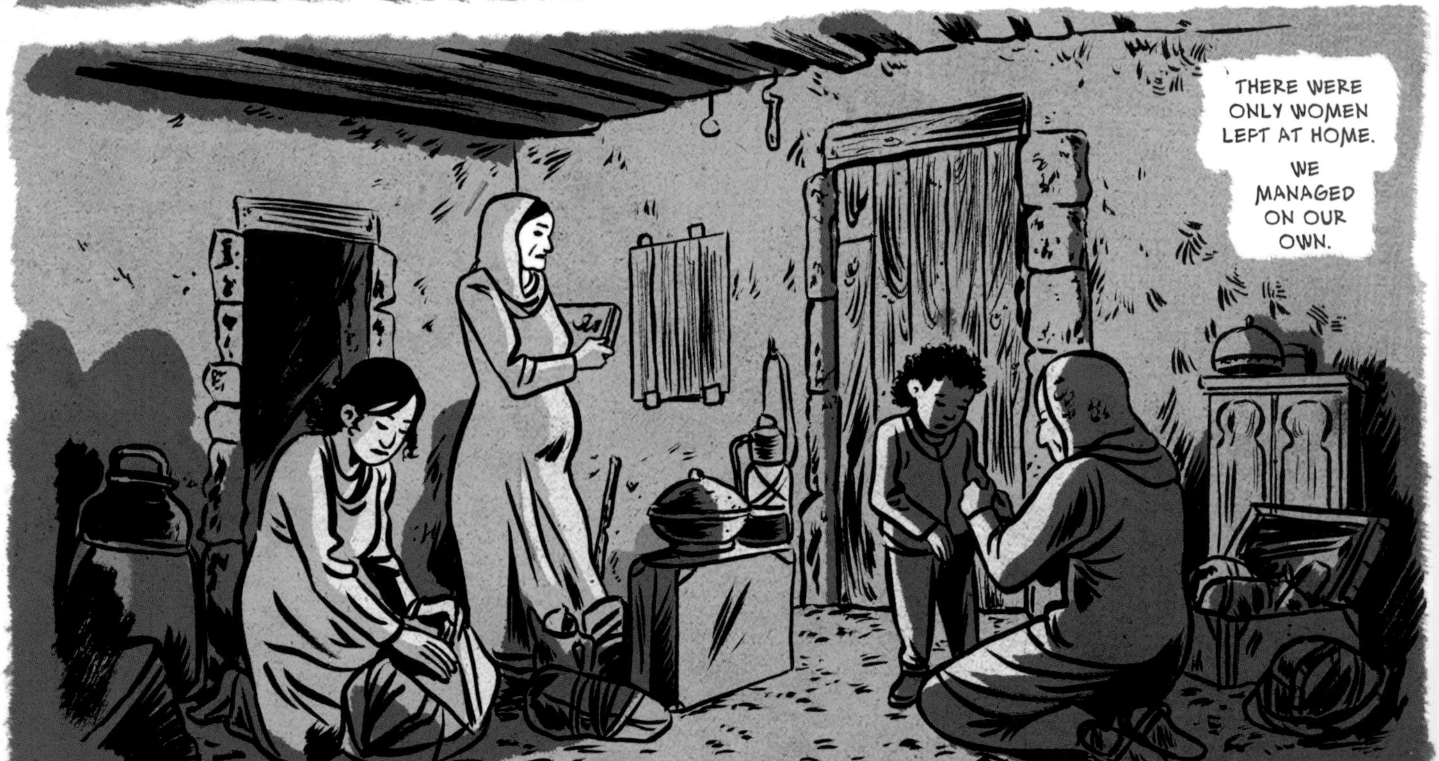
THERE WERE ONLY WOMEN LEFT AT HOME.
WE MANAGED ON OUR OWN.

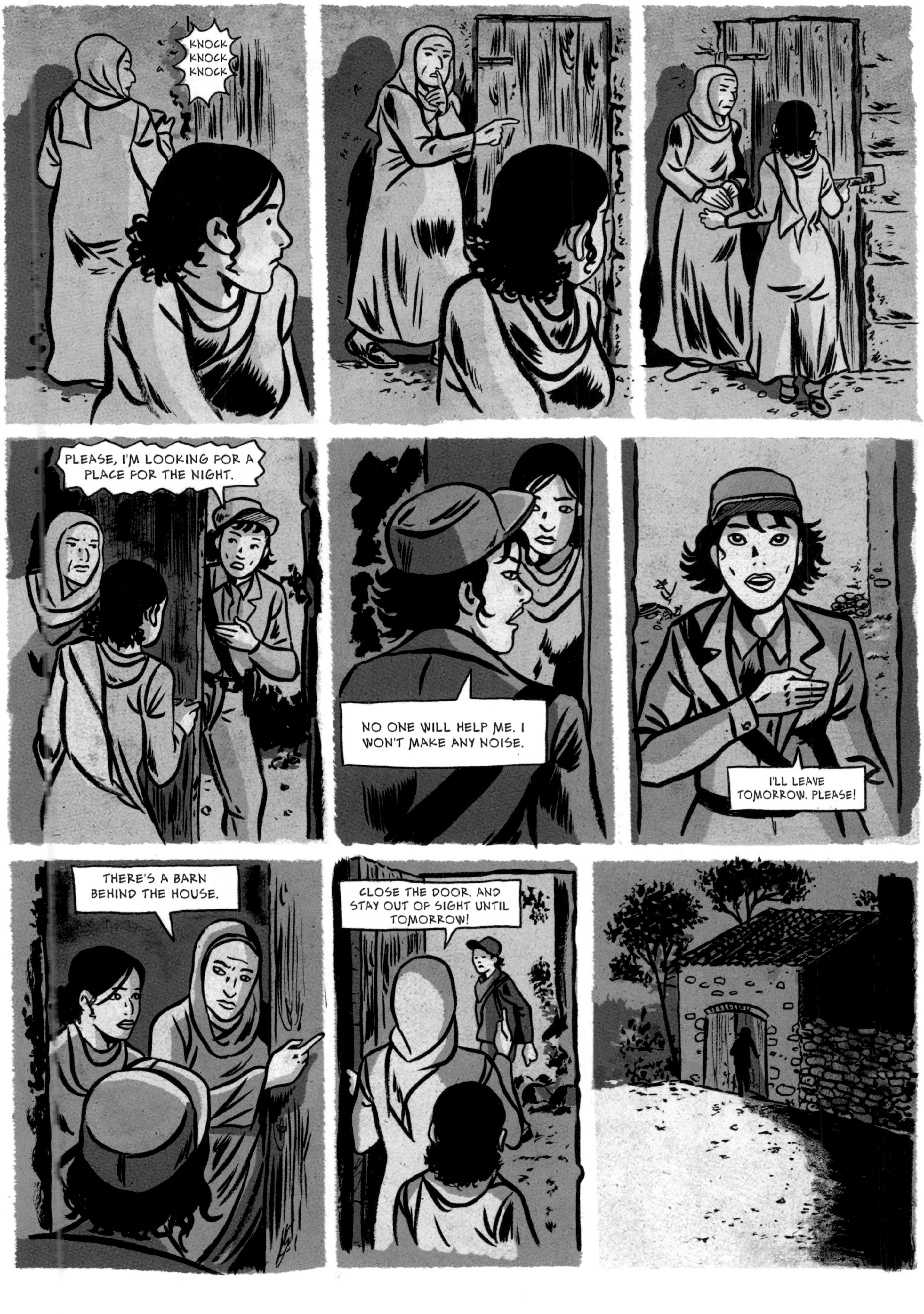
KNOCK KNOCK KNOCK
PLEASE, I'M LOOKING FOR A PLACE FOR THE NIGHT.
NO ONE WILL HELP ME. I WON'T MAKE ANY NOISE.
I'LL LEAVE TOMORROW. PLEASE!
THERE'S A BARN BEHIND THE HOUSE.
CLOSE THE DOOR. AND STAY OUT OF SIGHT UNTIL TOMORROW!

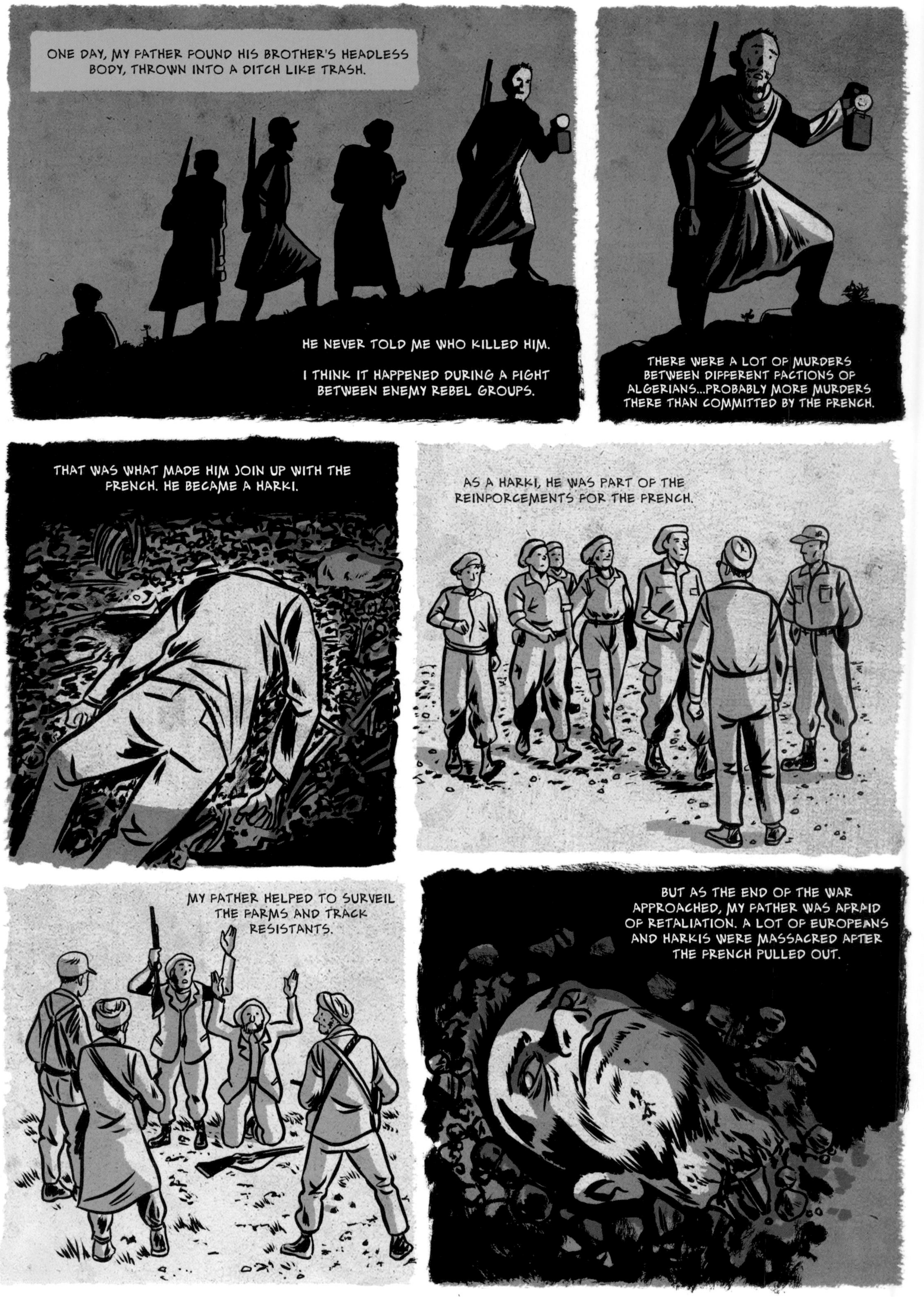
ONE DAY, MY FATHER FOUND HIS BROTHER'S HEADLESS BODY, THROWN INTO A DITCH LIKE TRASH.
HE NEVER TOLD ME WHO KILLED HIM.
I THINK IT HAPPENED DURING A FIGHT BETWEEN ENEMY REBEL GROUPS.
THERE WERE A LOT OF MURDERS BETWEEN DIFFERENT FACTIONS OF ALGERIANS...PROBABLY MORE MURDERS THERE THAN COMMITTED BY THE FRENCH.
THAT WAS WHAT MADE HIM JOIN UP WITH THE FRENCH. HE BECAME A HARKI.
AS A HARKI, HE WAS PART OF THE REINFORCEMENTS FOR THE FRENCH.
MY FATHER HELPED TO SURVEIL THE FARMS AND TRACK RESISTANTS.
BUT AS THE END OF THE WAR APPROACHED, MY FATHER WAS AFRAID OF RETALIATION. A LOT OF EUROPEANS AND HARKIS WERE MASSACRED AFTER THE FRENCH PULLED OUT.

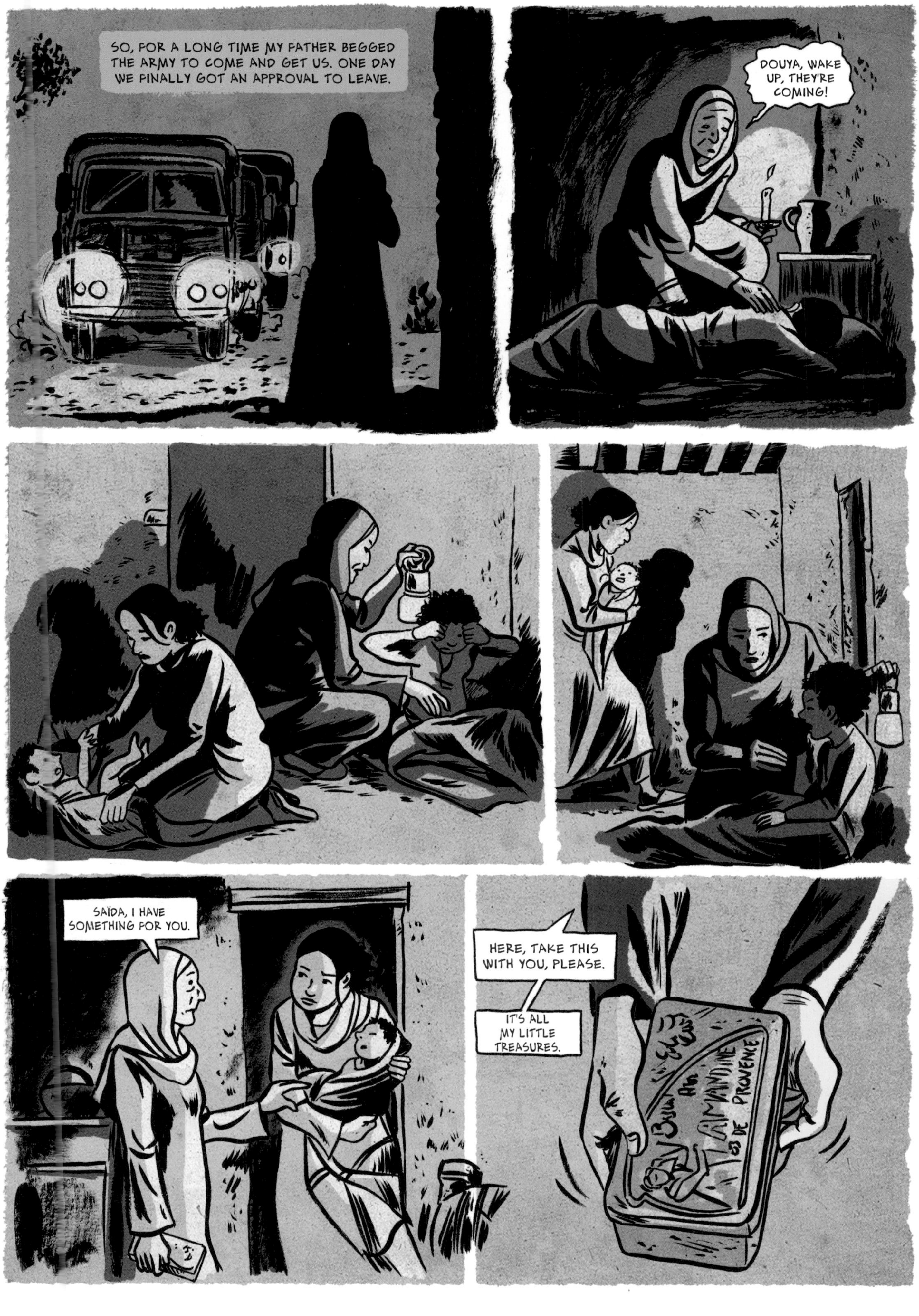
SO, FOR A LONG TIME MY FATHER BEGGED THE ARMY TO COME AND GET US. ONE DAY WE FINALLY GOT AN APPROVAL TO LEAVE.
DOUYA, WAKE UP, THEY'RE COMING!
SAÏDA, I HAVE SOMETHING FOR YOU.
HERE, TAKE THIS WITH YOU, PLEASE.
IT'S ALL MY LITTLE TREASURES.
AMANDINE DE PROVENCE

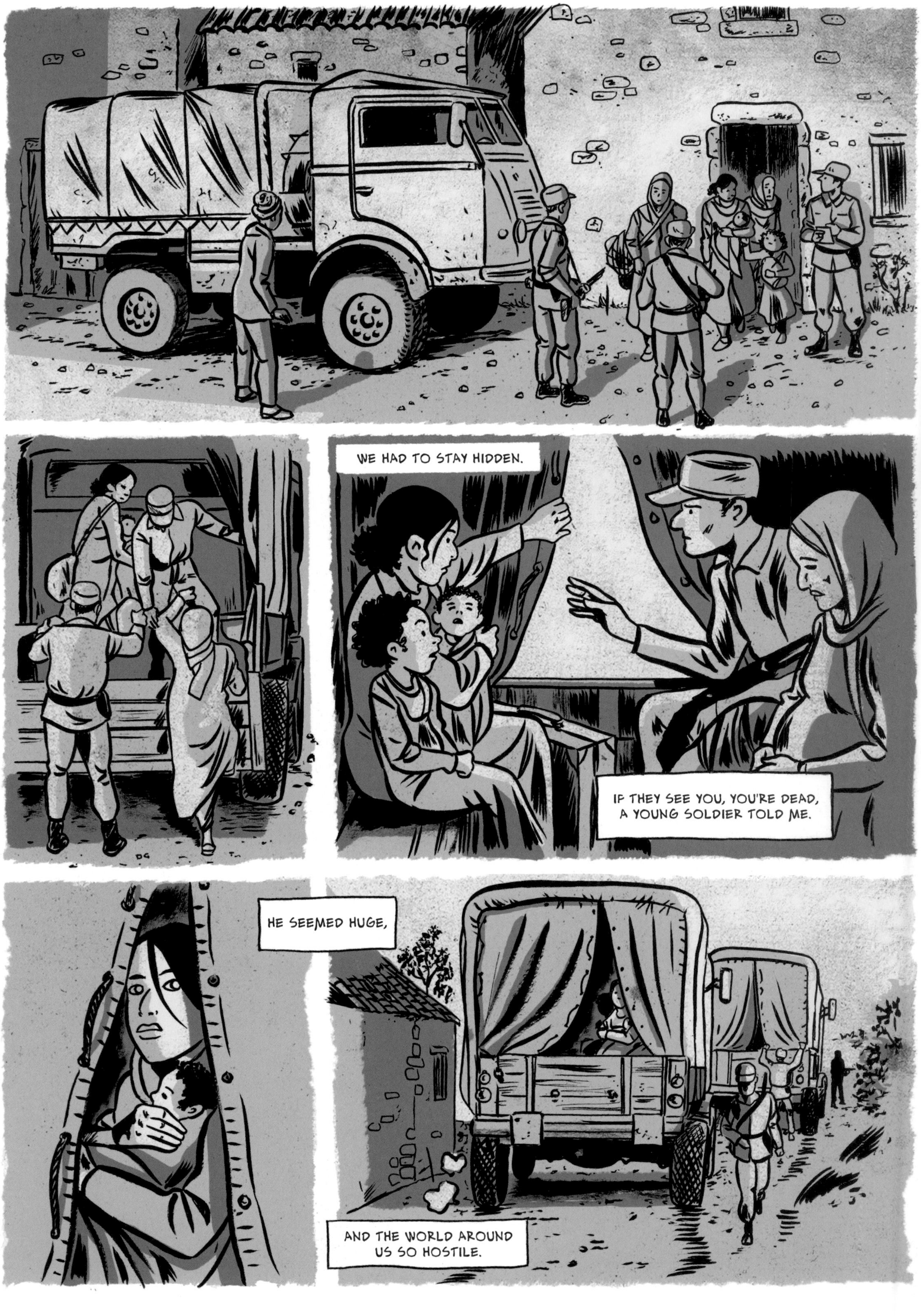
WE HAD TO STAY HIDDEN.
IF THEY SEE YOU, YOU'RE DEAD, A YOUNG SOLDIER TOLD ME.
HE SEEMED HUGE,
AND THE WORLD AROUND US SO HOSTILE.

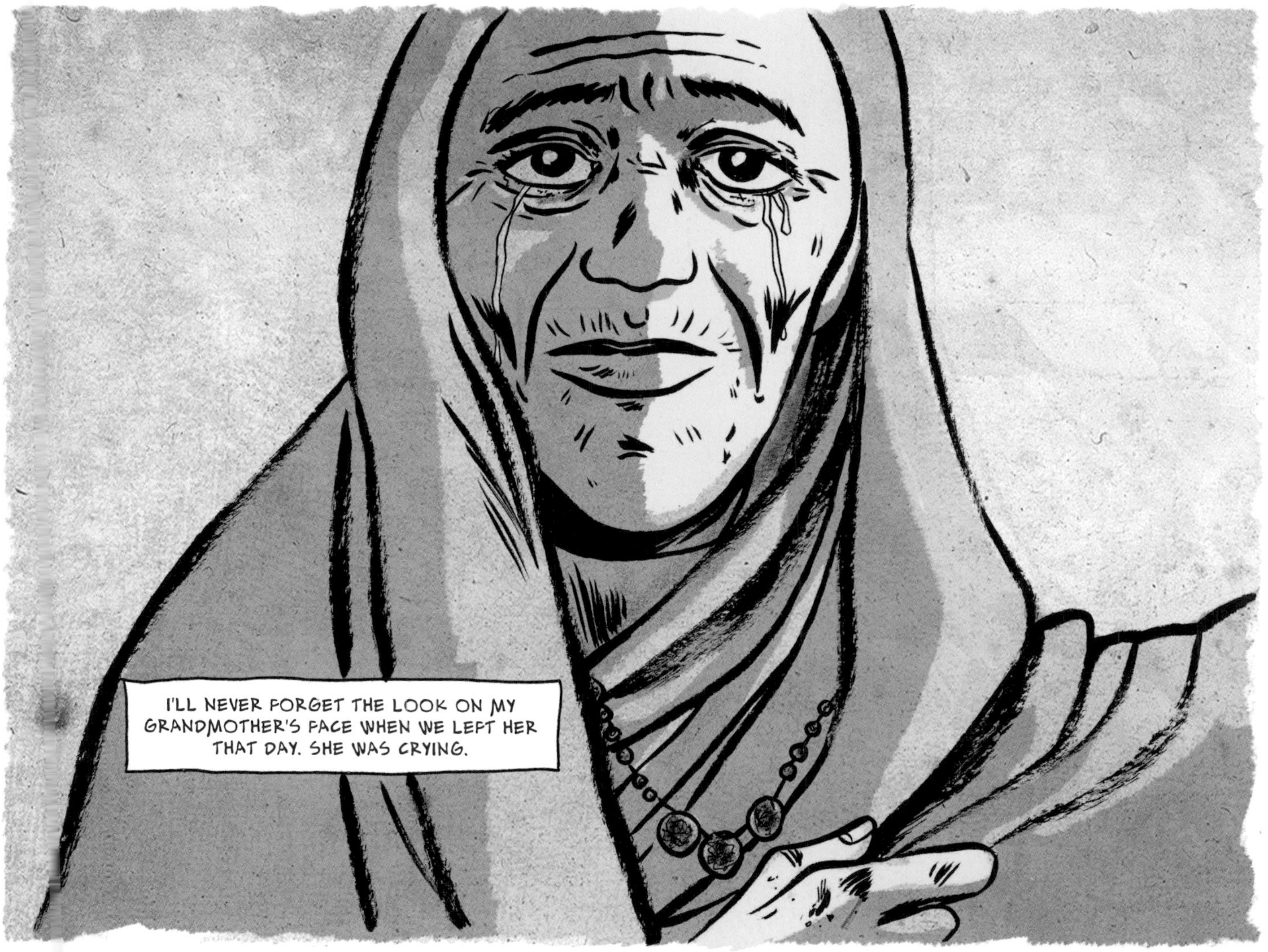
I'LL NEVER FORGET THE LOOK ON MY GRANDMOTHER'S FACE WHEN WE LEFT HER THAT DAY. SHE WAS CRYING.

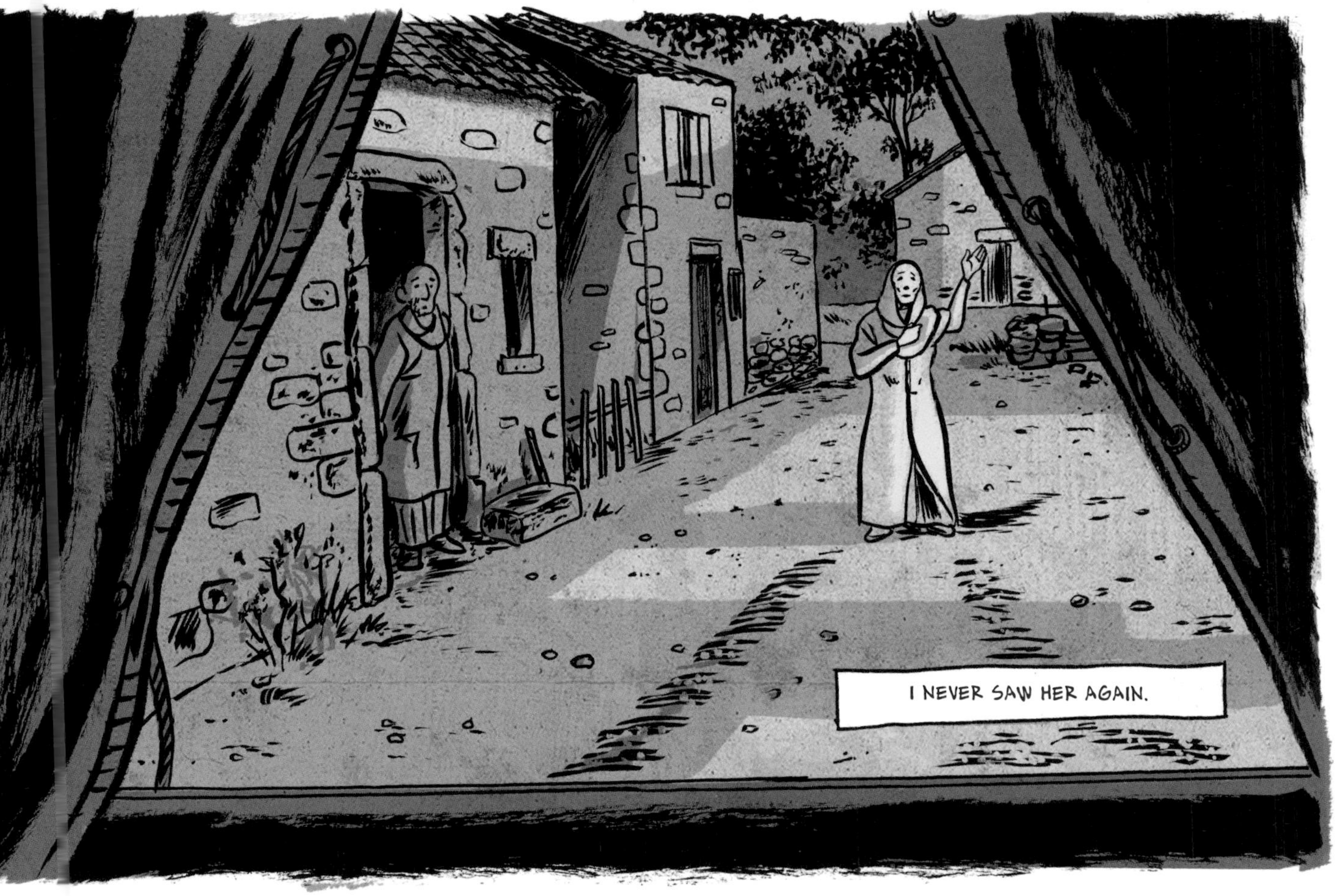
I NEVER SAW HER AGAIN.

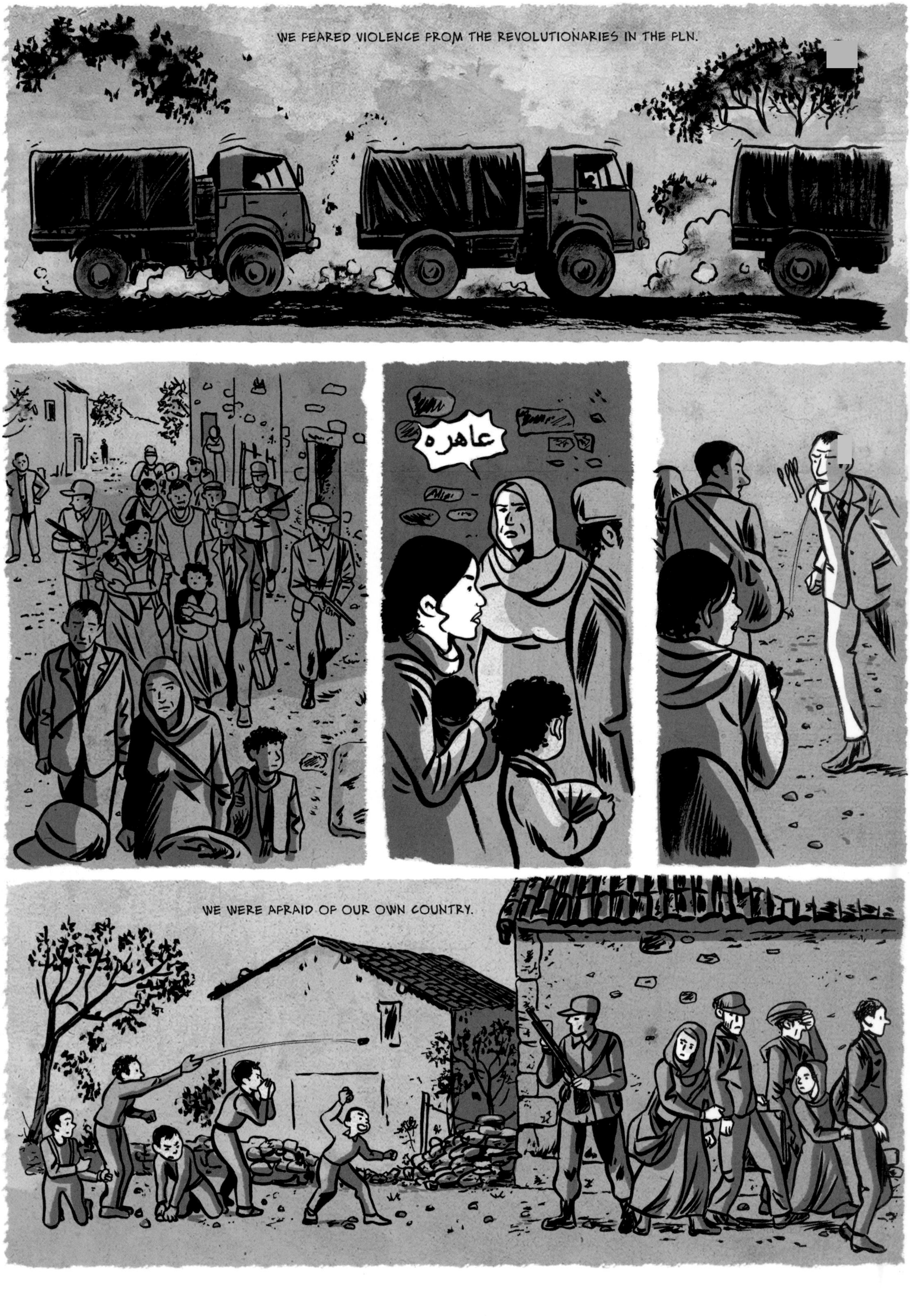
WE FEARED VIOLENCE FROM THE REVOLUTIONARIES IN THE FLN.
عاهره
WE WERE AFRAID OF OUR OWN COUNTRY.

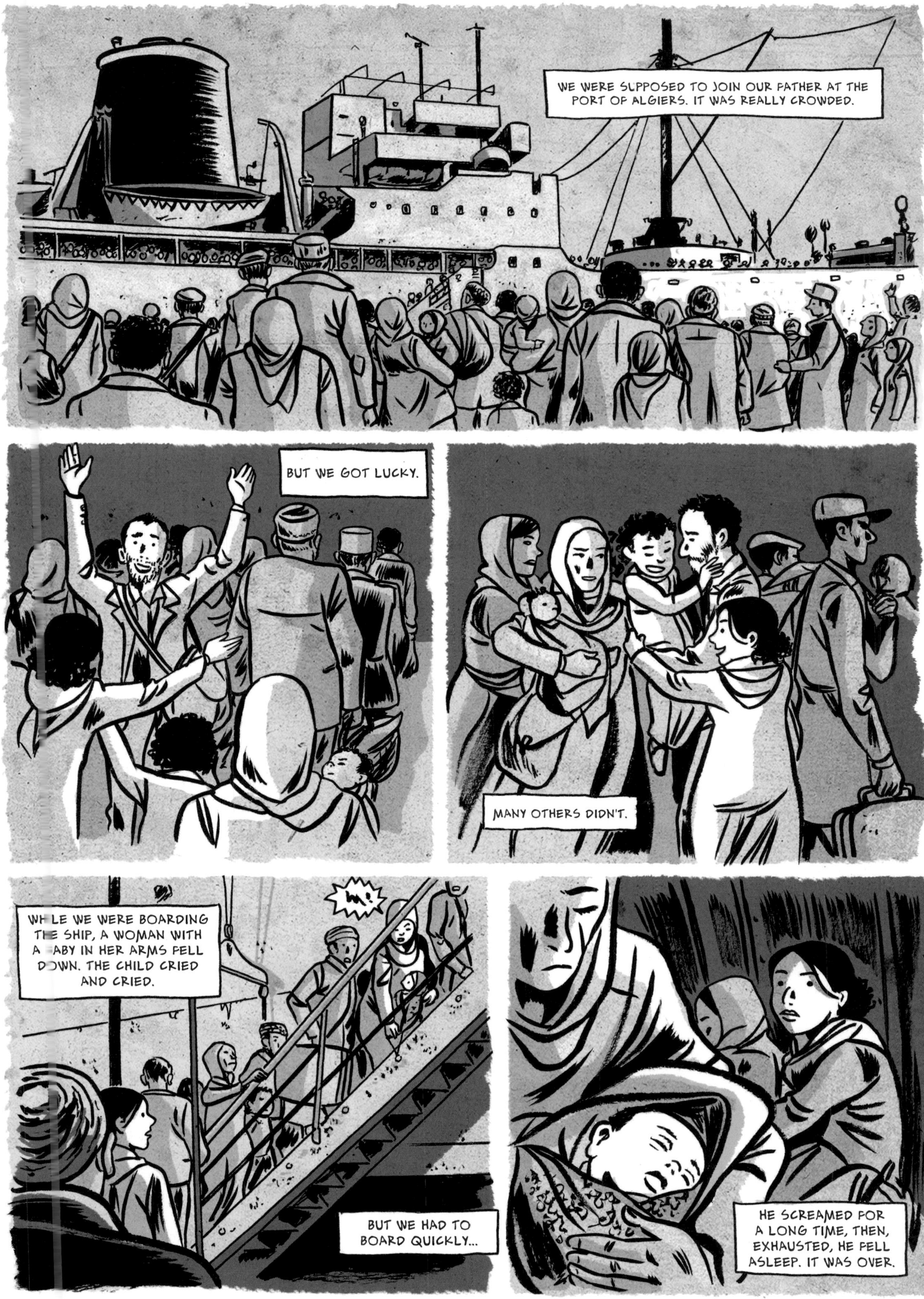
WE WERE SUPPOSED TO JOIN OUR FATHER AT THE PORT OF ALGIERS. IT WAS REALLY CROWDED.
BUT WE GOT LUCKY.
MANY OTHERS DIDN'T.
WHILE WE WERE BOARDING THE SHIP, A WOMAN WITH A BABY IN HER ARMS FELL DOWN. THE CHILD CRIED AND CRIED.
BUT WE HAD TO BOARD QUICKLY...
HE SCREAMED FOR A LONG TIME, THEN, EXHAUSTED, HE FELL ASLEEP. IT WAS OVER.

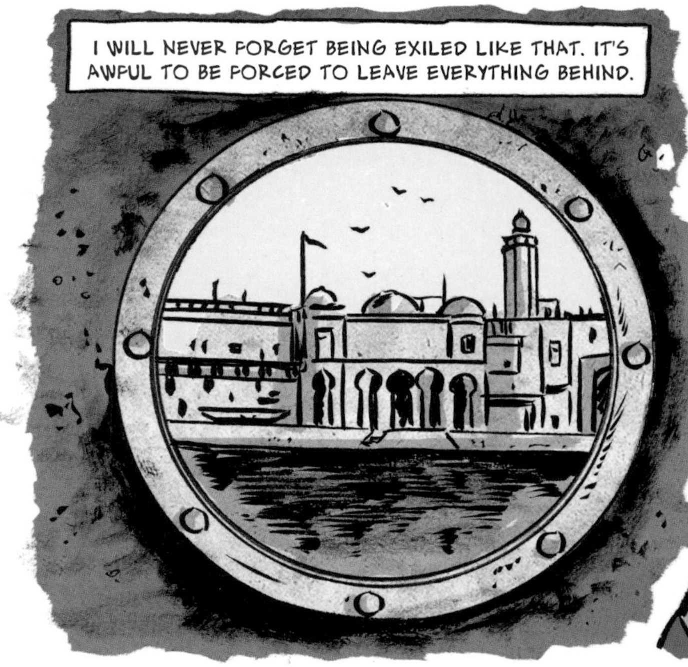
I WILL NEVER FORGET BEING EXILED LIKE THAT. IT'S AWFUL TO BE FORCED TO LEAVE EVERYTHING BEHIND.

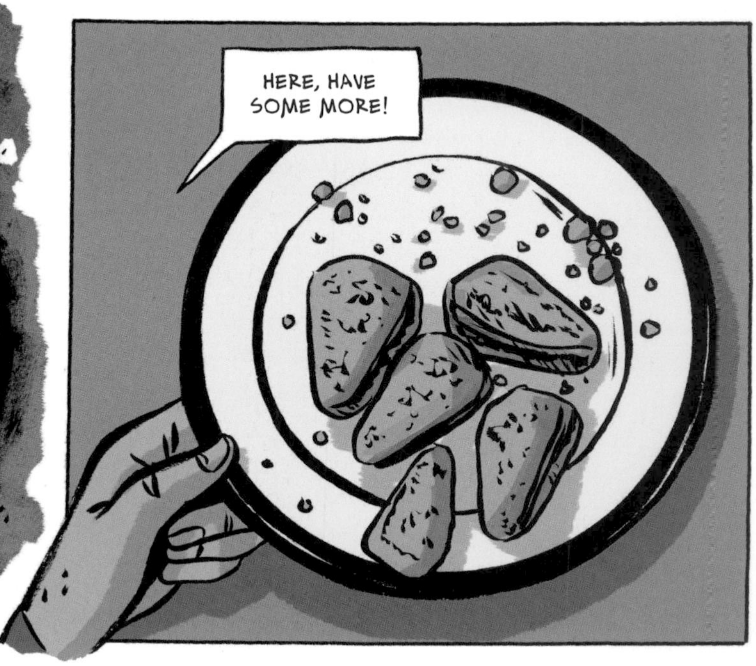
HERE, HAVE SOME MORE!

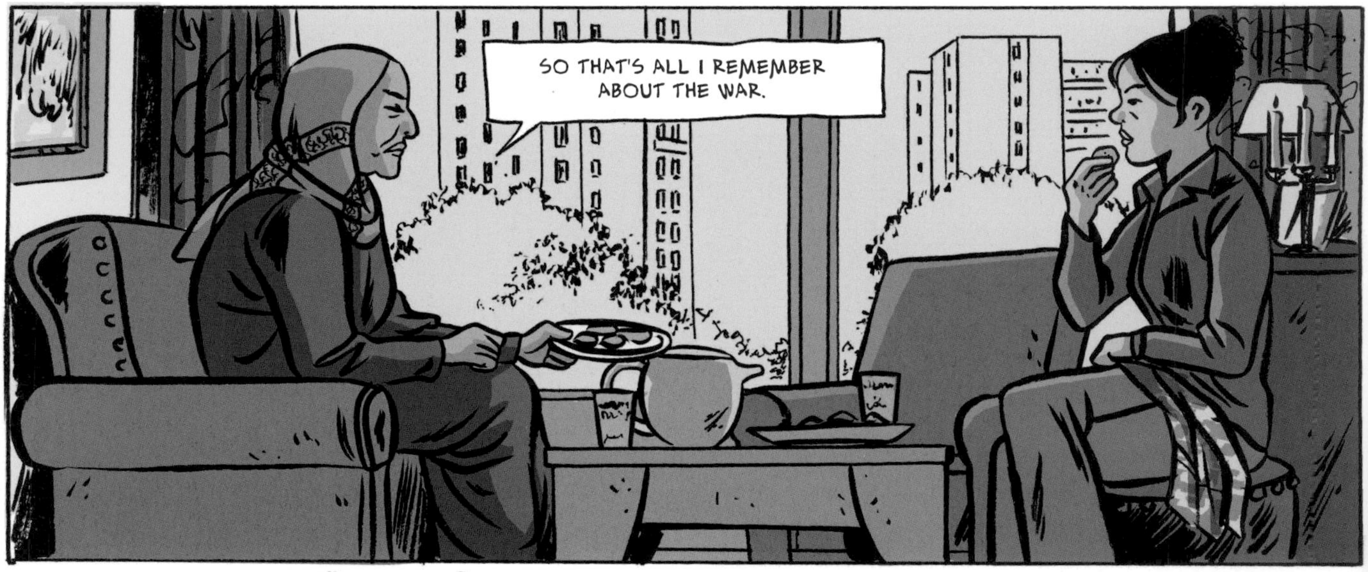
SO THAT'S ALL I REMEMBER ABOUT THE WAR.

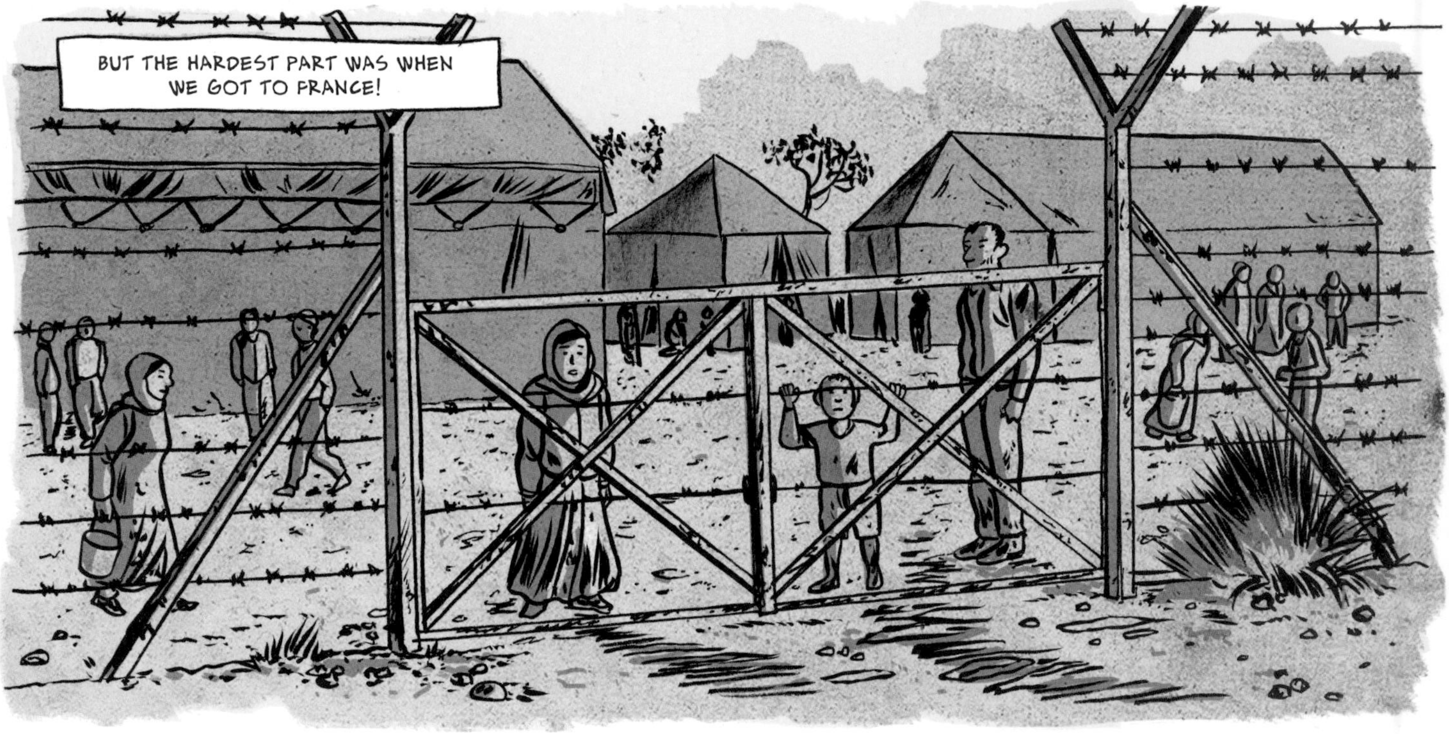
BUT THE HARDEST PART WAS WHEN WE GOT TO FRANCE!

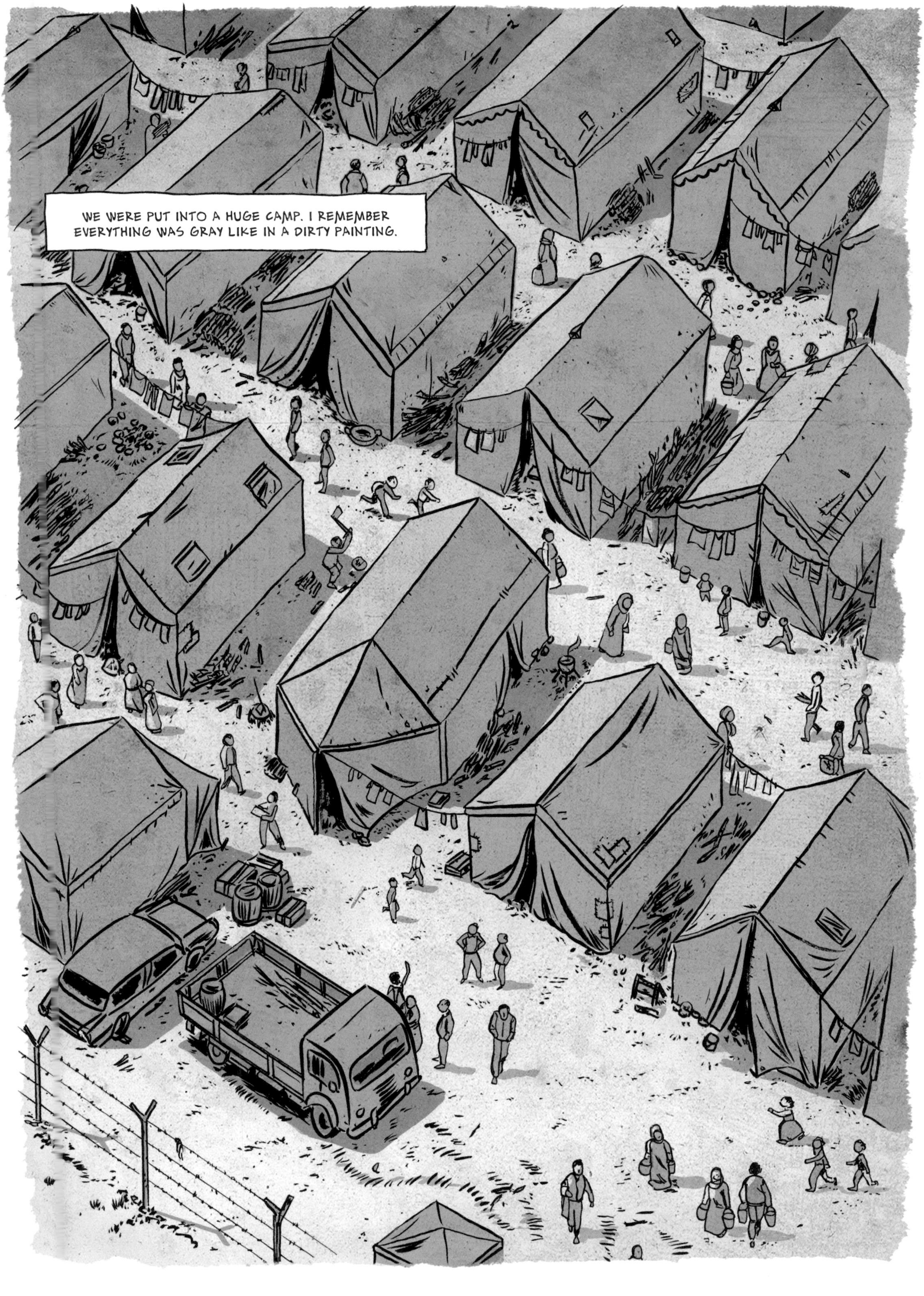
WE WERE PUT INTO A HUGE CAMP. I REMEMBER EVERYTHING WAS GRAY LIKE IN A DIRTY PAINTING.

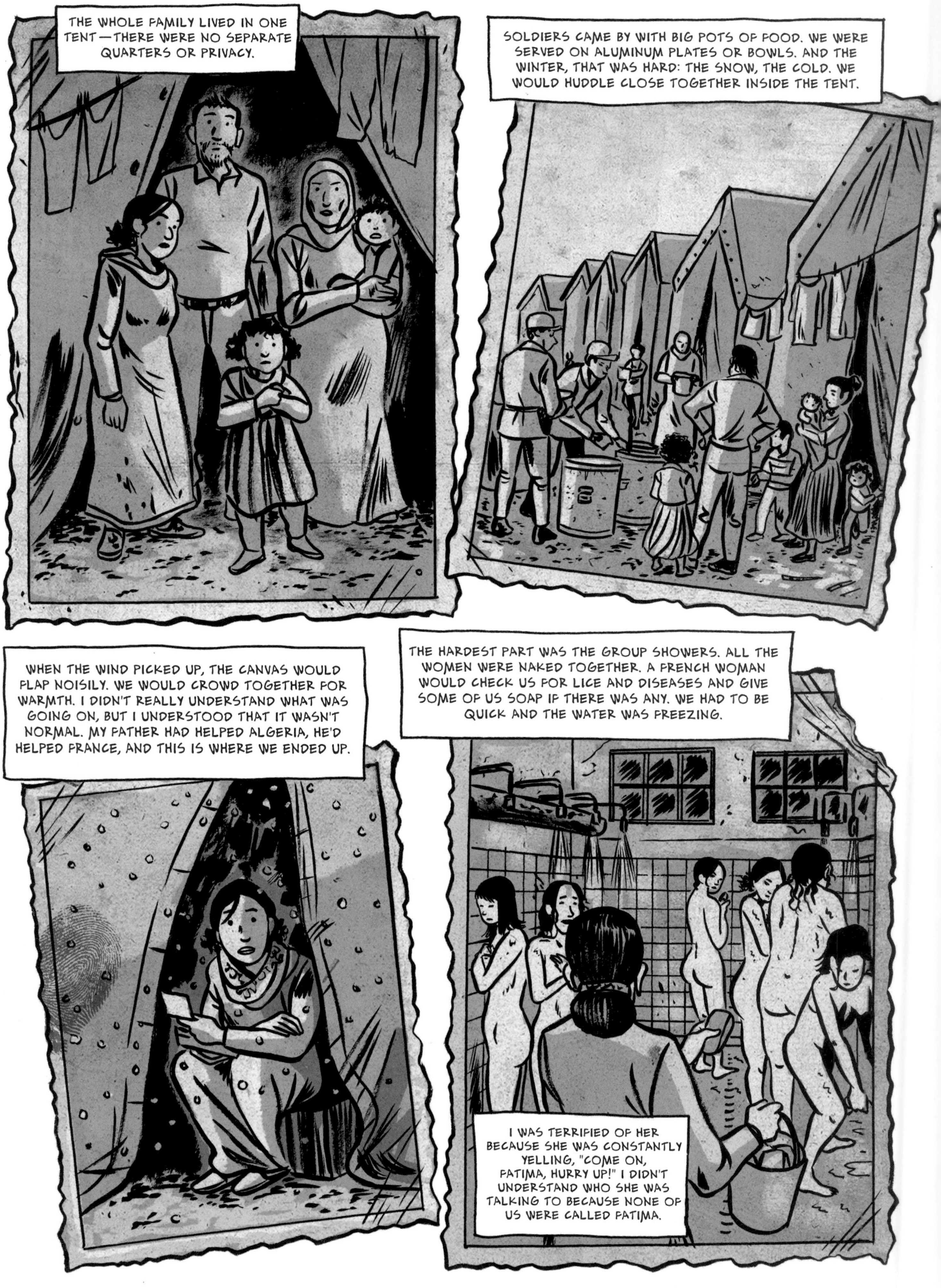
THE WHOLE FAMILY LIVED IN ONE TENT—THERE WERE NO SEPARATE QUARTERS OR PRIVACY.
SOLDIERS CAME BY WITH BIG POTS OF FOOD. WE WERE SERVED ON ALUMINUM PLATES OR BOWLS. AND THE WINTER, THAT WAS HARD: THE SNOW, THE COLD. WE WOULD HUDDLE CLOSE TOGETHER INSIDE THE TENT.
WHEN THE WIND PICKED UP, THE CANVAS WOULD FLAP NOISILY. WE WOULD CROWD TOGETHER FOR WARMTH. I DIDN'T REALLY UNDERSTAND WHAT WAS GOING ON, BUT I UNDERSTOOD THAT IT WASN'T NORMAL. MY FATHER HAD HELPED ALGERIA, HE'D HELPED FRANCE, AND THIS IS WHERE WE ENDED UP.
THE HARDEST PART WAS THE GROUP SHOWERS. ALL THE WOMEN WERE NAKED TOGETHER. A FRENCH WOMAN WOULD CHECK US FOR LICE AND DISEASES AND GIVE SOME OF US SOAP IF THERE WAS ANY. WE HAD TO BE QUICK AND THE WATER WAS FREEZING.
I WAS TERRIFIED OF HER BECAUSE SHE WAS CONSTANTLY YELLING, "COME ON, FATIMA, HURRY UP!" I DIDN'T UNDERSTAND WHO SHE WAS TALKING TO BECAUSE NONE OF US WERE CALLED FATIMA.

WE WEREN'T ALLOWED TO LEAVE THE CAMP, ESPECIALLY THE WOMEN! ONE MORNING, I WENT OFF WITH THE BOYS TO CHASE SQUIRRELS AND SELL THEM AT THE MARKET. WHEN I GOT BACK, MY FATHER WAS FURIOUS BECAUSE I HAD LEFT THE CAMP.

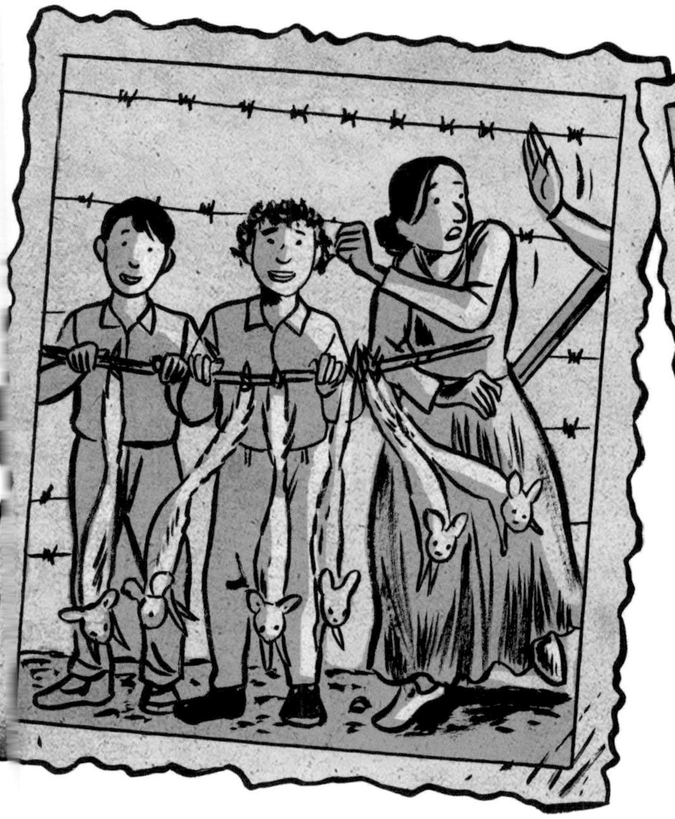

THE LIVING CONDITIONS WERE SO HARSH THAT ONE DAY A GUY CAME OUT OF HIS TENT WITH A GUN AND STARTED SHOOTING AT EVERYTHING. HE'D SNAPPED.

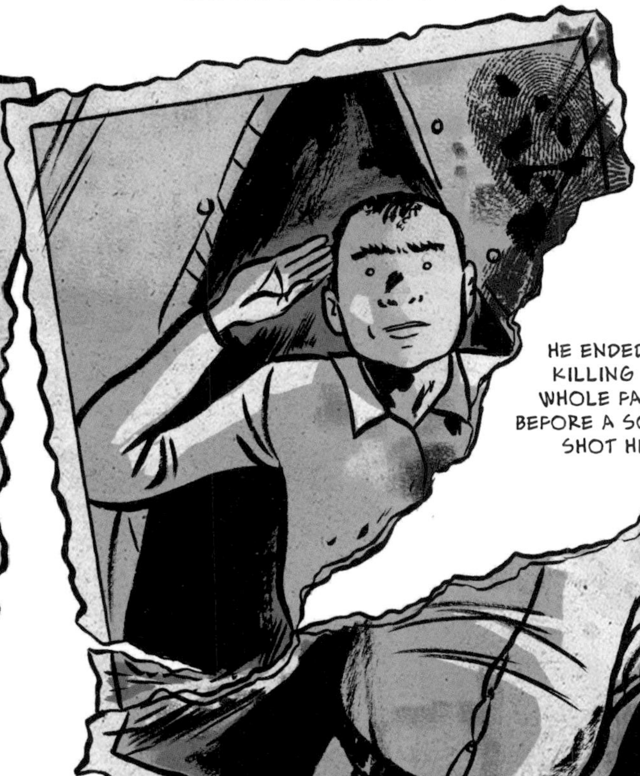

HE ENDED UP KILLING HIS WHOLE FAMILY BEFORE A SOLDIER SHOT HIM.

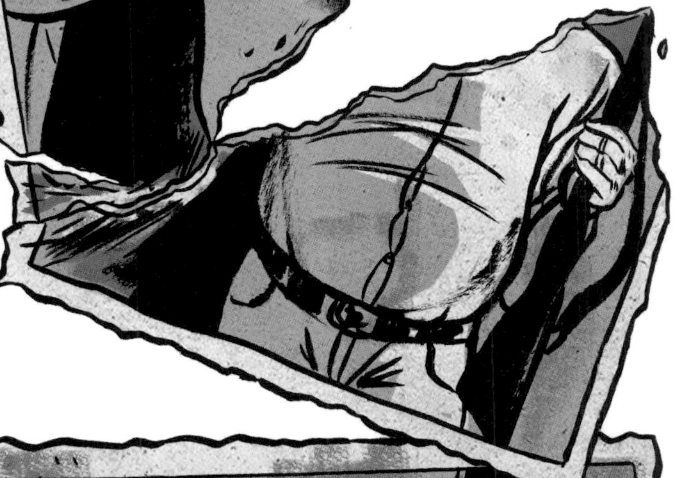

THE WOMEN NATURALLY HELPED EACH OTHER. THEY WOULD GET TOGETHER TO TALK OR TO SHARE CLOTHES. WHEN ONE OF THEM WAS TO GIVE BIRTH, THE OTHERS WOULD WORK TOGETHER TO ASSIST. WE LIVED TOGETHER LIKE A BIG FAMILY.

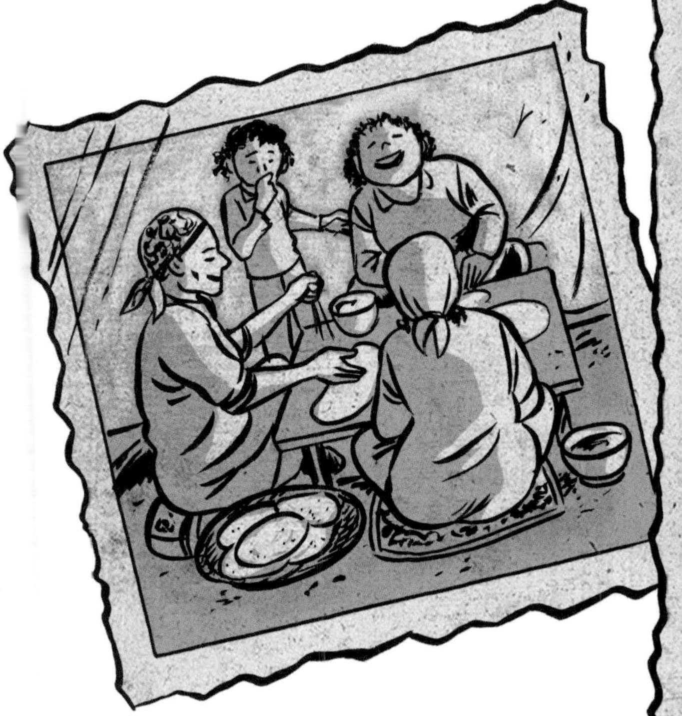

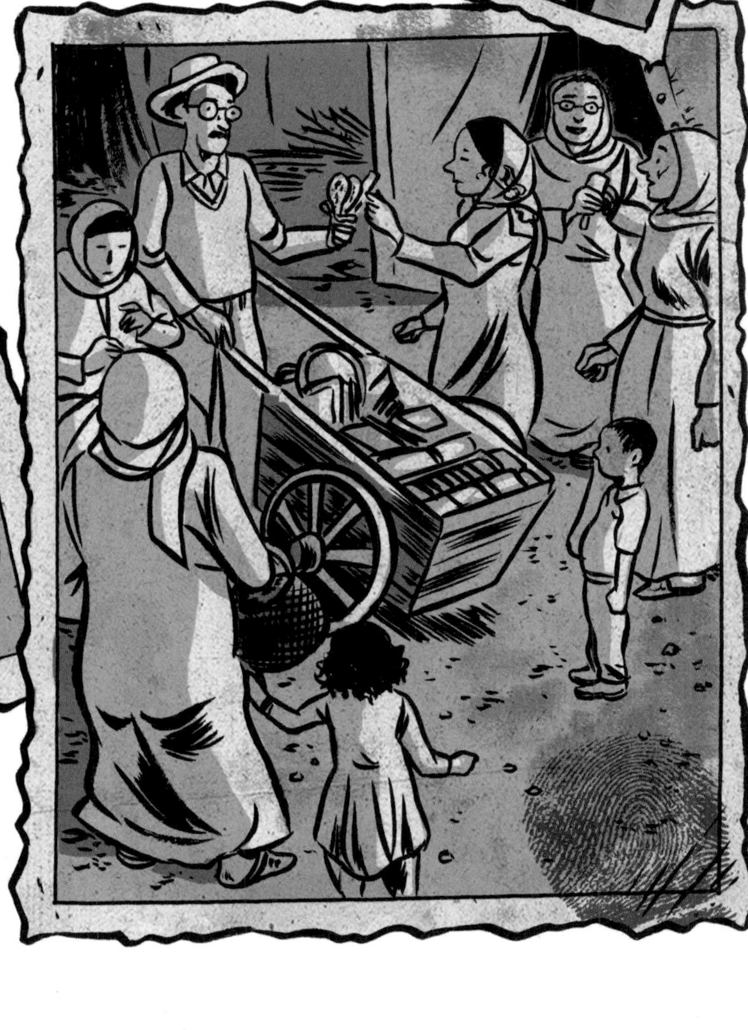

WHEN THE TRAVELING SALESMAN PASSED, THEY WOULD CALL TO ONE ANOTHER TO COME SHOP. BRUSHES, CLOTHES. AND WE OFTEN GOT TOGETHER TO SHARE FOOD.

LUCKILY THERE WERE PEOPLE WHO HELPED US. ESPECIALLY A NUN FROM THE CIMADE,* WHO WOULD GIVE US NEWS FROM HOME.

*"COMITÉ INTER MOUVEMENTS AUPRÈS DES ÉVACUÉS," A SOLIDARITY ORGANIZATION WORKING WITH MIGRANTS, REFUGEES, AND ASYLUM SEEKERS, FOUNDED IN 1939.

SHE TAUGHT COURSES IN FRENCH, KNITTING, AND ETIQUETTE. ALL THE WOMEN WENT—IT WAS LIKE A MINI-PARTY EACH TIME!

A FEW MONTHS LATER WE WERE ALL SENT TO AN EVEN BIGGER CAMP IN BOURG-LASTIC. LIKE ALL THE OTHER CHILDREN, I DIDN'T UNDERSTAND WHY WE WERE CONFINED LIKE THIS AND MOVED FROM CAMP TO CAMP, ALL OF WHICH LOOKED PRETTY MUCH THE SAME.

IN OUR NEW CAMP, WE HAD TO LIVE WITH THE SHAME OF BEING HARKIS. SO MANY FELT THE PAIN OF KNOWING THEY WOULD NEVER SEE THEIR FAMILIES AGAIN. SO MANY FRIENDS HAD TO GO TO THERAPY TO DEAL WITH IT, REJECTED AS THEY WERE FROM BOTH SIDES OF THE MEDITERRANEAN.

I NEVER WENT BACK TO ALGERIA FOR FEAR OF REPRISAL.

BUT MOST IMPORTANTLY, WE STAYED TOGETHER.

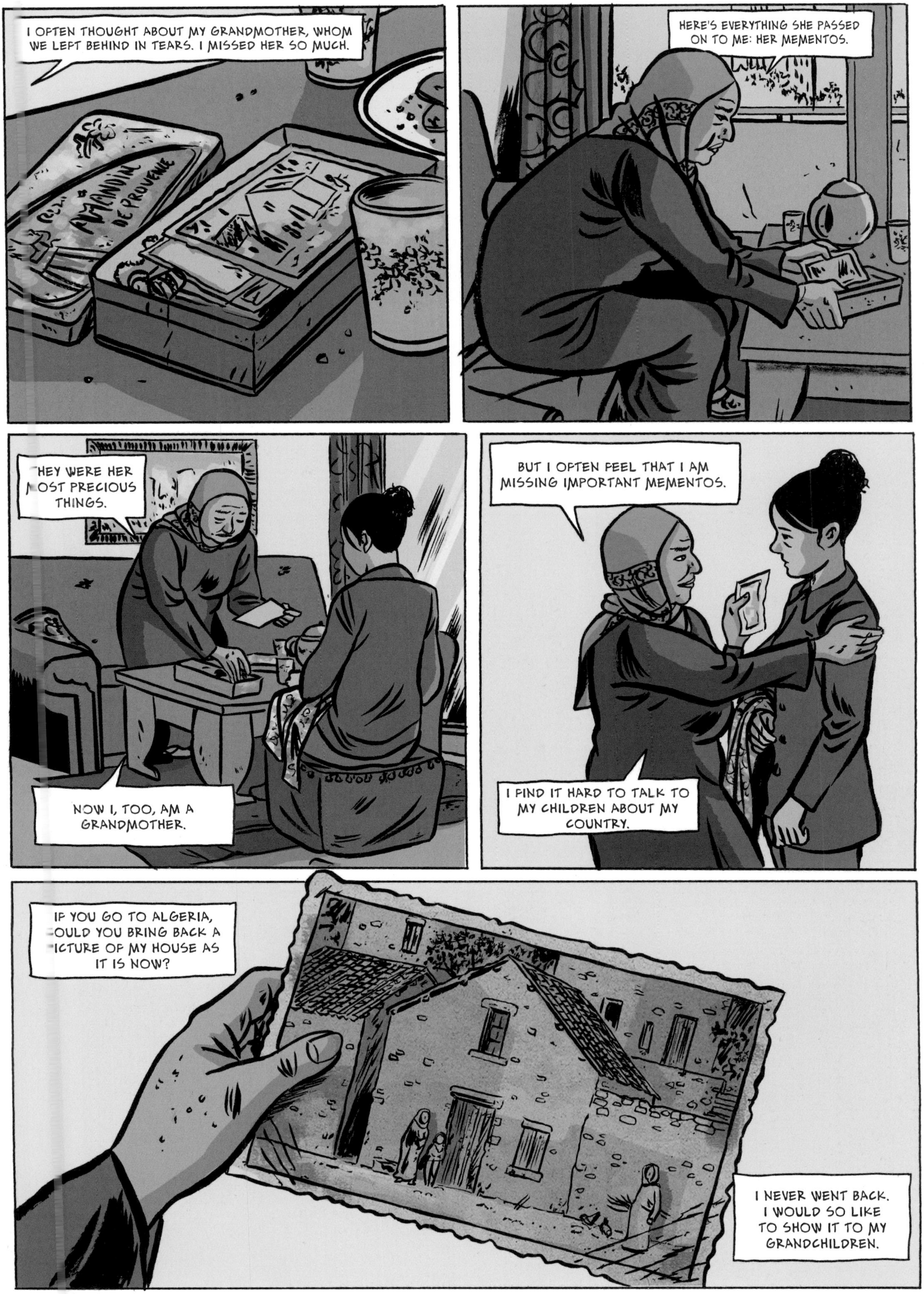

I OFTEN THOUGHT ABOUT MY GRANDMOTHER, WHOM WE LEFT BEHIND IN TEARS. I MISSED HER SO MUCH.
HERE'S EVERYTHING SHE PASSED ON TO ME: HER MEMENTOS.
THEY WERE HER MOST PRECIOUS THINGS.
NOW I, TOO, AM A GRANDMOTHER.
BUT I OFTEN FEEL THAT I AM MISSING IMPORTANT MEMENTOS.
I FIND IT HARD TO TALK TO MY CHILDREN ABOUT MY COUNTRY.
IF YOU GO TO ALGERIA, COULD YOU BRING BACK A PICTURE OF MY HOUSE AS IT IS NOW?
I NEVER WENT BACK. I WOULD SO LIKE TO SHOW IT TO MY GRANDCHILDREN.

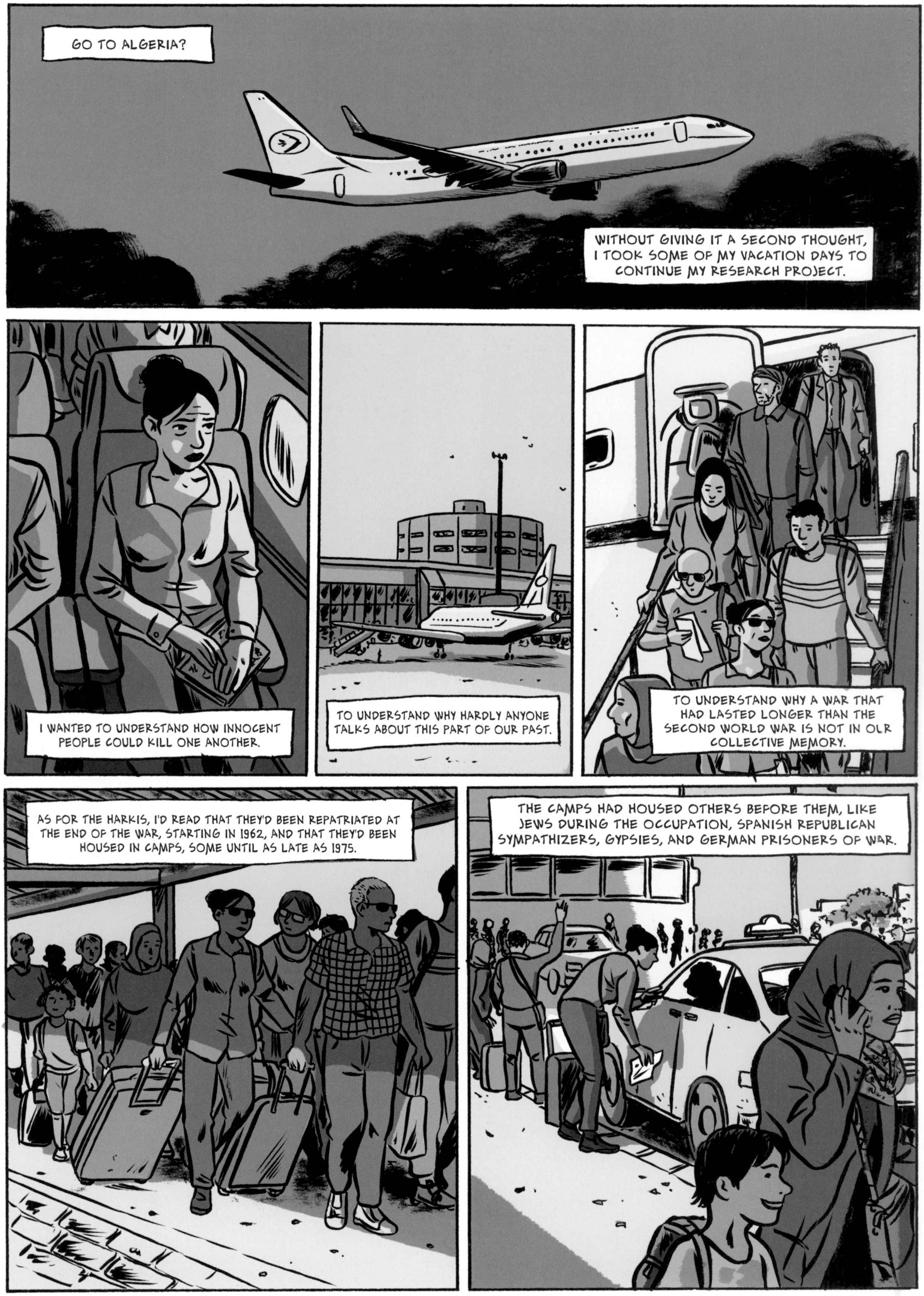
GO TO ALGERIA?
WITHOUT GIVING IT A SECOND THOUGHT, I TOOK SOME OF MY VACATION DAYS TO CONTINUE MY RESEARCH PROJECT.
I WANTED TO UNDERSTAND HOW INNOCENT PEOPLE COULD KILL ONE ANOTHER.
TO UNDERSTAND WHY HARDLY ANYONE TALKS ABOUT THIS PART OF OUR PAST.
TO UNDERSTAND WHY A WAR THAT HAD LASTED LONGER THAN THE SECOND WORLD WAR IS NOT IN OUR COLLECTIVE MEMORY.
AS FOR THE HARKIS, I'D READ THAT THEY'D BEEN REPATRIATED AT THE END OF THE WAR, STARTING IN 1962, AND THAT THEY'D BEEN HOUSED IN CAMPS, SOME UNTIL AS LATE AS 1975.
THE CAMPS HAD HOUSED OTHERS BEFORE THEM, LIKE JEWS DURING THE OCCUPATION, SPANISH REPUBLICAN SYMPATHIZERS, GYPSIES, AND GERMAN PRISONERS OF WAR.

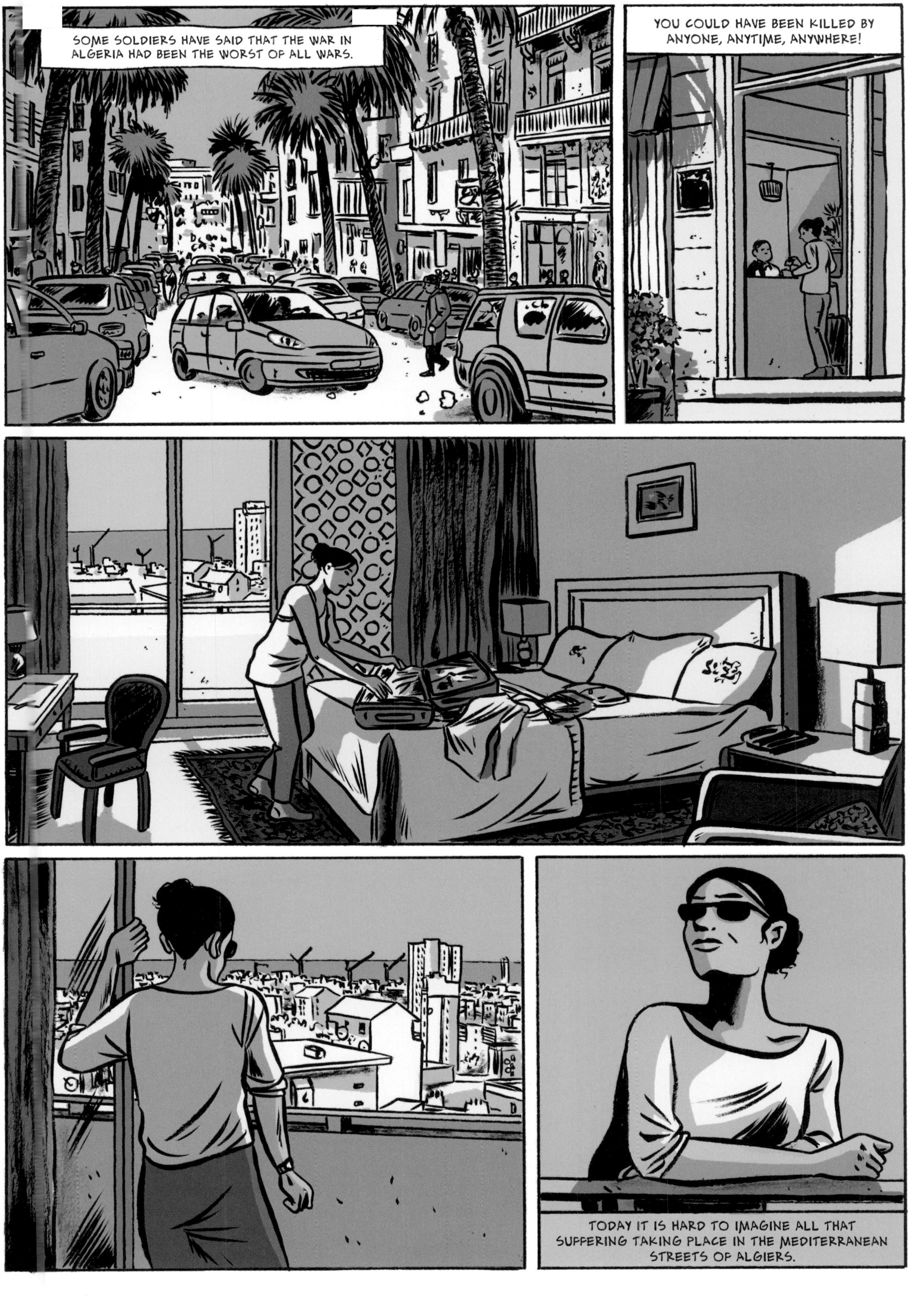
SOME SOLDIERS HAVE SAID THAT THE WAR IN ALGERIA HAD BEEN THE WORST OF ALL WARS.
YOU COULD HAVE BEEN KILLED BY ANYONE, ANYTIME, ANYWHERE!
TODAY IT IS HARD TO IMAGINE ALL THAT SUFFERING TAKING PLACE IN THE MEDITERRANEAN STREETS OF ALGIERS.

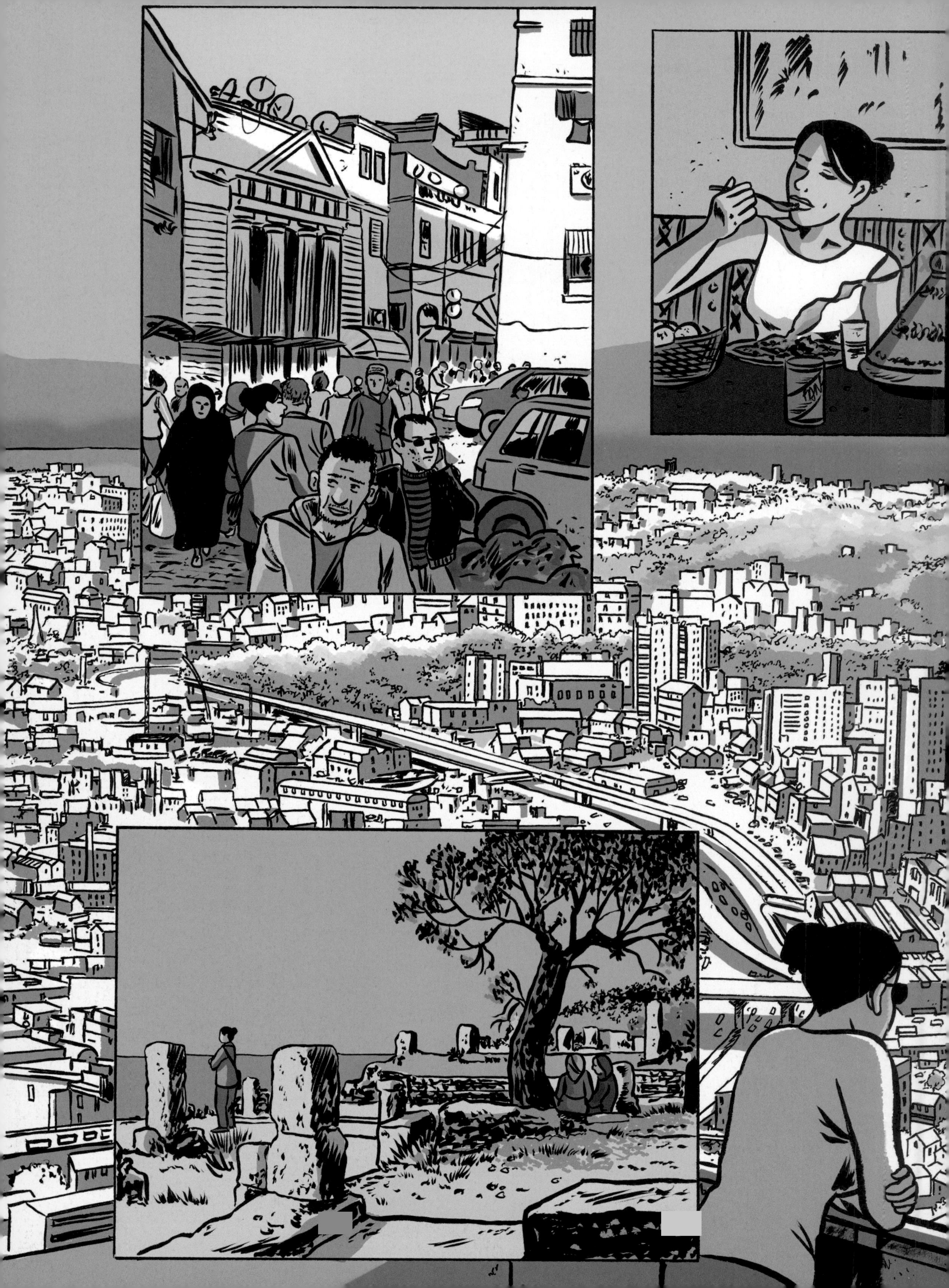

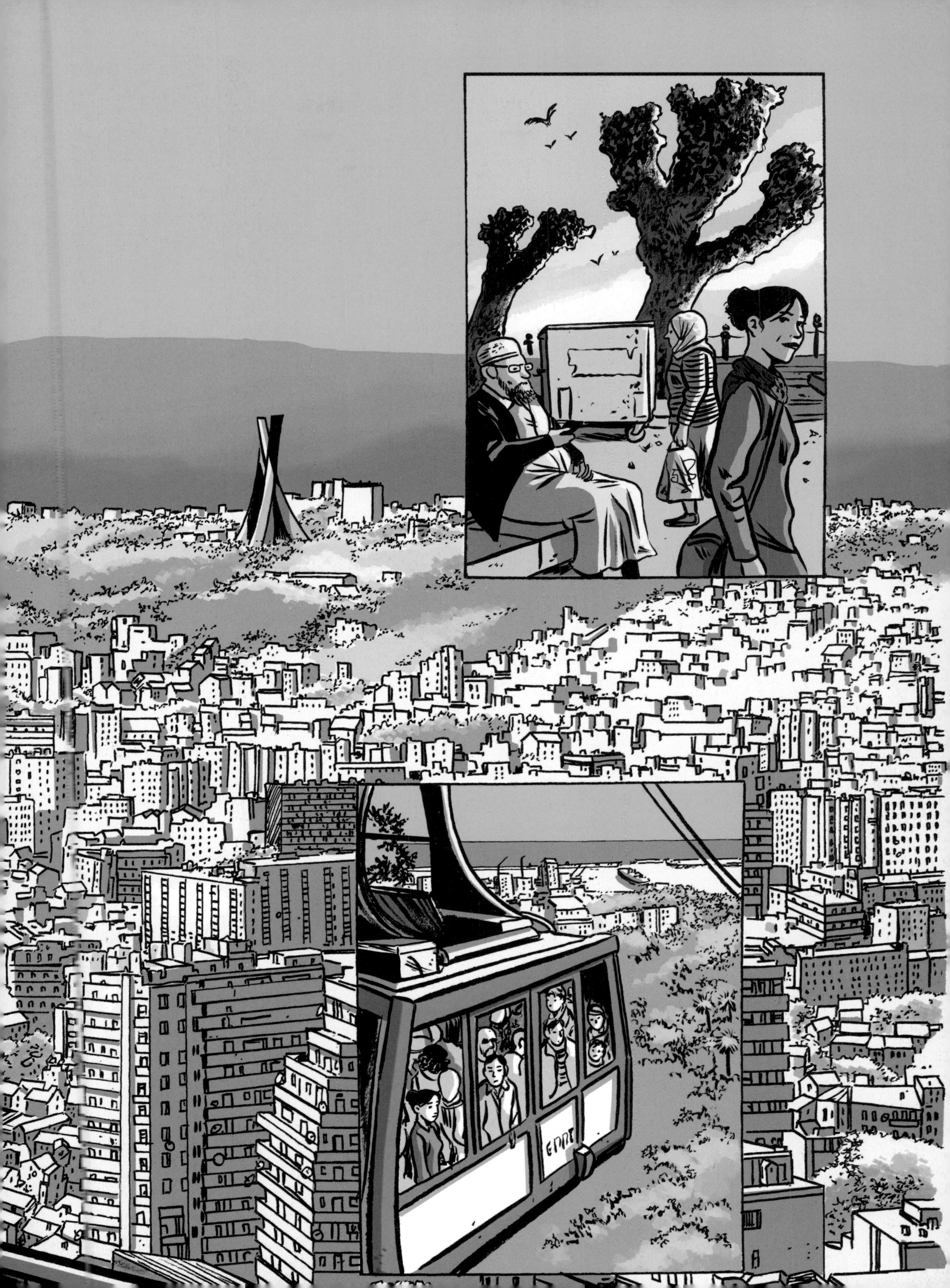

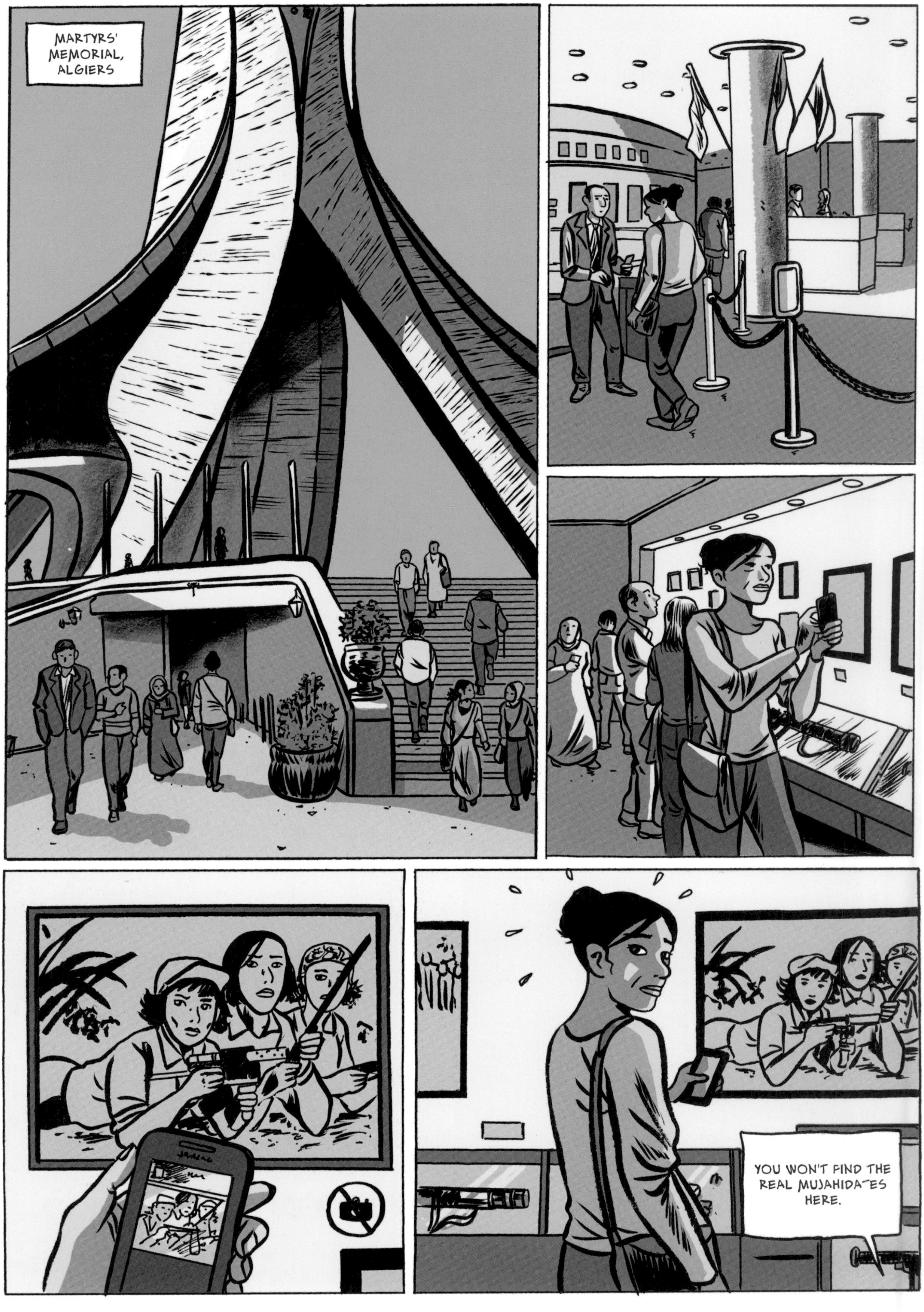
MARTYRS' MEMORIAL, ALGIERS
YOU WON'T FIND THE REAL MUJAHIDATES HERE.

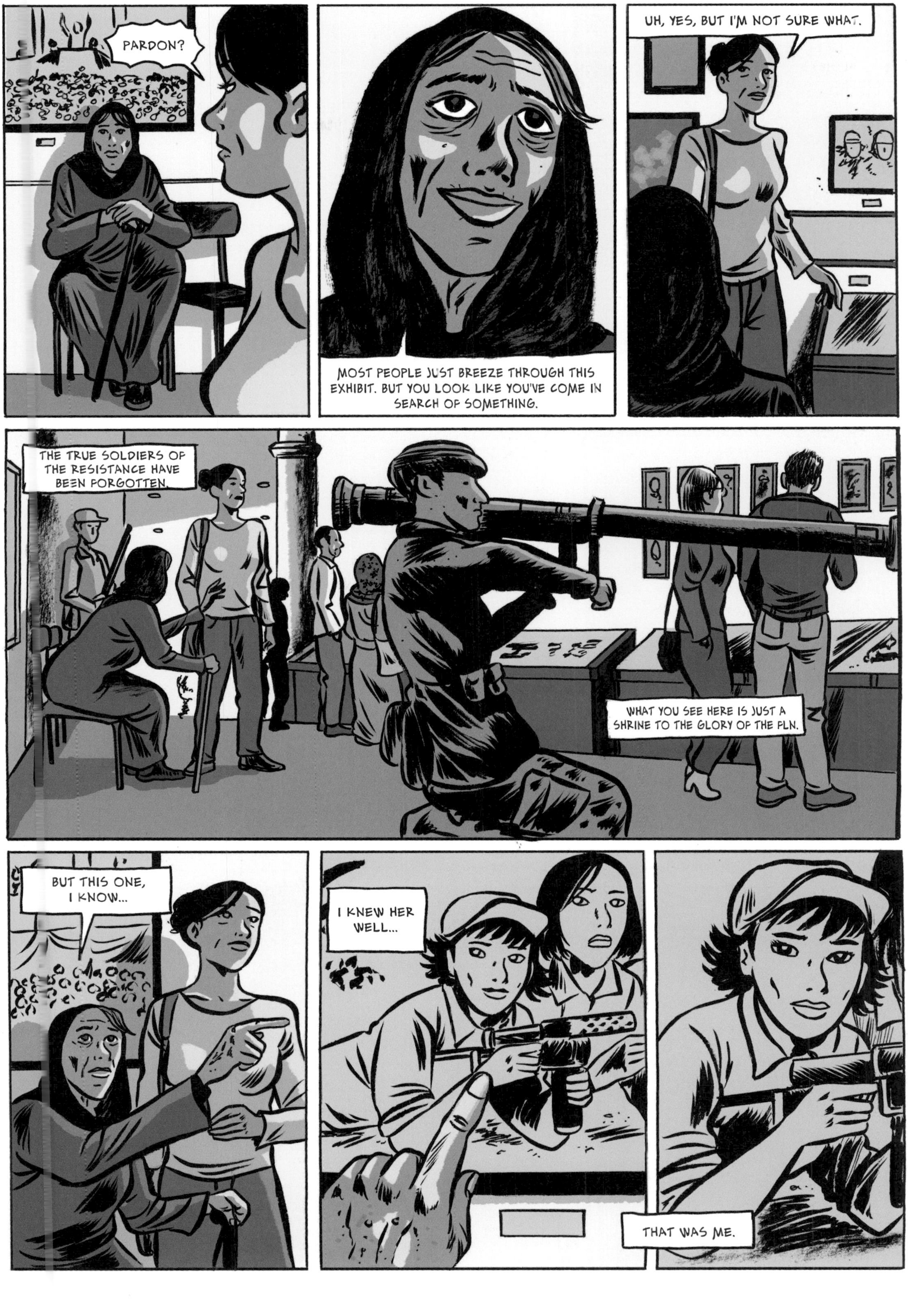
PARDON?
MOST PEOPLE JUST BREEZE THROUGH THIS EXHIBIT. BUT YOU LOOK LIKE YOU'VE COME IN SEARCH OF SOMETHING.
UH, YES, BUT I'M NOT SURE WHAT.
THE TRUE SOLDIERS OF THE RESISTANCE HAVE BEEN FORGOTTEN.
WHAT YOU SEE HERE IS JUST A SHRINE TO THE GLORY OF THE FLN.
BUT THIS ONE, I KNOW...
I KNEW HER WELL...
THAT WAS ME.

HERE, EVERYTHING IS BLACK OR WHITE. BUT FORGOTTEN ARE ALL THE MASSACRES COMMITTED BY THE ALGERIANS.

AND THERE'S HARDLY ANY SPACE HERE DEDICATED TO US, THE WOMEN.

SO, YOU WERE IN THE RESISTANCE?

I GUESS SO, YES, BUT I'M NOT SO SURE ANYMORE.

I'M TRYING TO FIND OUT MORE ABOUT THE WAR. I WENT TO THE MEMORIAL TO UNDERSTAND WHAT HAPPENED.

IS THERE NO MEMORIAL IN FRANCE FOR THE FRENCH SOLDIERS?

YOU WANT TO KNOW MORE, BUT IN THERE YOU'LL ONLY FIND MEDALS AND PHOTOS OF WEAPONS.

I'LL MAKE YOU A DEAL, OK?

YOU HELP AN OLD LADY HOME, AND SHE'LL TELL YOU HER STORY.

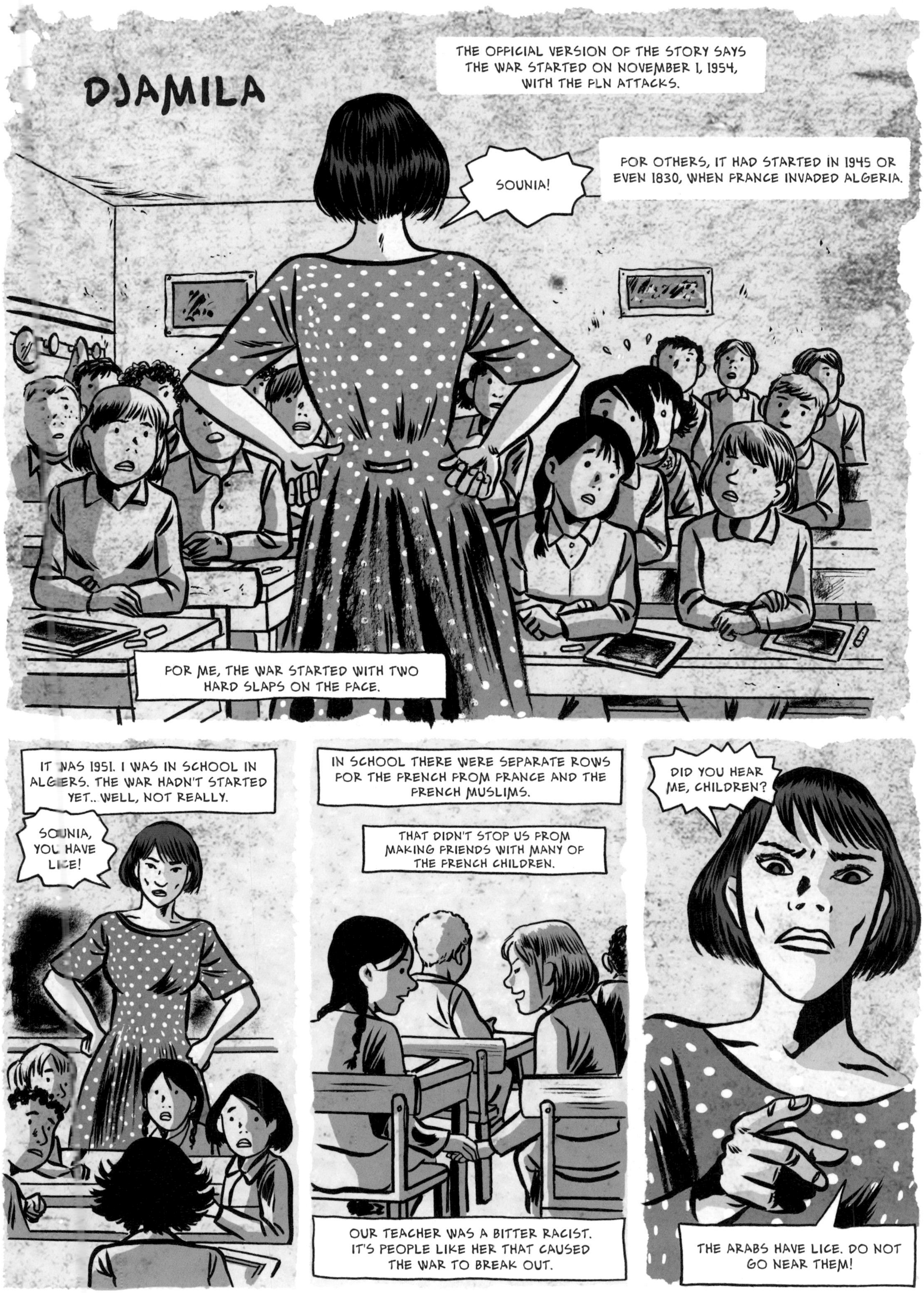
DJAMILA
THE OFFICIAL VERSION OF THE STORY SAYS THE WAR STARTED ON NOVEMBER 1, 1954, WITH THE FLN ATTACKS.
SOUNIA!
FOR OTHERS, IT HAD STARTED IN 1945 OR EVEN 1830, WHEN FRANCE INVADED ALGERIA.
FOR ME, THE WAR STARTED WITH TWO HARD SLAPS ON THE FACE.
IT WAS 1951. I WAS IN SCHOOL IN ALGIERS. THE WAR HADN'T STARTED YET... WELL, NOT REALLY.
SOUNIA, YOU HAVE LICE!
IN SCHOOL THERE WERE SEPARATE ROWS FOR THE FRENCH FROM FRANCE AND THE FRENCH MUSLIMS.
THAT DIDN'T STOP US FROM MAKING FRIENDS WITH MANY OF THE FRENCH CHILDREN.
OUR TEACHER WAS A BITTER RACIST. IT'S PEOPLE LIKE HER THAT CAUSED THE WAR TO BREAK OUT.
DID YOU HEAR ME, CHILDREN?
THE ARABS HAVE LICE. DO NOT GO NEAR THEM!

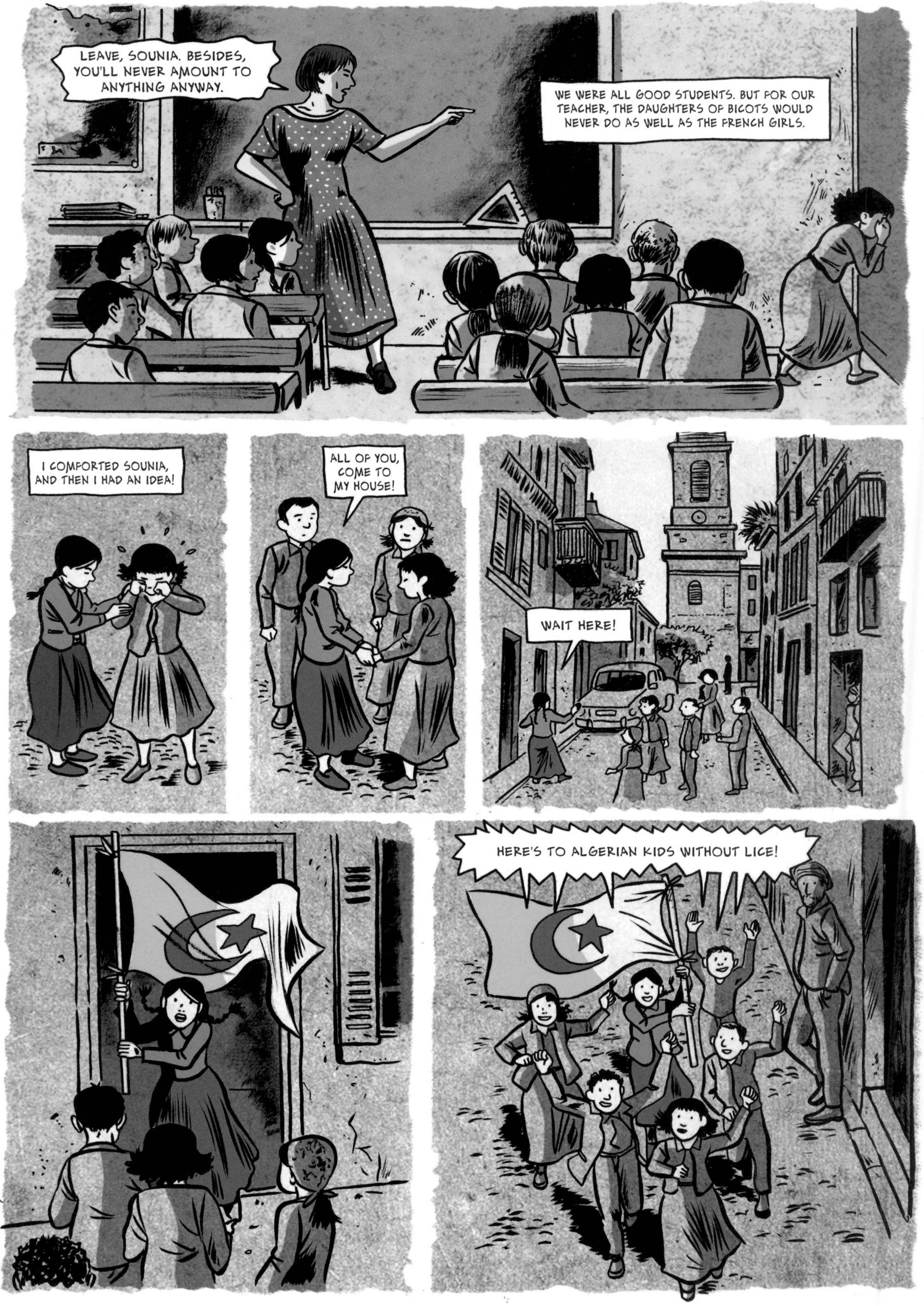
LEAVE, SOUNIA. BESIDES, YOU'LL NEVER AMOUNT TO ANYTHING ANYWAY.
WE WERE ALL GOOD STUDENTS. BUT FOR OUR TEACHER, THE DAUGHTERS OF BICOTS WOULD NEVER DO AS WELL AS THE FRENCH GIRLS.
I COMFORTED SOUNIA, AND THEN I HAD AN IDEA!
ALL OF YOU, COME TO MY HOUSE!
WAIT HERE!
HERE'S TO ALGERIAN KIDS WITHOUT LICE!

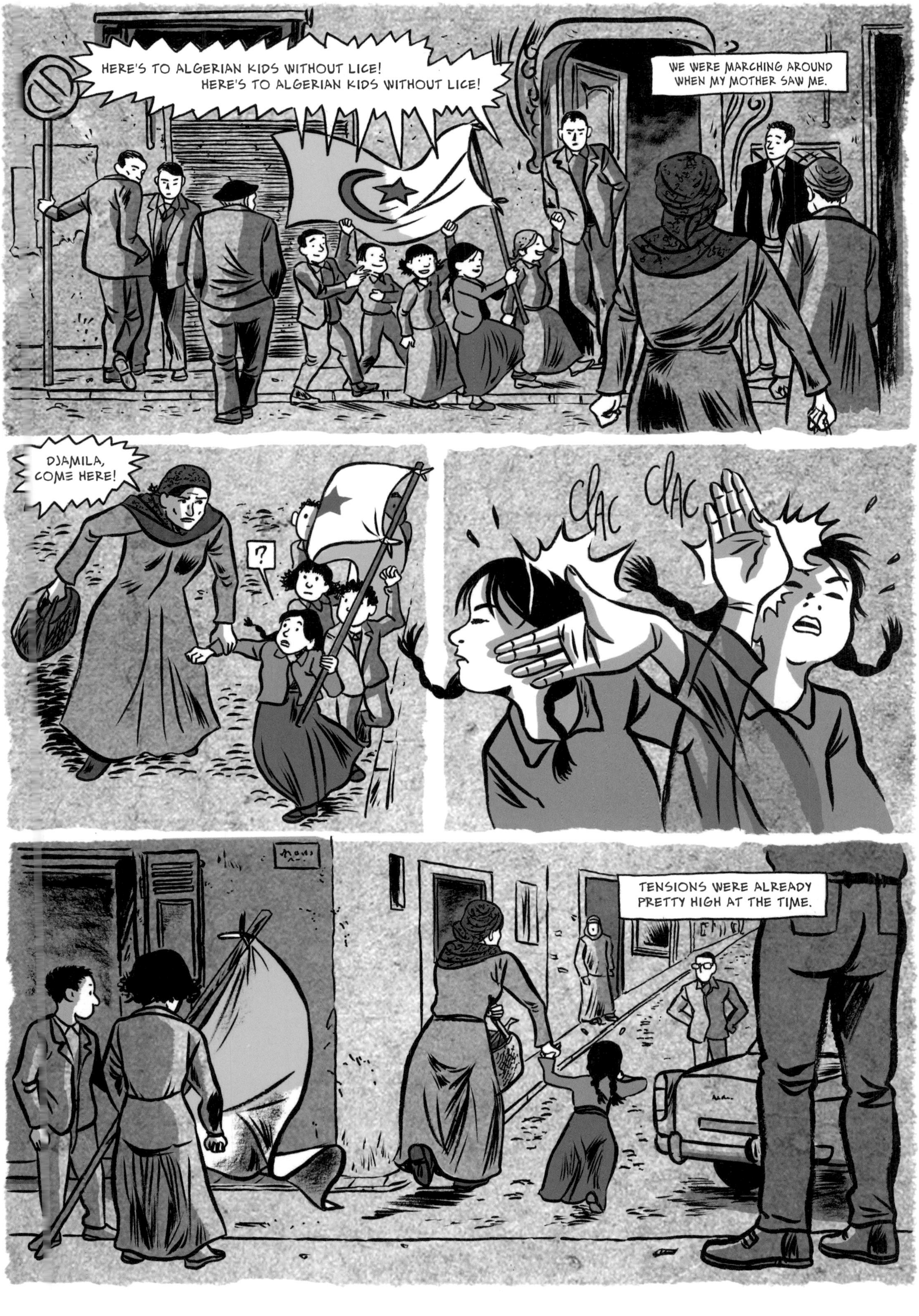
HERE'S TO ALGERIAN KIDS WITHOUT LICE!
HERE'S TO ALGERIAN KIDS WITHOUT LICE!
WE WERE MARCHING AROUND WHEN MY MOTHER SAW ME.
DJAMILA, COME HERE!
?
CLAC CLAC
TENSIONS WERE ALREADY PRETTY HIGH AT THE TIME.

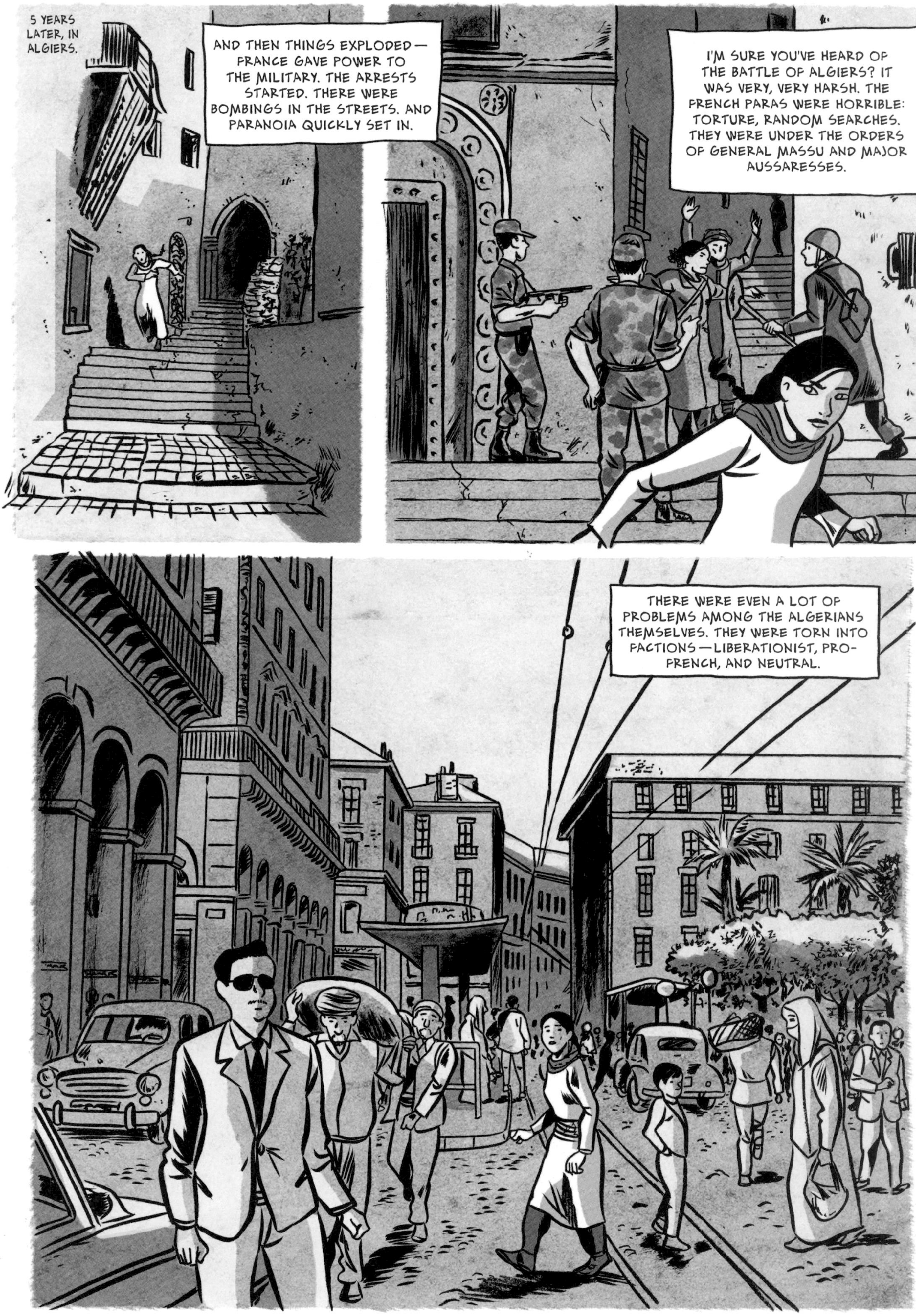
5 YEARS LATER, IN ALGIERS.
AND THEN THINGS EXPLODED—FRANCE GAVE POWER TO THE MILITARY. THE ARRESTS STARTED. THERE WERE BOMBINGS IN THE STREETS. AND PARANOIA QUICKLY SET IN.
I'M SURE YOU'VE HEARD OF THE BATTLE OF ALGIERS? IT WAS VERY, VERY HARSH. THE FRENCH PARAS WERE HORRIBLE: TORTURE, RANDOM SEARCHES. THEY WERE UNDER THE ORDERS OF GENERAL MASSU AND MAJOR AUSSARESSES.
THERE WERE EVEN A LOT OF PROBLEMS AMONG THE ALGERIANS THEMSELVES. THEY WERE TORN INTO FACTIONS—LIBERATIONIST, PRO-FRENCH, AND NEUTRAL.

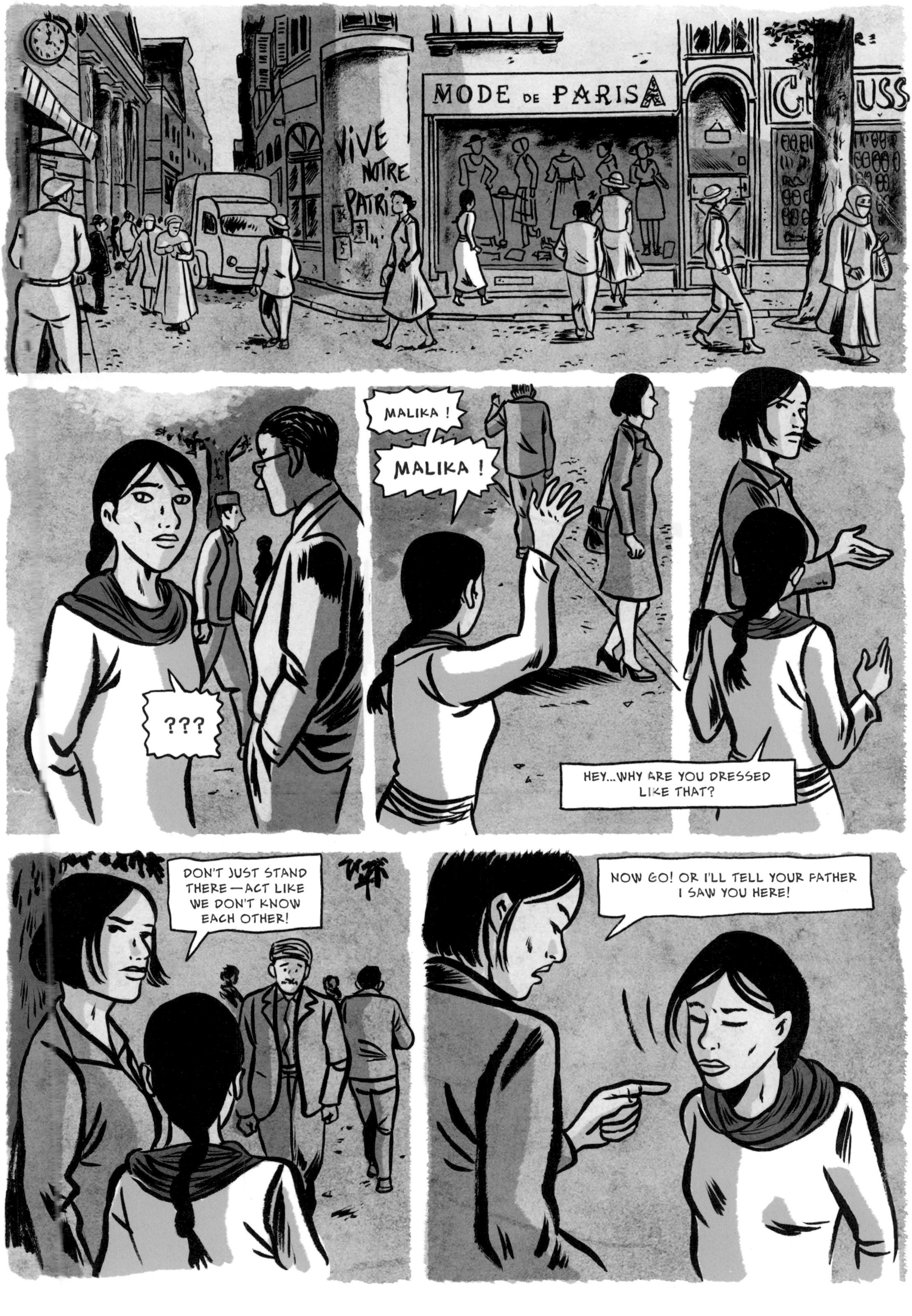
MODE DE PARIS
VIVE NOTRE PATRI
???
MALIKA !
MALIKA !
HEY...WHY ARE YOU DRESSED LIKE THAT?
DON'T JUST STAND THERE—ACT LIKE WE DON'T KNOW EACH OTHER!
NOW GO! OR I'LL TELL YOUR FATHER I SAW YOU HERE!

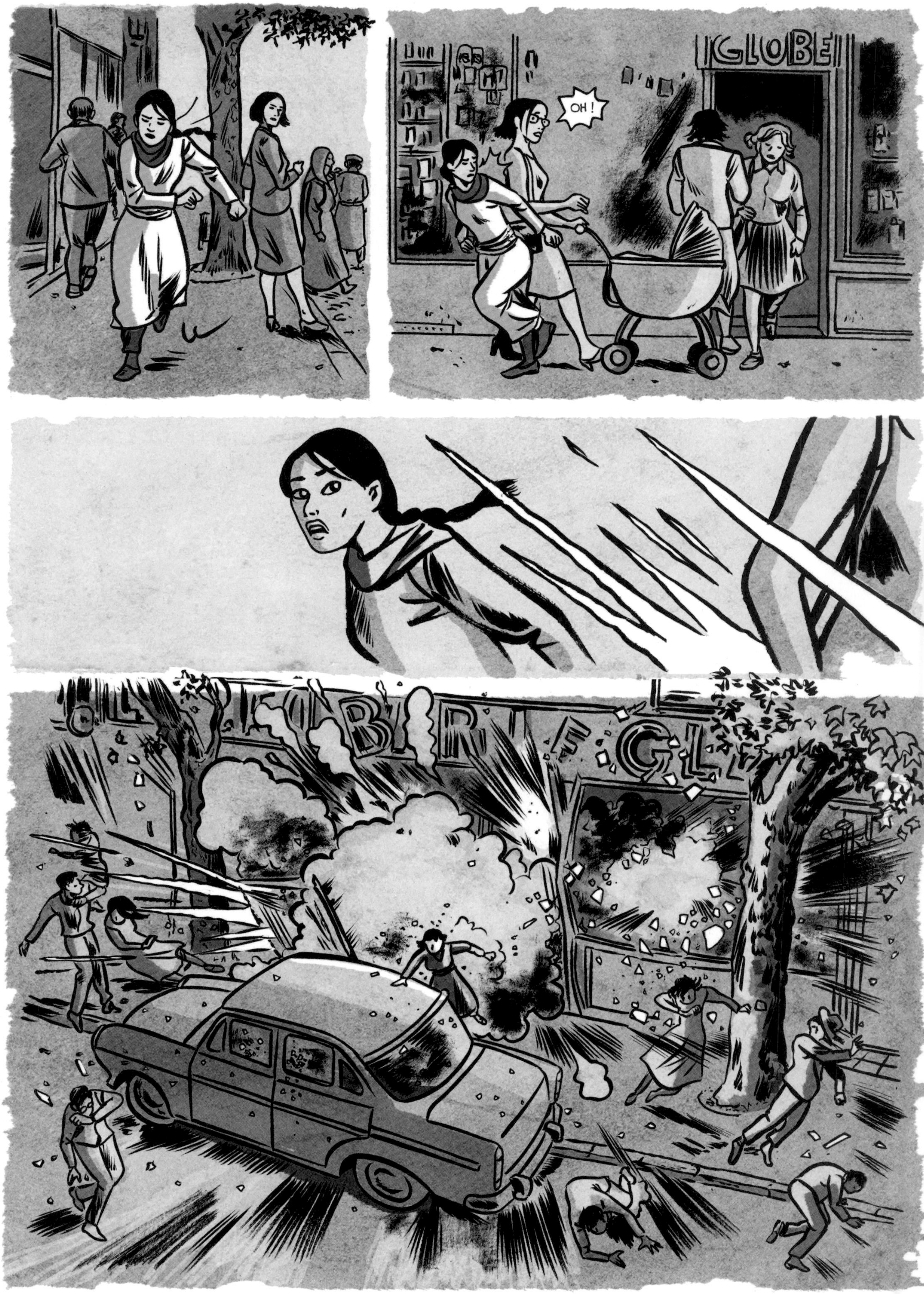
GLOBE
OH !

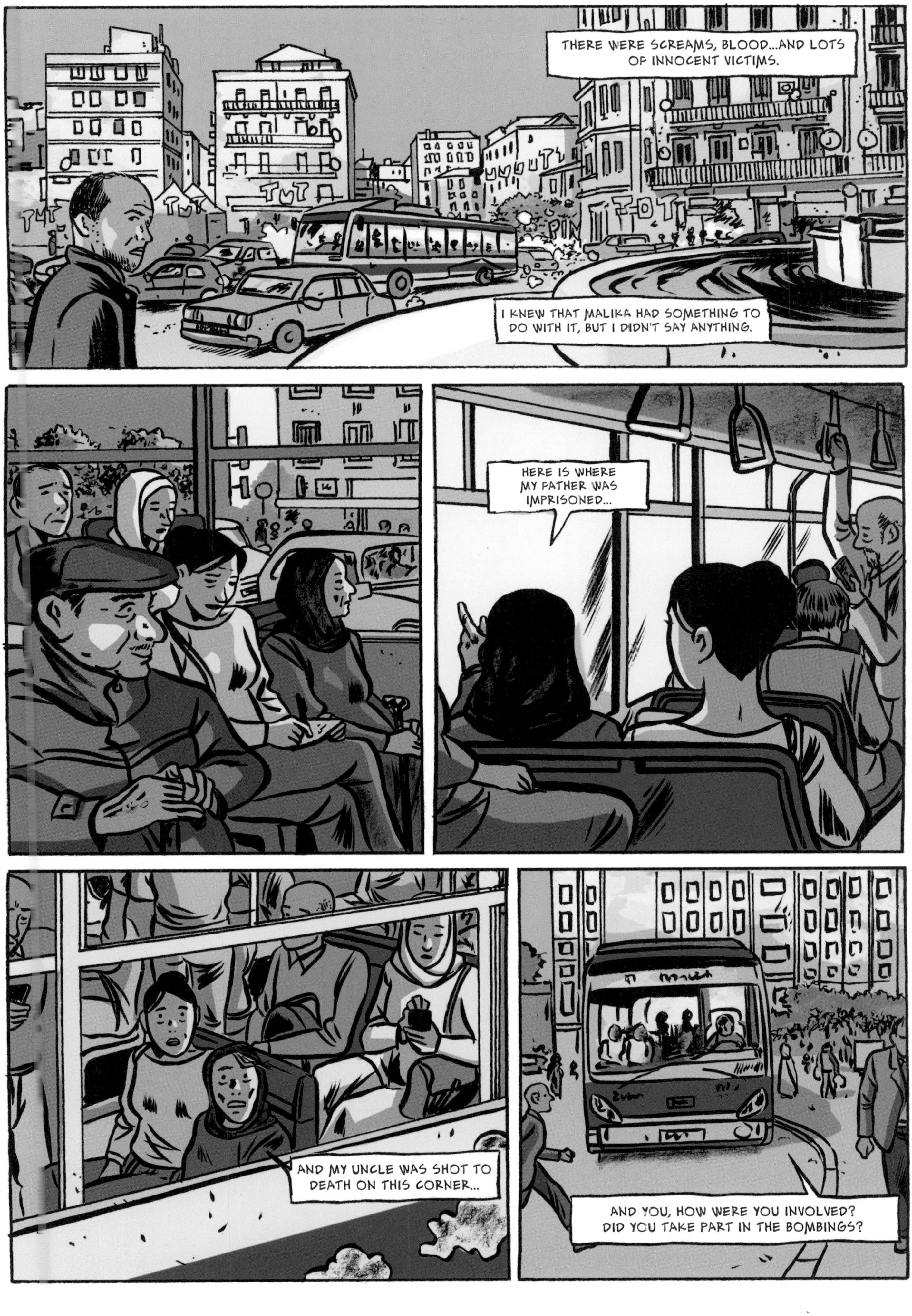
THERE WERE SCREAMS, BLOOD...AND LOTS OF INNOCENT VICTIMS.
I KNEW THAT MALIKA HAD SOMETHING TO DO WITH IT, BUT I DIDN'T SAY ANYTHING.
HERE IS WHERE MY FATHER WAS IMPRISONED...
AND MY UNCLE WAS SHOT TO DEATH ON THIS CORNER...
AND YOU, HOW WERE YOU INVOLVED? DID YOU TAKE PART IN THE BOMBINGS?

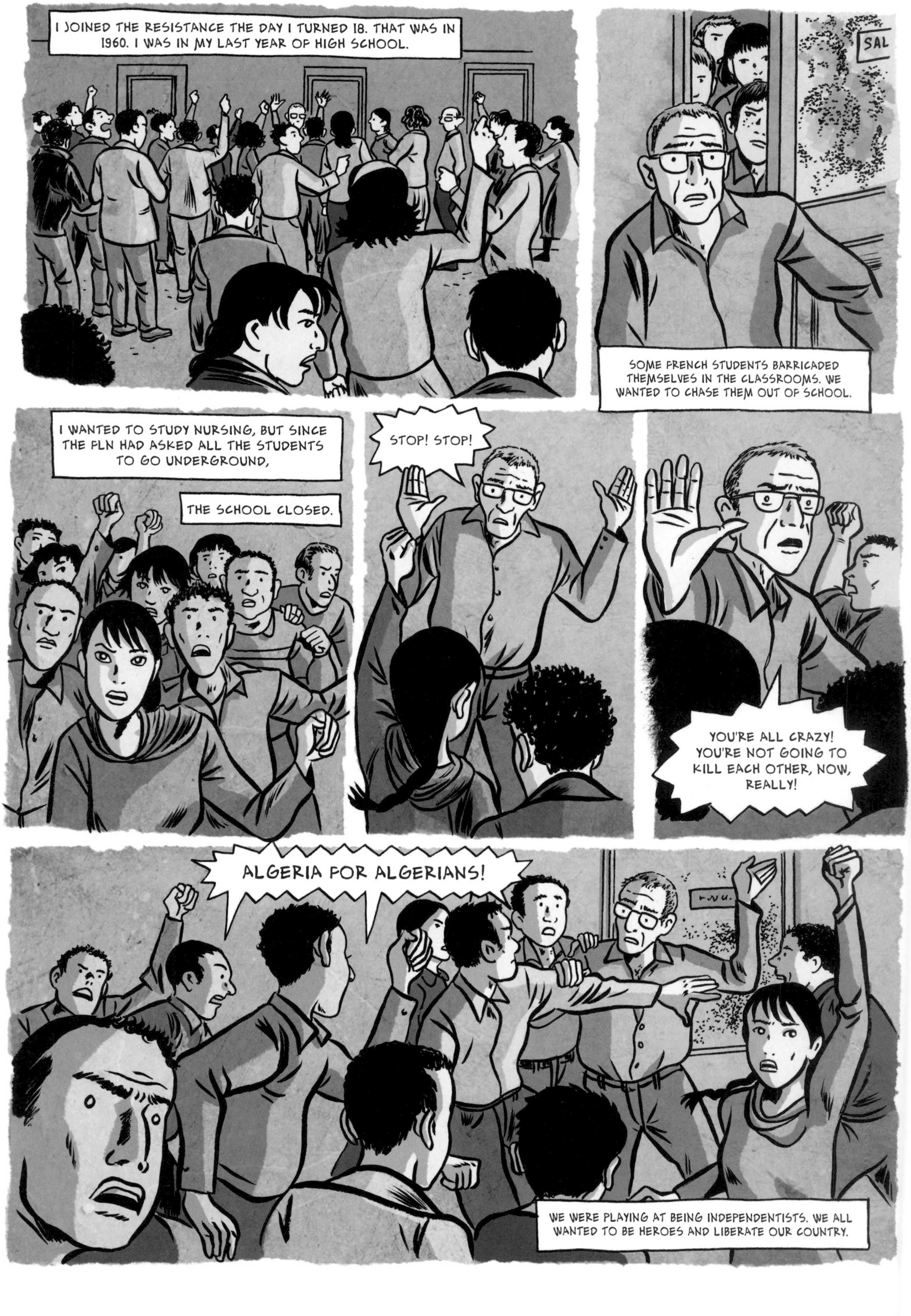
I JOINED THE RESISTANCE THE DAY I TURNED 18. THAT WAS IN 1960. I WAS IN MY LAST YEAR OF HIGH SCHOOL.
SAL
SOME FRENCH STUDENTS BARRICADED THEMSELVES IN THE CLASSROOMS. WE WANTED TO CHASE THEM OUT OF SCHOOL.
I WANTED TO STUDY NURSING, BUT SINCE THE FLN HAD ASKED ALL THE STUDENTS TO GO UNDERGROUND,
THE SCHOOL CLOSED.
STOP! STOP!
YOU'RE ALL CRAZY! YOU'RE NOT GOING TO KILL EACH OTHER, NOW, REALLY!
ALGERIA FOR ALGERIANS!
WE WERE PLAYING AT BEING INDEPENDENTISTS. WE ALL WANTED TO BE HEROES AND LIBERATE OUR COUNTRY.

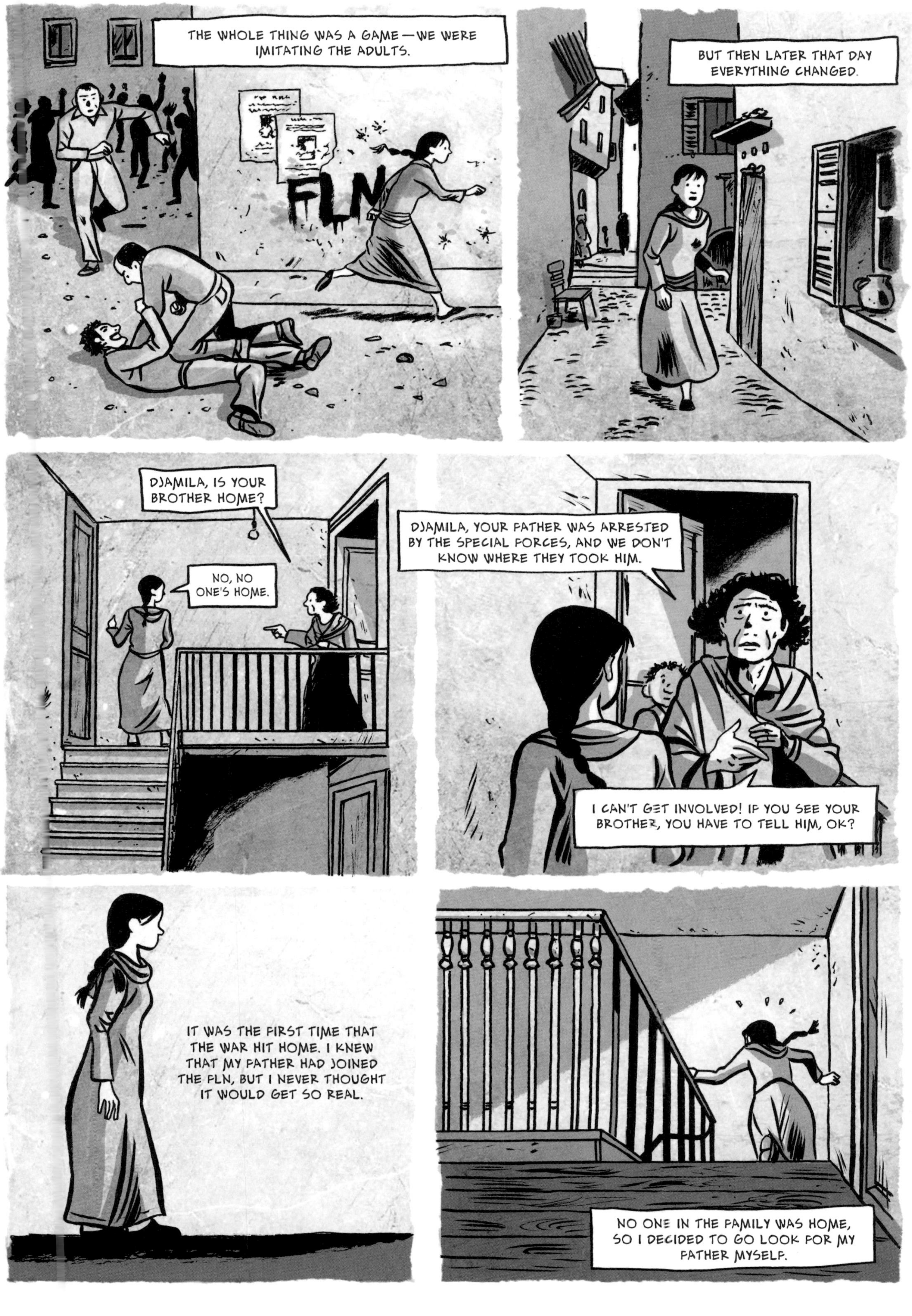

THE WHOLE THING WAS A GAME—WE WERE IMITATING THE ADULTS.
FLN
BUT THEN LATER THAT DAY EVERYTHING CHANGED.
DJAMILA, IS YOUR BROTHER HOME?
NO, NO ONE'S HOME.
DJAMILA, YOUR FATHER WAS ARRESTED BY THE SPECIAL FORCES, AND WE DON'T KNOW WHERE THEY TOOK HIM.
I CAN'T GET INVOLVED! IF YOU SEE YOUR BROTHER, YOU HAVE TO TELL HIM, OK?
IT WAS THE FIRST TIME THAT THE WAR HIT HOME. I KNEW THAT MY FATHER HAD JOINED THE FLN, BUT I NEVER THOUGHT IT WOULD GET SO REAL.
NO ONE IN THE FAMILY WAS HOME, SO I DECIDED TO GO LOOK FOR MY FATHER MYSELF.

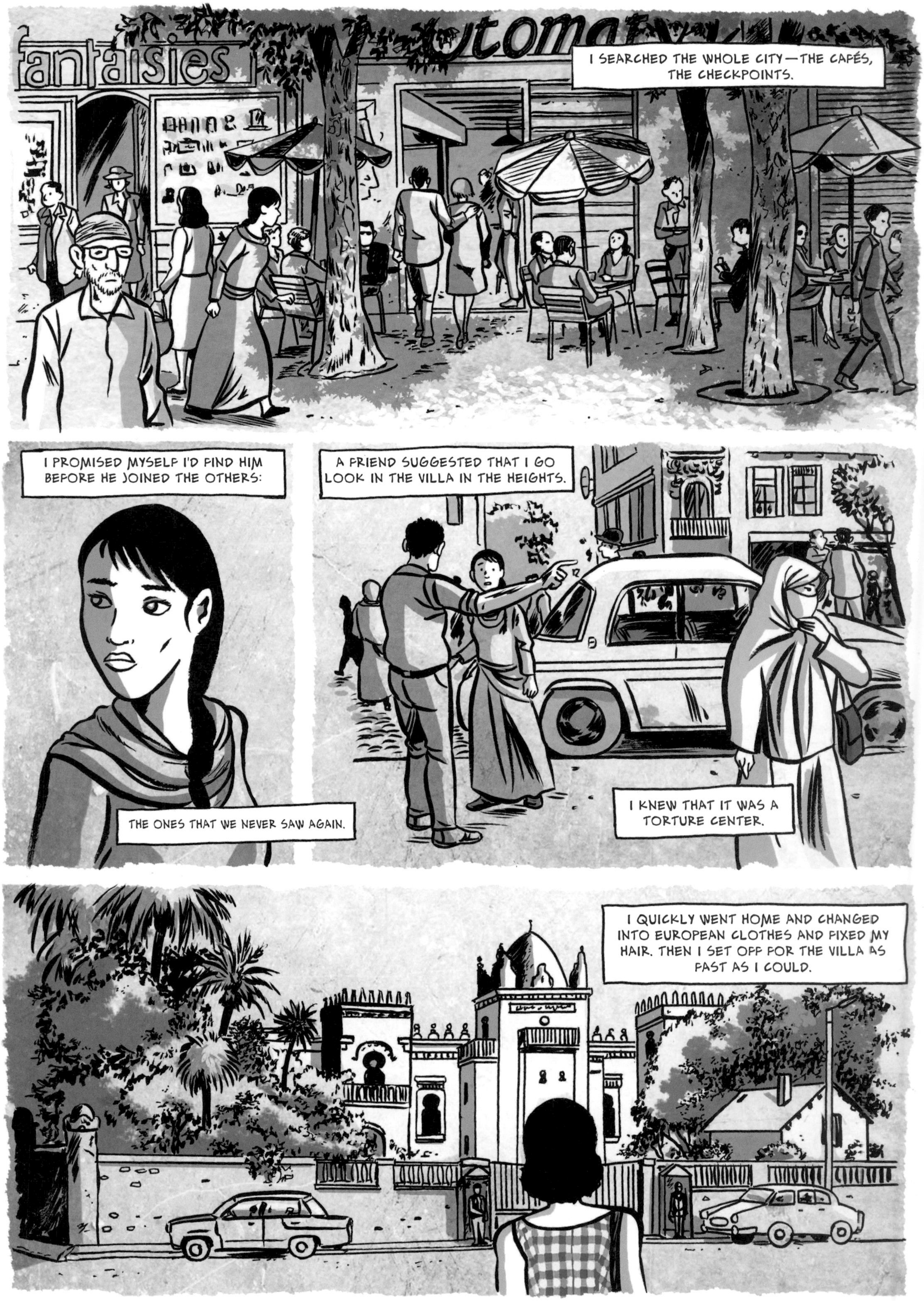
fantaisies
I SEARCHED THE WHOLE CITY—THE CAFÉS, THE CHECKPOINTS.
I PROMISED MYSELF I'D FIND HIM BEFORE HE JOINED THE OTHERS:
THE ONES THAT WE NEVER SAW AGAIN.
A FRIEND SUGGESTED THAT I GO LOOK IN THE VILLA IN THE HEIGHTS.
I KNEW THAT IT WAS A TORTURE CENTER.
I QUICKLY WENT HOME AND CHANGED INTO EUROPEAN CLOTHES AND FIXED MY HAIR. THEN I SET OFF FOR THE VILLA AS FAST AS I COULD.

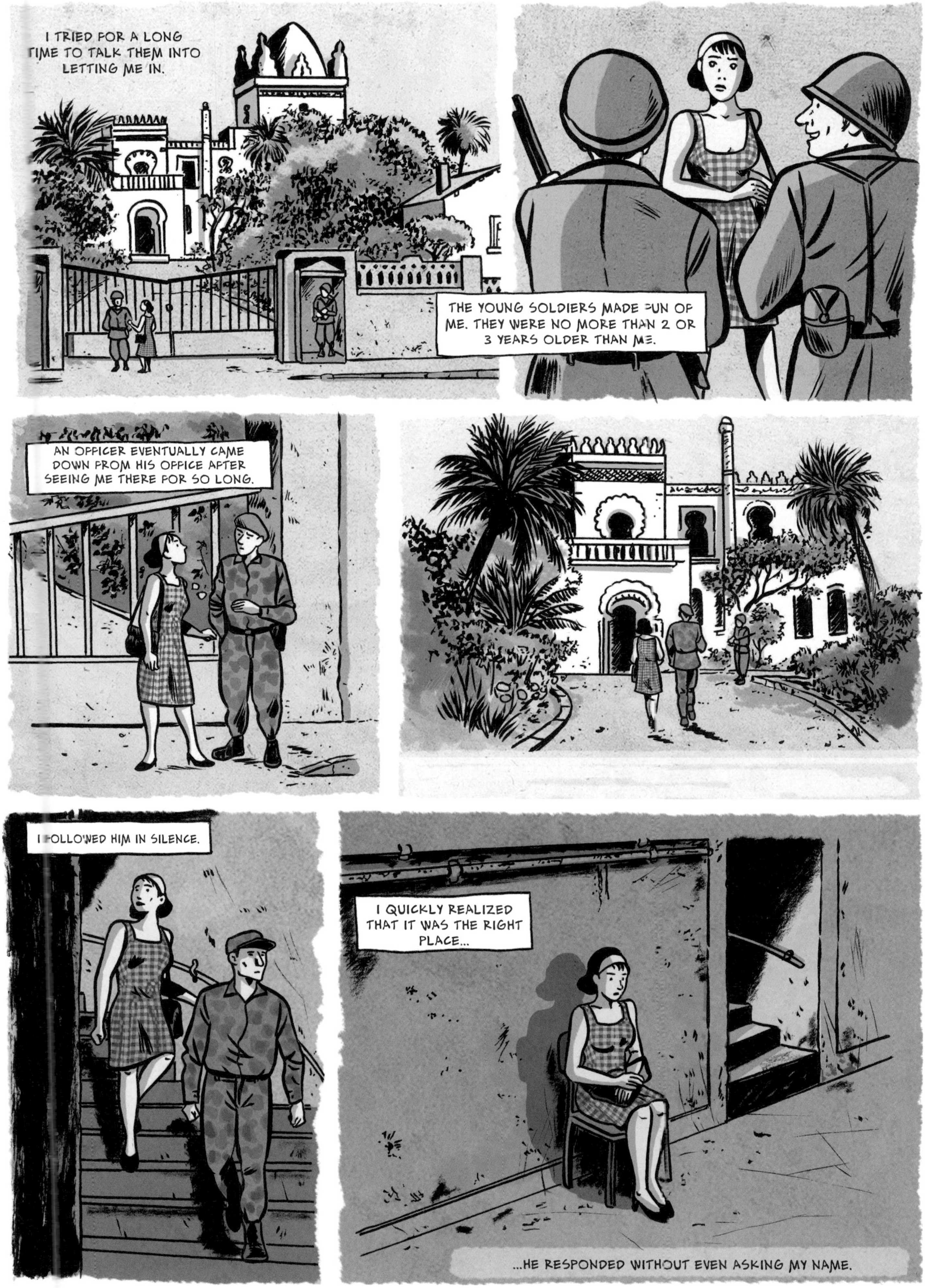
I TRIED FOR A LONG TIME TO TALK THEM INTO LETTING ME IN.
THE YOUNG SOLDIERS MADE FUN OF ME. THEY WERE NO MORE THAN 2 OR 3 YEARS OLDER THAN ME.
AN OFFICER EVENTUALLY CAME DOWN FROM HIS OFFICE AFTER SEEING ME THERE FOR SO LONG.
I FOLLOWED HIM IN SILENCE.
I QUICKLY REALIZED THAT IT WAS THE RIGHT PLACE...
...HE RESPONDED WITHOUT EVEN ASKING MY NAME.

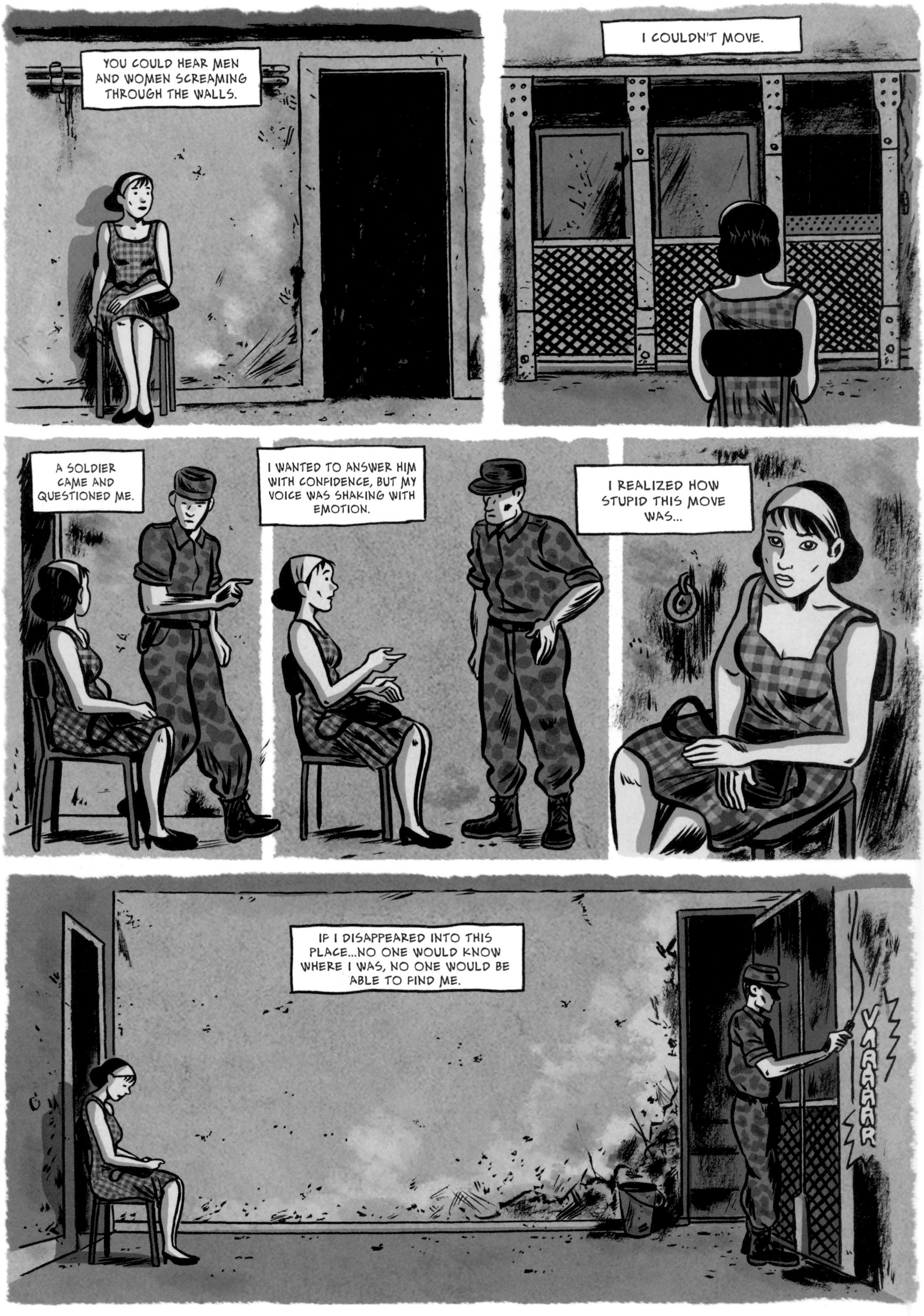
YOU COULD HEAR MEN AND WOMEN SCREAMING THROUGH THE WALLS.
I COULDN'T MOVE.
A SOLDIER CAME AND QUESTIONED ME.
I WANTED TO ANSWER HIM WITH CONFIDENCE, BUT MY VOICE WAS SHAKING WITH EMOTION.
I REALIZED HOW STUPID THIS MOVE WAS...
IF I DISAPPEARED INTO THIS PLACE...NO ONE WOULD KNOW WHERE I WAS, NO ONE WOULD BE ABLE TO FIND ME.
VRRRRRRR

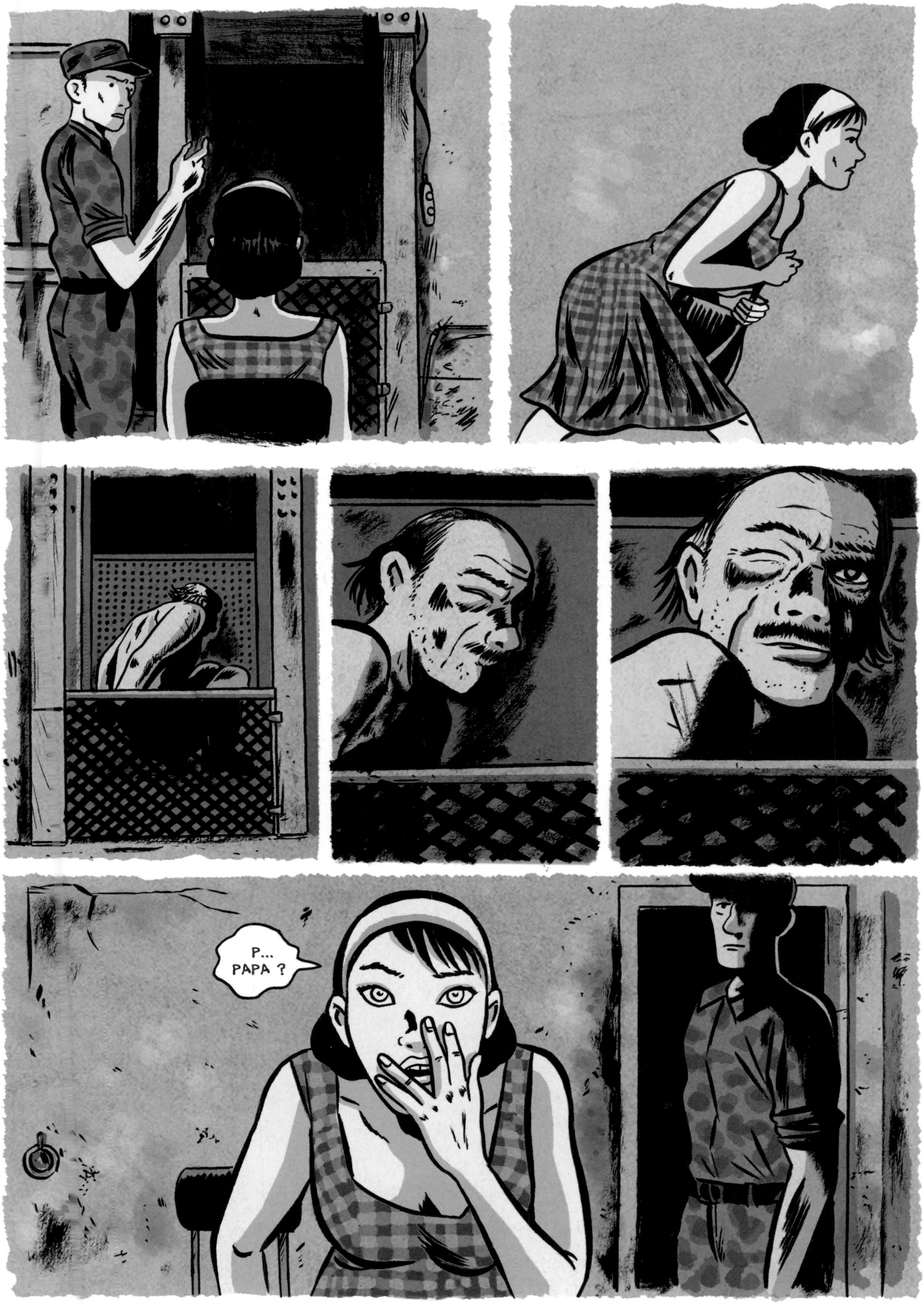
P...
PAPA ?

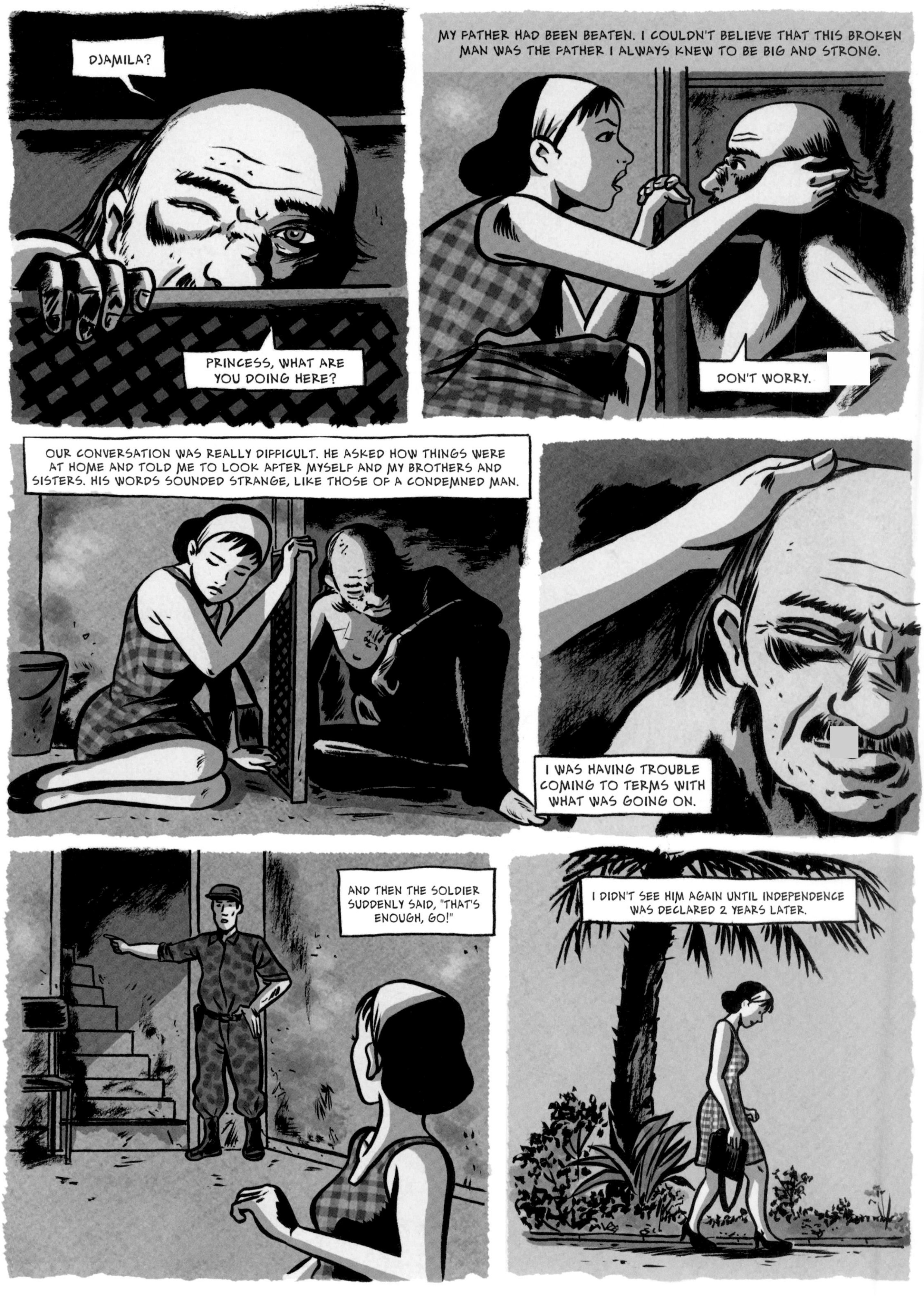
DJAMILA?
PRINCESS, WHAT ARE YOU DOING HERE?
MY FATHER HAD BEEN BEATEN. I COULDN'T BELIEVE THAT THIS BROKEN MAN WAS THE FATHER I ALWAYS KNEW TO BE BIG AND STRONG.
DON'T WORRY.
OUR CONVERSATION WAS REALLY DIFFICULT. HE ASKED HOW THINGS WERE AT HOME AND TOLD ME TO LOOK AFTER MYSELF AND MY BROTHERS AND SISTERS. HIS WORDS SOUNDED STRANGE, LIKE THOSE OF A CONDEMNED MAN.
I WAS HAVING TROUBLE COMING TO TERMS WITH WHAT WAS GOING ON.
AND THEN THE SOLDIER SUDDENLY SAID, "THAT'S ENOUGH, GO!"
I DIDN'T SEE HIM AGAIN UNTIL INDEPENDENCE WAS DECLARED 2 YEARS LATER.

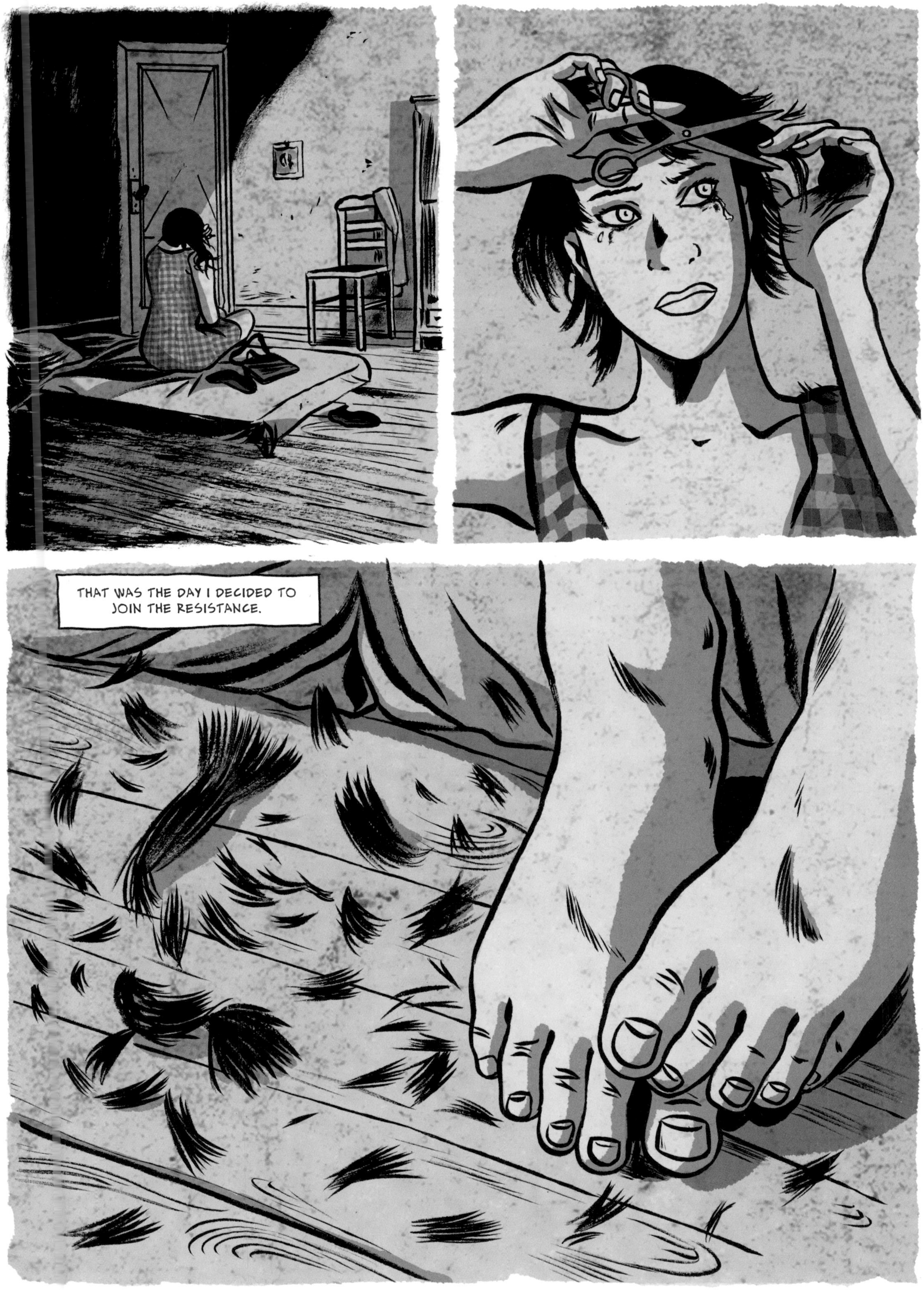
THAT WAS THE DAY I DECIDED TO
JOIN THE RESISTANCE.

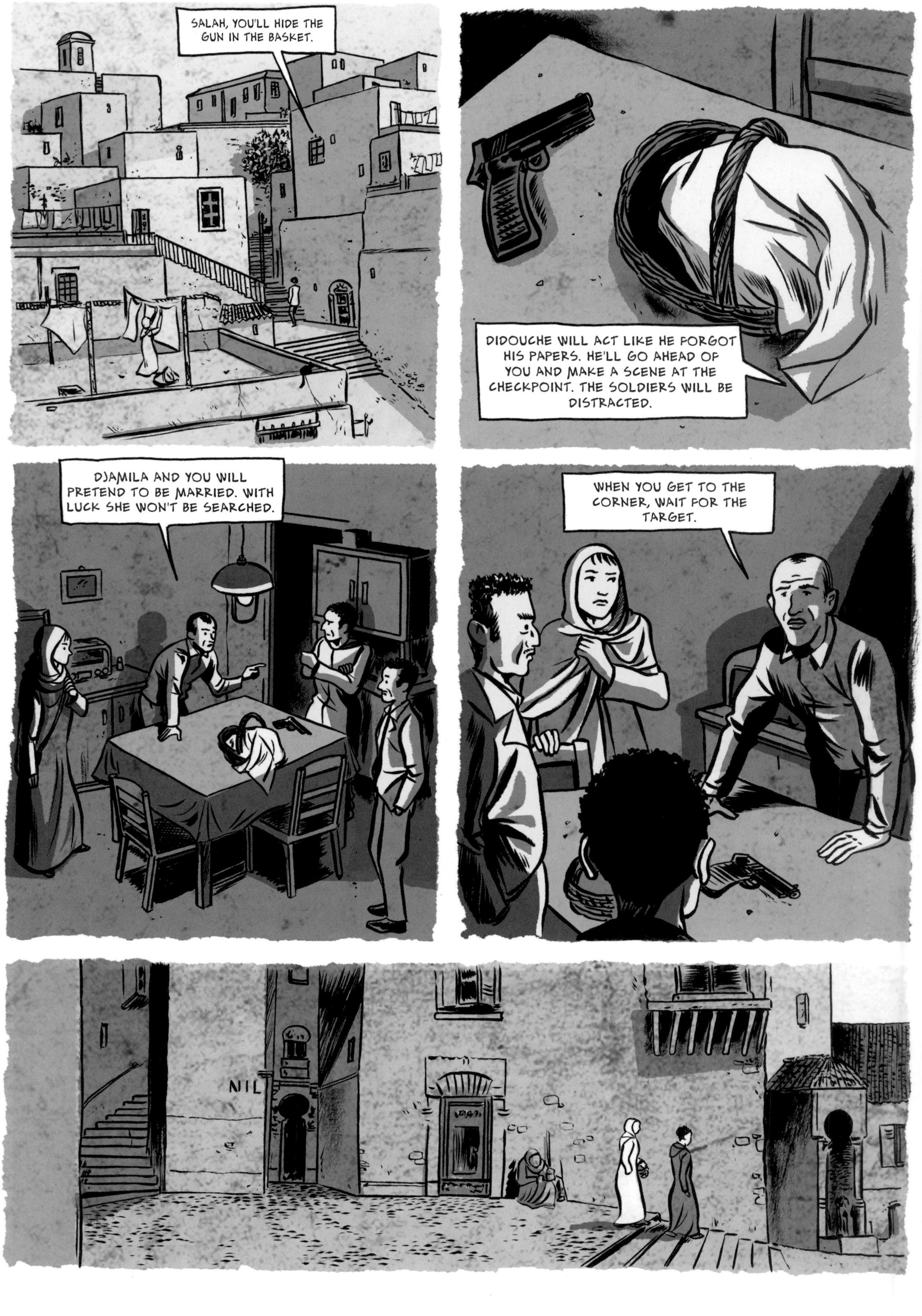
SALAH, YOU'LL HIDE THE GUN IN THE BASKET.
DIDOUCHE WILL ACT LIKE HE FORGOT HIS PAPERS. HE'LL GO AHEAD OF YOU AND MAKE A SCENE AT THE CHECKPOINT. THE SOLDIERS WILL BE DISTRACTED.
DJAMILA AND YOU WILL PRETEND TO BE MARRIED. WITH LUCK SHE WON'T BE SEARCHED.
WHEN YOU GET TO THE CORNER, WAIT FOR THE TARGET.
NIL

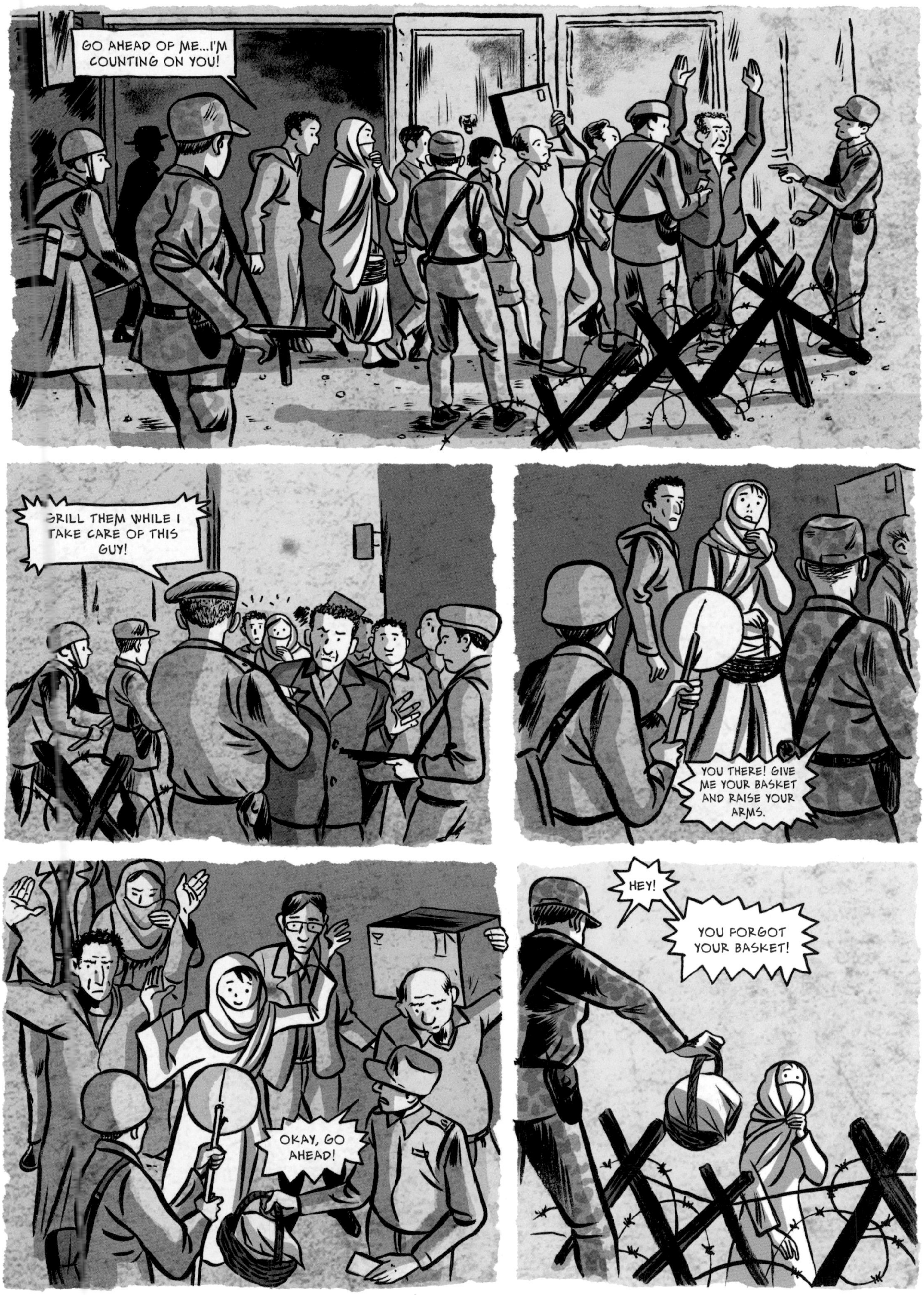
GO AHEAD OF ME...I'M COUNTING ON YOU!
GRILL THEM WHILE I TAKE CARE OF THIS GUY!
YOU THERE! GIVE ME YOUR BASKET AND RAISE YOUR ARMS.
OKAY, GO AHEAD!
HEY!
YOU FORGOT YOUR BASKET!

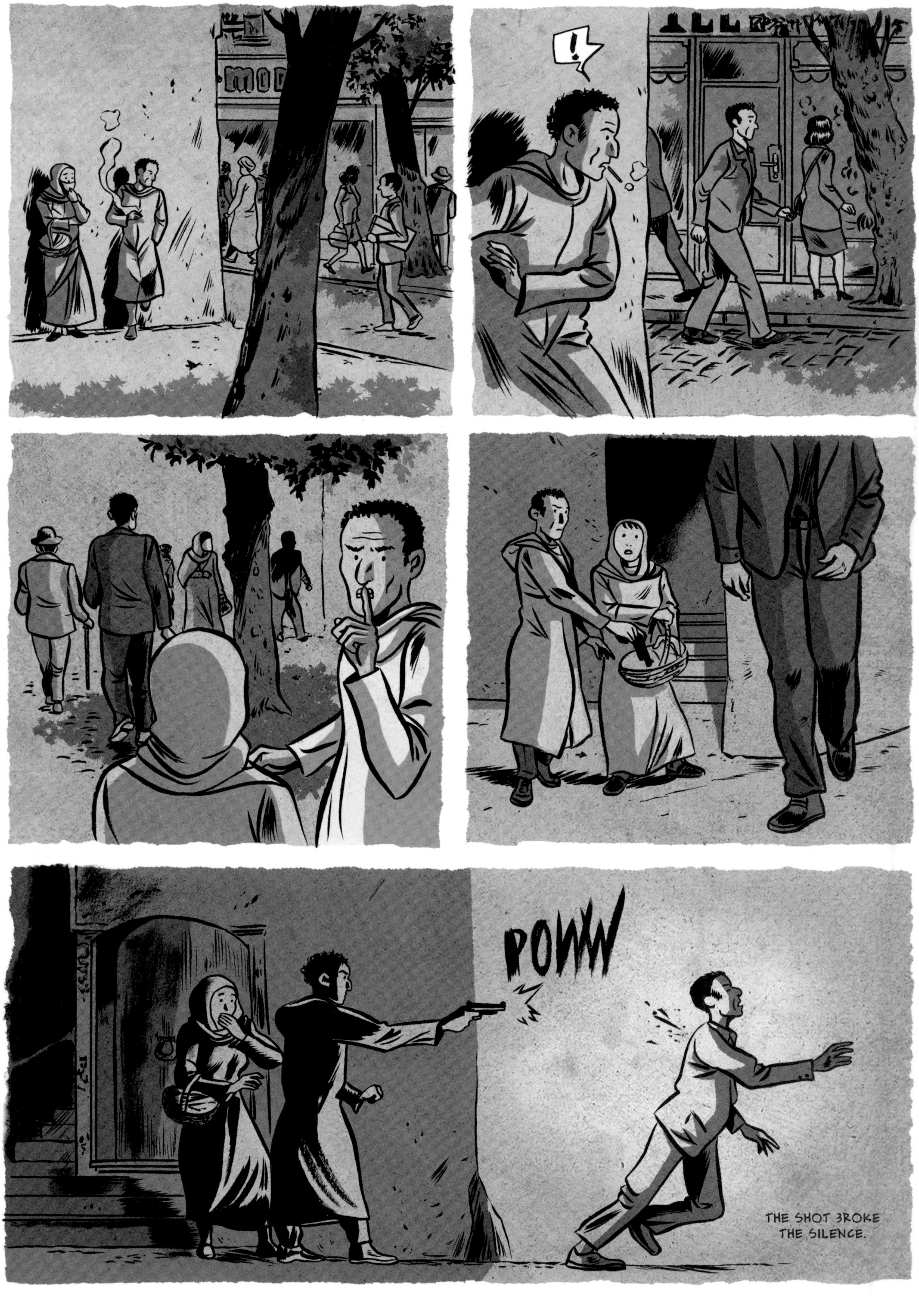
!
POWW
THE SHOT BROKE
THE SILENCE.

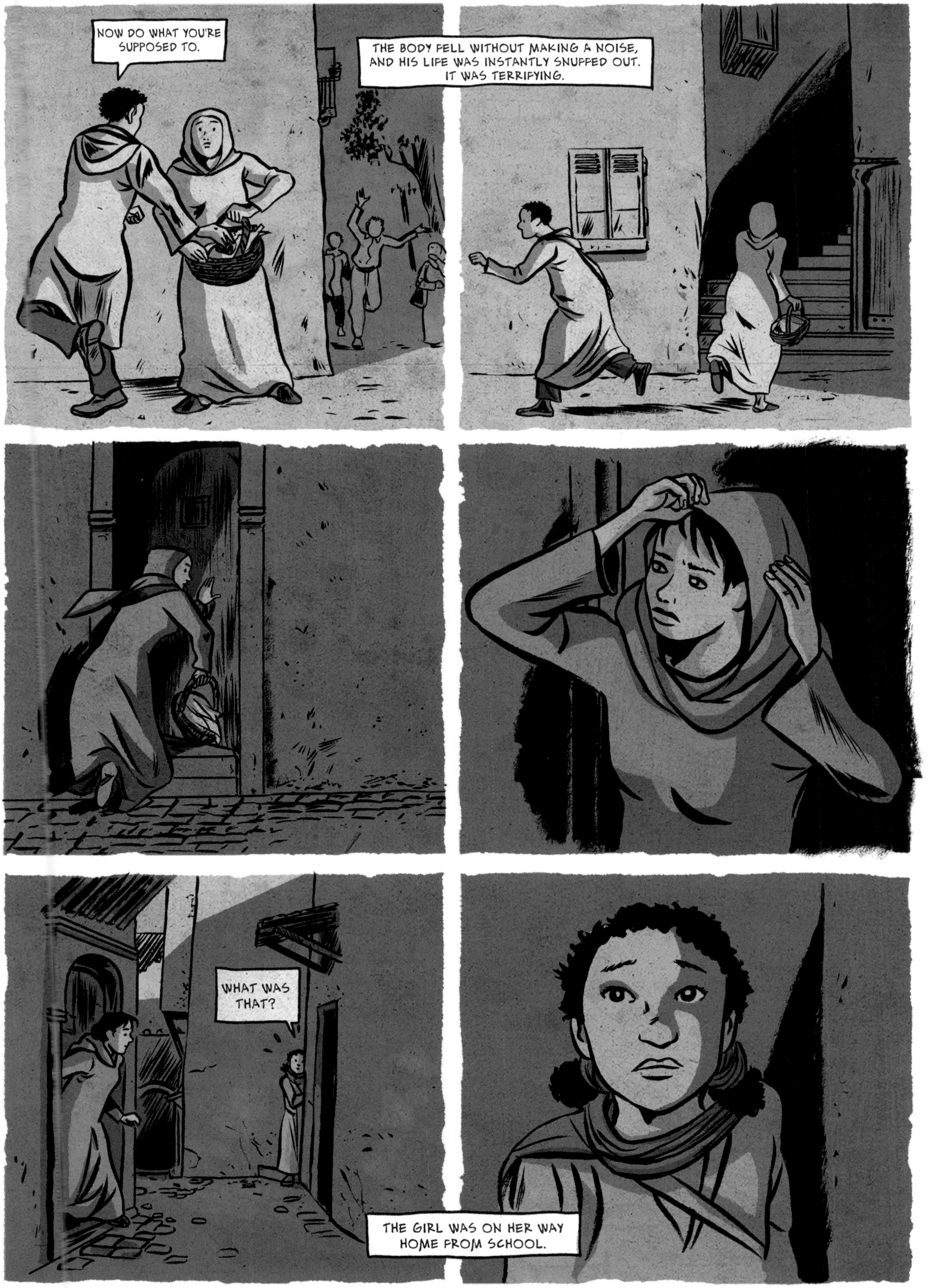
NOW DO WHAT YOU'RE SUPPOSED TO.
THE BODY FELL WITHOUT MAKING A NOISE, AND HIS LIFE WAS INSTANTLY SNUFFED OUT. IT WAS TERRIFYING.
WHAT WAS THAT?
THE GIRL WAS ON HER WAY HOME FROM SCHOOL.

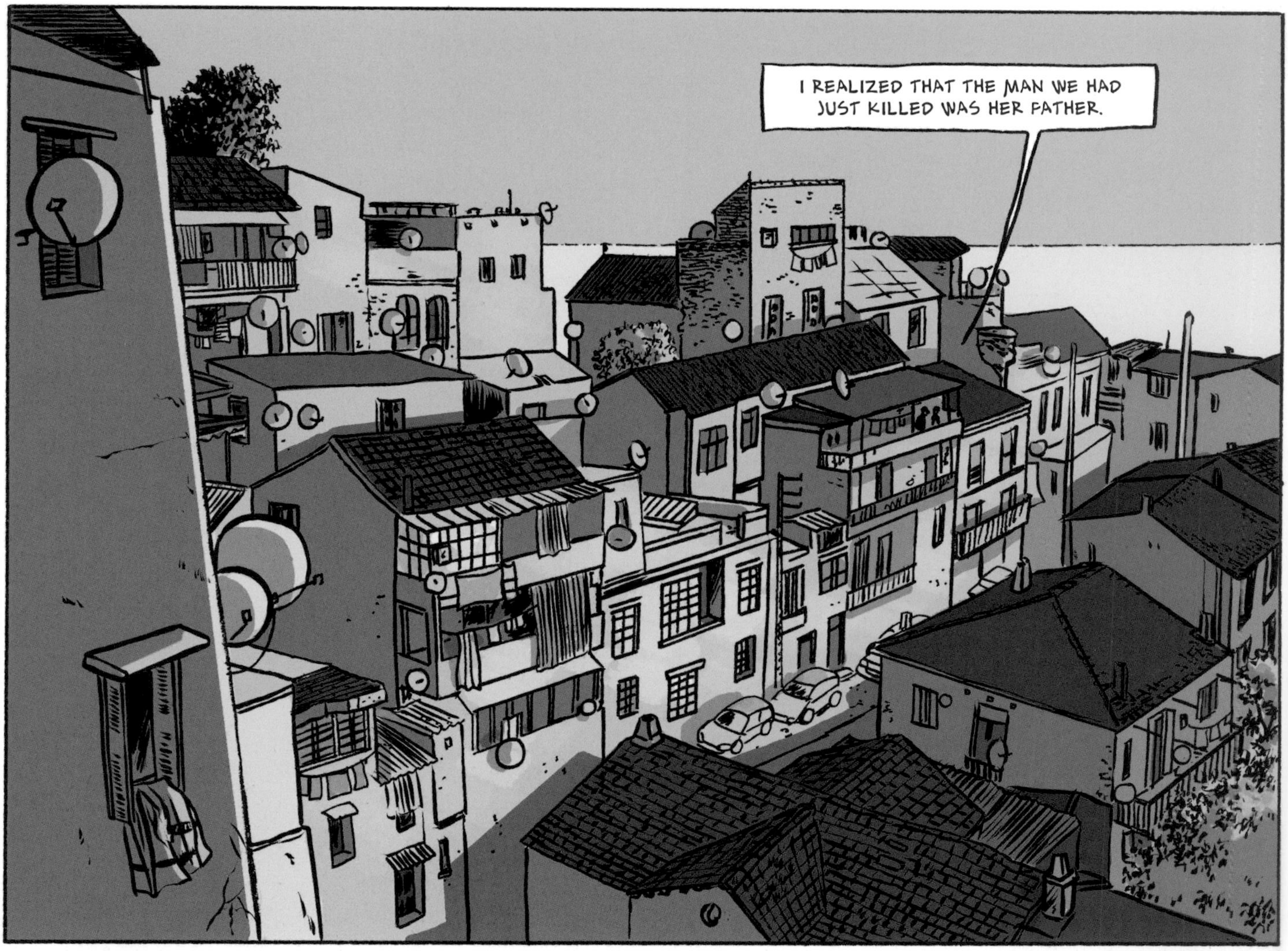
I REALIZED THAT THE MAN WE HAD JUST KILLED WAS HER FATHER.

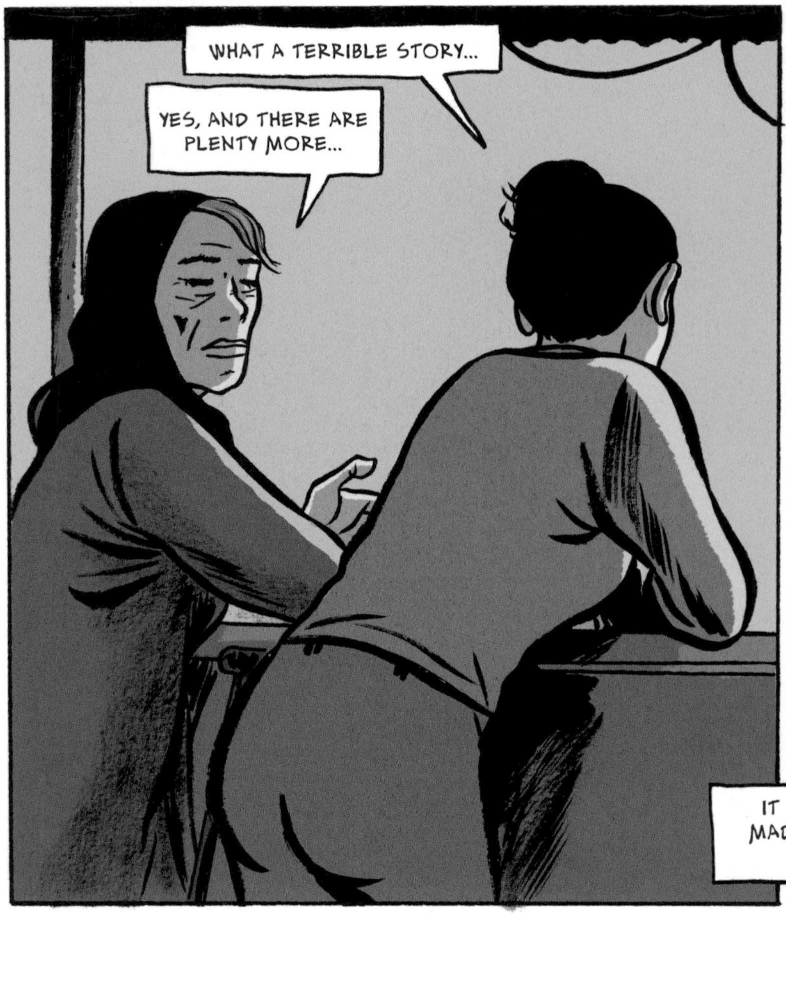
WHAT A TERRIBLE STORY...
YES, AND THERE ARE PLENTY MORE...

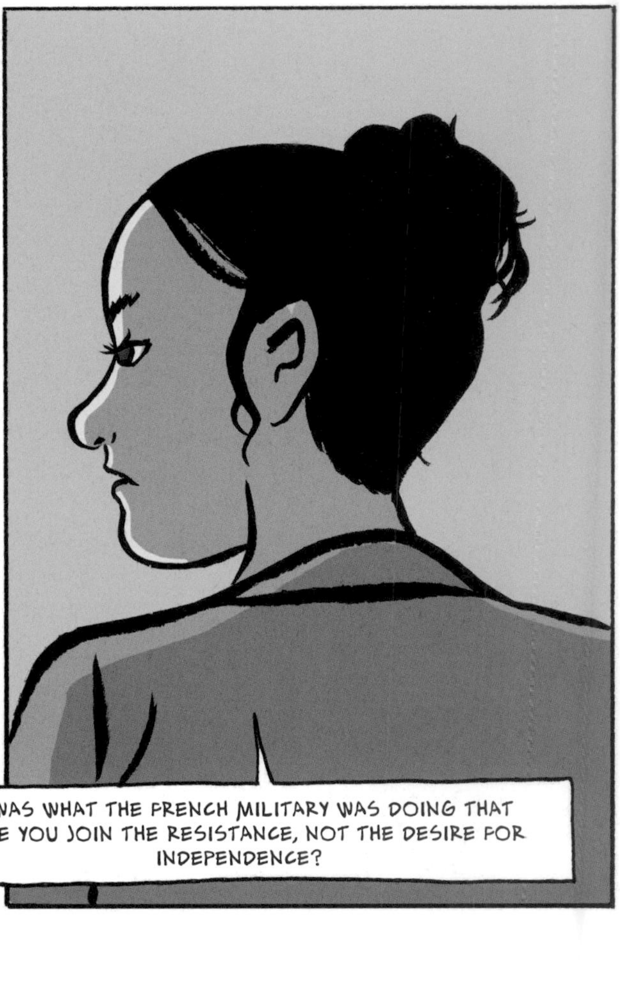
IT WAS WHAT THE FRENCH MILITARY WAS DOING THAT MADE YOU JOIN THE RESISTANCE, NOT THE DESIRE FOR INDEPENDENCE?

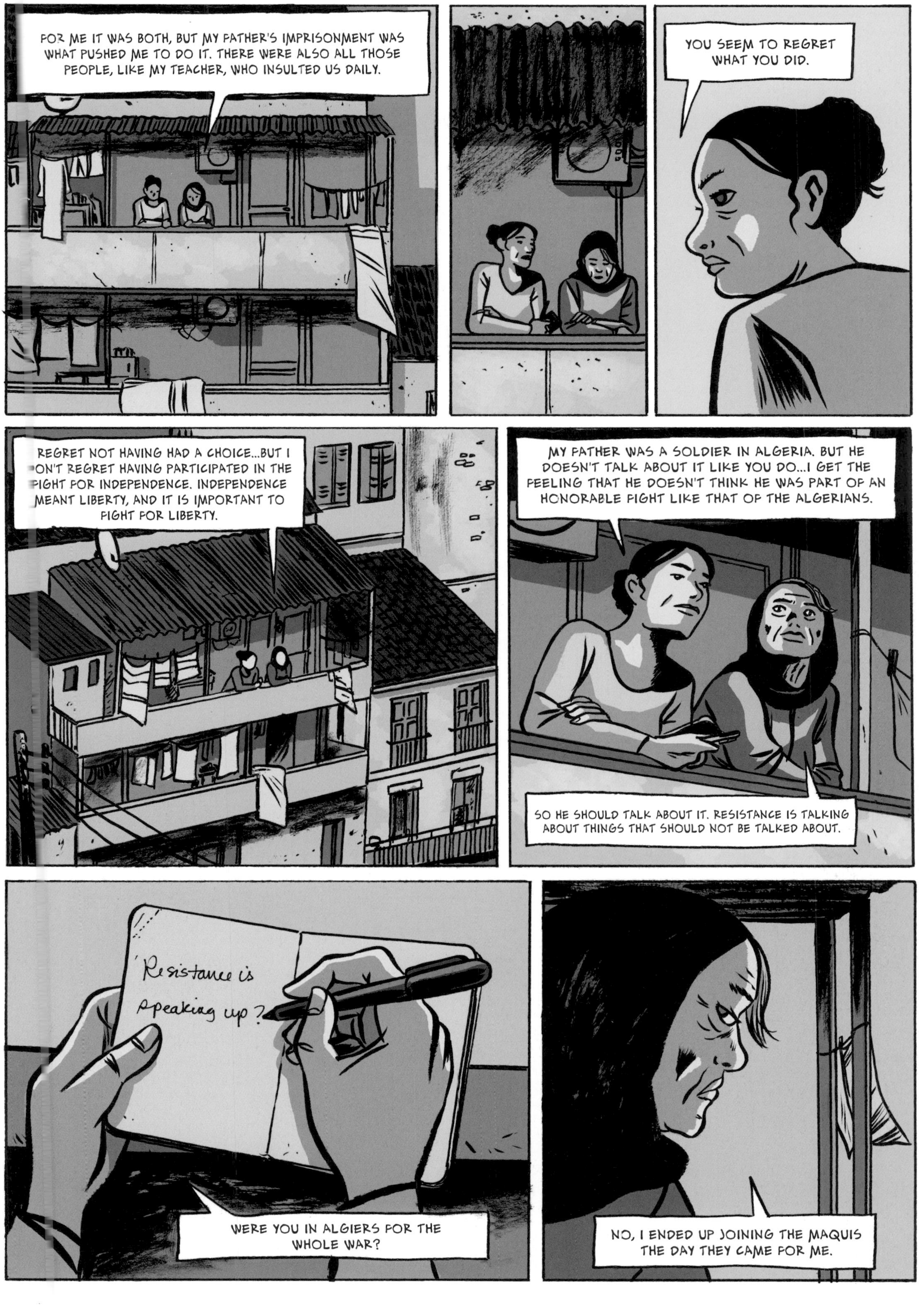
FOR ME IT WAS BOTH, BUT MY FATHER'S IMPRISONMENT WAS WHAT PUSHED ME TO DO IT. THERE WERE ALSO ALL THOSE PEOPLE, LIKE MY TEACHER, WHO INSULTED US DAILY.
YOU SEEM TO REGRET WHAT YOU DID.
I REGRET NOT HAVING HAD A CHOICE...BUT I DON'T REGRET HAVING PARTICIPATED IN THE FIGHT FOR INDEPENDENCE. INDEPENDENCE MEANT LIBERTY, AND IT IS IMPORTANT TO FIGHT FOR LIBERTY.
MY FATHER WAS A SOLDIER IN ALGERIA. BUT HE DOESN'T TALK ABOUT IT LIKE YOU DO...I GET THE FEELING THAT HE DOESN'T THINK HE WAS PART OF AN HONORABLE FIGHT LIKE THAT OF THE ALGERIANS.
SO HE SHOULD TALK ABOUT IT. RESISTANCE IS TALKING ABOUT THINGS THAT SHOULD NOT BE TALKED ABOUT.
Resistance is
speaking up?
WERE YOU IN ALGIERS FOR THE WHOLE WAR?
NO, I ENDED UP JOINING THE MAQUIS THE DAY THEY CAME FOR ME.

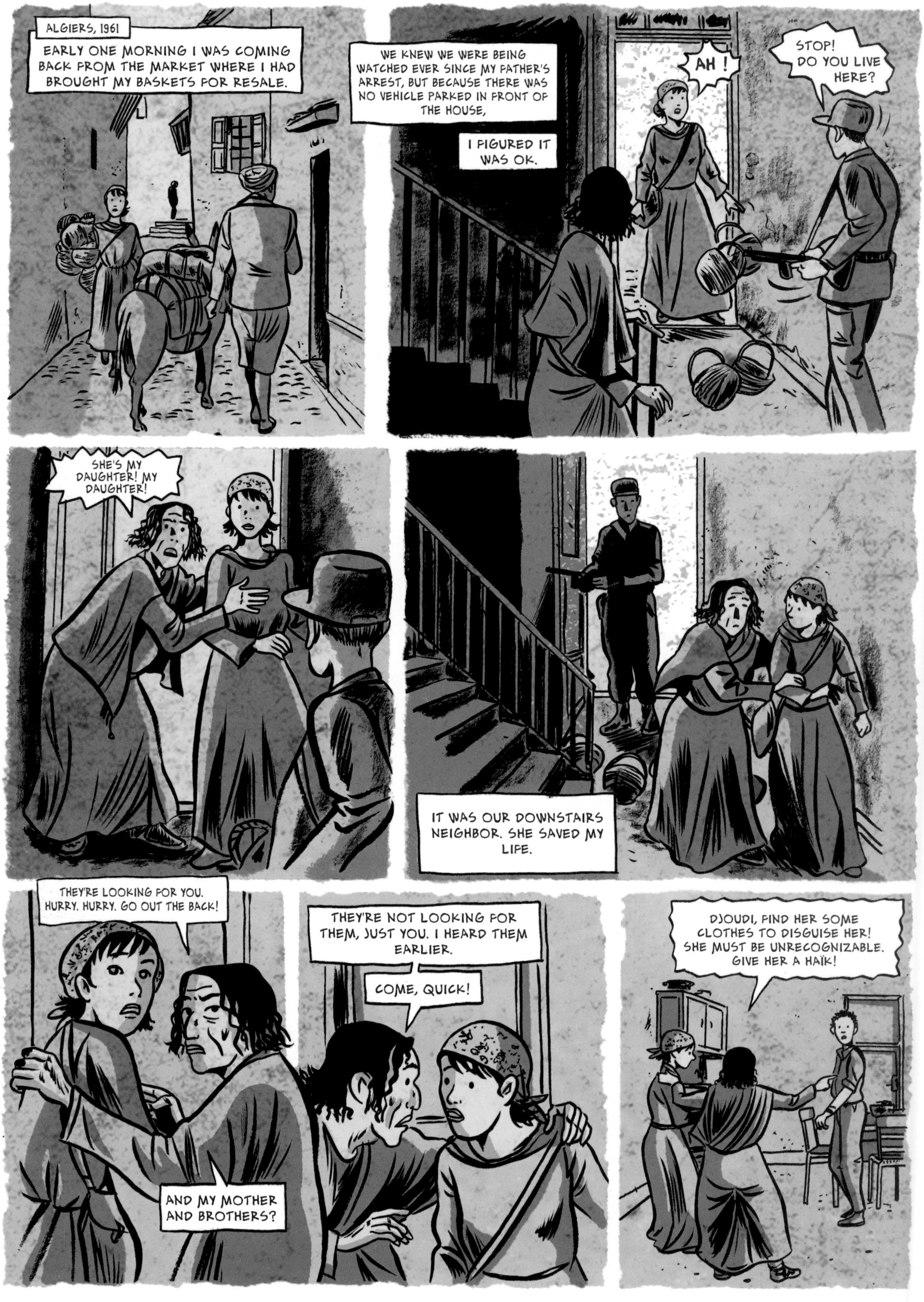
ALGIERS, 1961
EARLY ONE MORNING I WAS COMING BACK FROM THE MARKET WHERE I HAD BROUGHT MY BASKETS FOR RESALE.
WE KNEW WE WERE BEING WATCHED EVER SINCE MY FATHER'S ARREST, BUT BECAUSE THERE WAS NO VEHICLE PARKED IN FRONT OF THE HOUSE,
I FIGURED IT WAS OK.
AH !
STOP! DO YOU LIVE HERE?
SHE'S MY DAUGHTER! MY DAUGHTER!
IT WAS OUR DOWNSTAIRS NEIGHBOR. SHE SAVED MY LIFE.
THEY'RE LOOKING FOR YOU. HURRY. HURRY. GO OUT THE BACK!
AND MY MOTHER AND BROTHERS?
THEY'RE NOT LOOKING FOR THEM, JUST YOU. I HEARD THEM EARLIER.
COME, QUICK!
DJOUDI, FIND HER SOME CLOTHES TO DISGUISE HER! SHE MUST BE UNRECOGNIZABLE. GIVE HER A HAÏK!

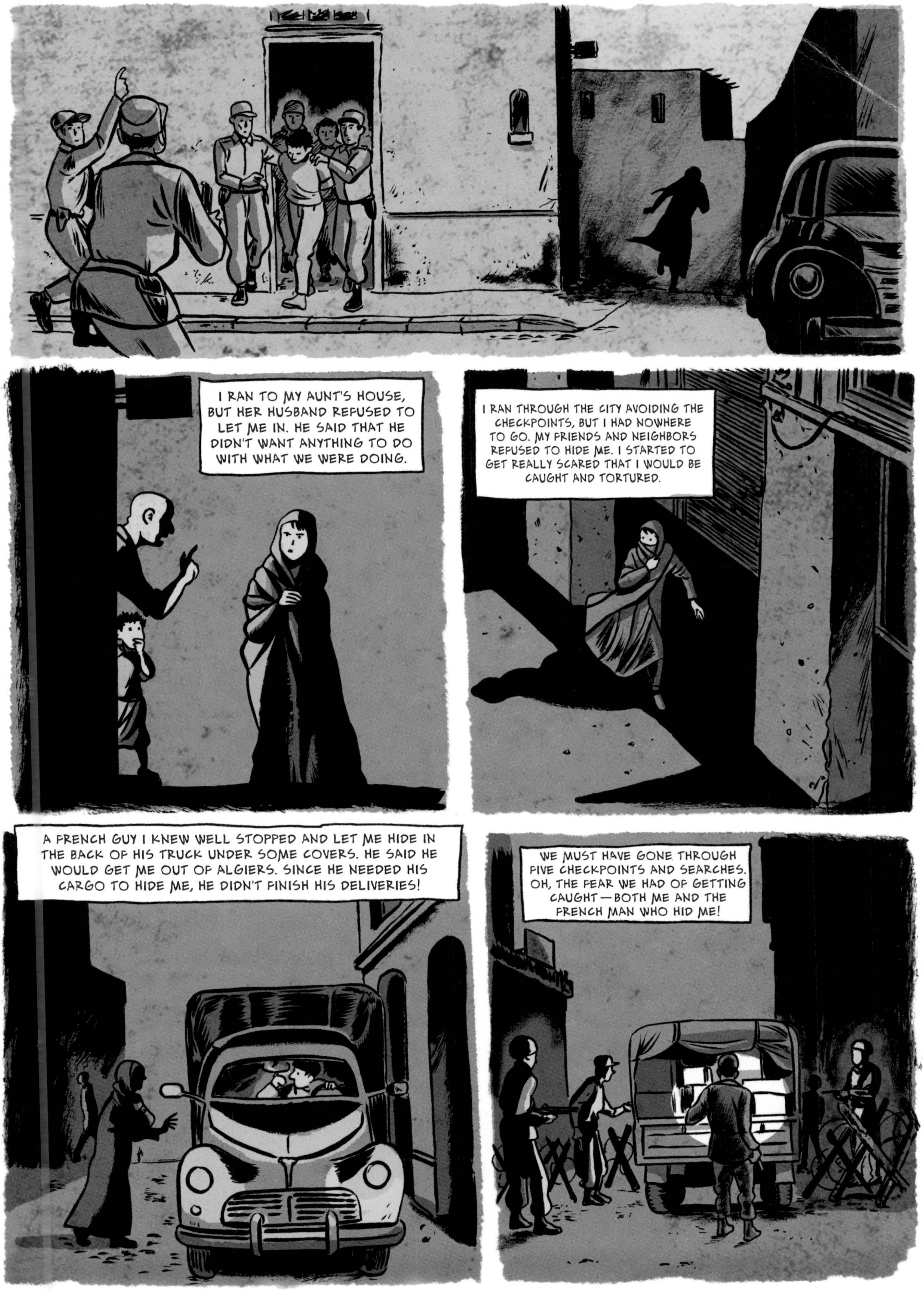
I RAN TO MY AUNT'S HOUSE, BUT HER HUSBAND REFUSED TO LET ME IN. HE SAID THAT HE DIDN'T WANT ANYTHING TO DO WITH WHAT WE WERE DOING.
I RAN THROUGH THE CITY AVOIDING THE CHECKPOINTS, BUT I HAD NOWHERE TO GO. MY FRIENDS AND NEIGHBORS REFUSED TO HIDE ME. I STARTED TO GET REALLY SCARED THAT I WOULD BE CAUGHT AND TORTURED.
A FRENCH GUY I KNEW WELL STOPPED AND LET ME HIDE IN THE BACK OF HIS TRUCK UNDER SOME COVERS. HE SAID HE WOULD GET ME OUT OF ALGIERS. SINCE HE NEEDED HIS CARGO TO HIDE ME, HE DIDN'T FINISH HIS DELIVERIES!
WE MUST HAVE GONE THROUGH FIVE CHECKPOINTS AND SEARCHES. OH, THE FEAR WE HAD OF GETTING CAUGHT—BOTH ME AND THE FRENCH MAN WHO HID ME!

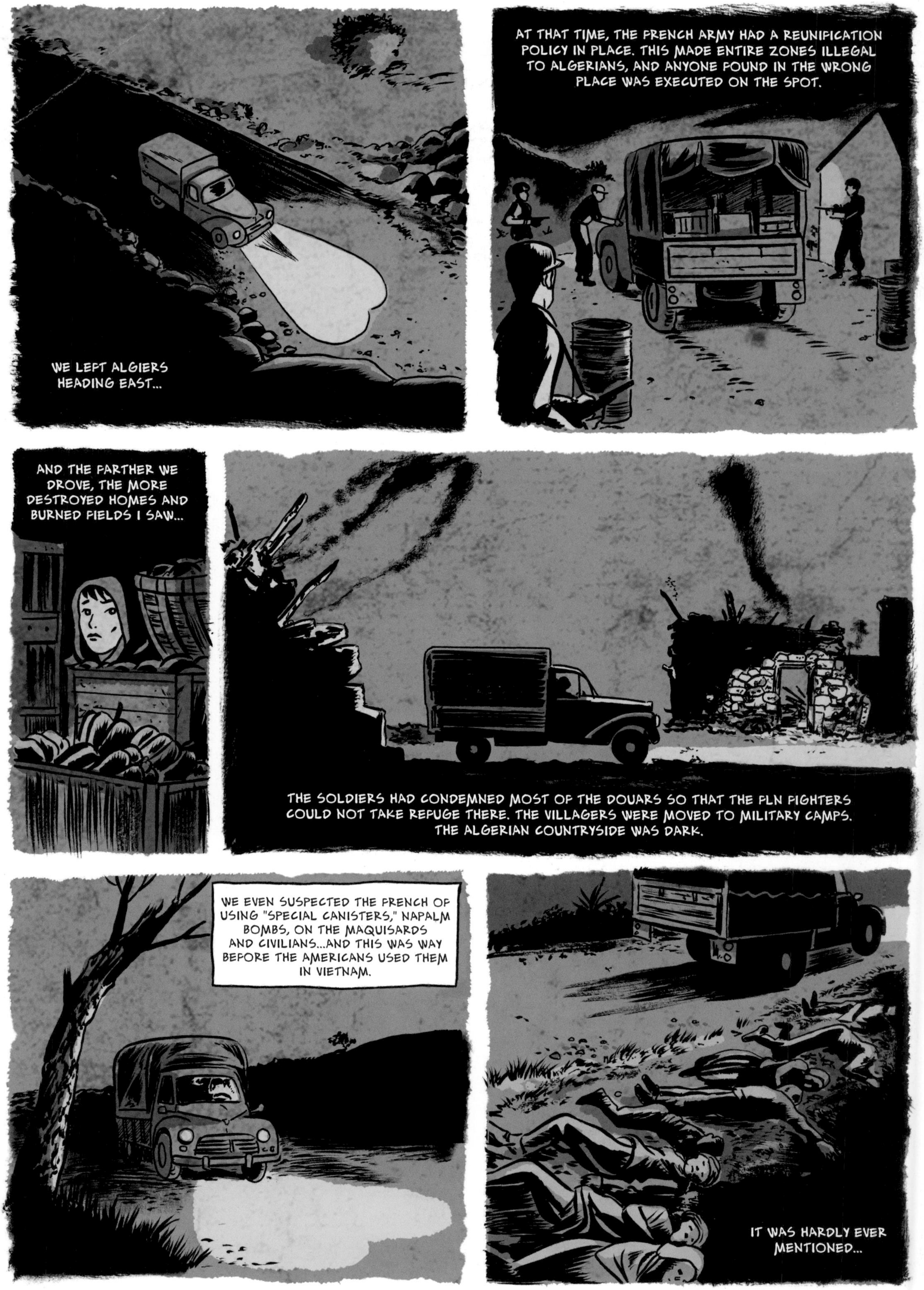
WE LEFT ALGIERS HEADING EAST...
AT THAT TIME, THE FRENCH ARMY HAD A REUNIFICATION POLICY IN PLACE. THIS MADE ENTIRE ZONES ILLEGAL TO ALGERIANS, AND ANYONE FOUND IN THE WRONG PLACE WAS EXECUTED ON THE SPOT.
AND THE FARTHER WE DROVE, THE MORE DESTROYED HOMES AND BURNED FIELDS I SAW...
THE SOLDIERS HAD CONDEMNED MOST OF THE DOUARS SO THAT THE FLN FIGHTERS COULD NOT TAKE REFUGE THERE. THE VILLAGERS WERE MOVED TO MILITARY CAMPS. THE ALGERIAN COUNTRYSIDE WAS DARK.
WE EVEN SUSPECTED THE FRENCH OF USING "SPECIAL CANISTERS," NAPALM BOMBS, ON THE MAQUISARDS AND CIVILIANS...AND THIS WAS WAY BEFORE THE AMERICANS USED THEM IN VIETNAM.
IT WAS HARDLY EVER MENTIONED...

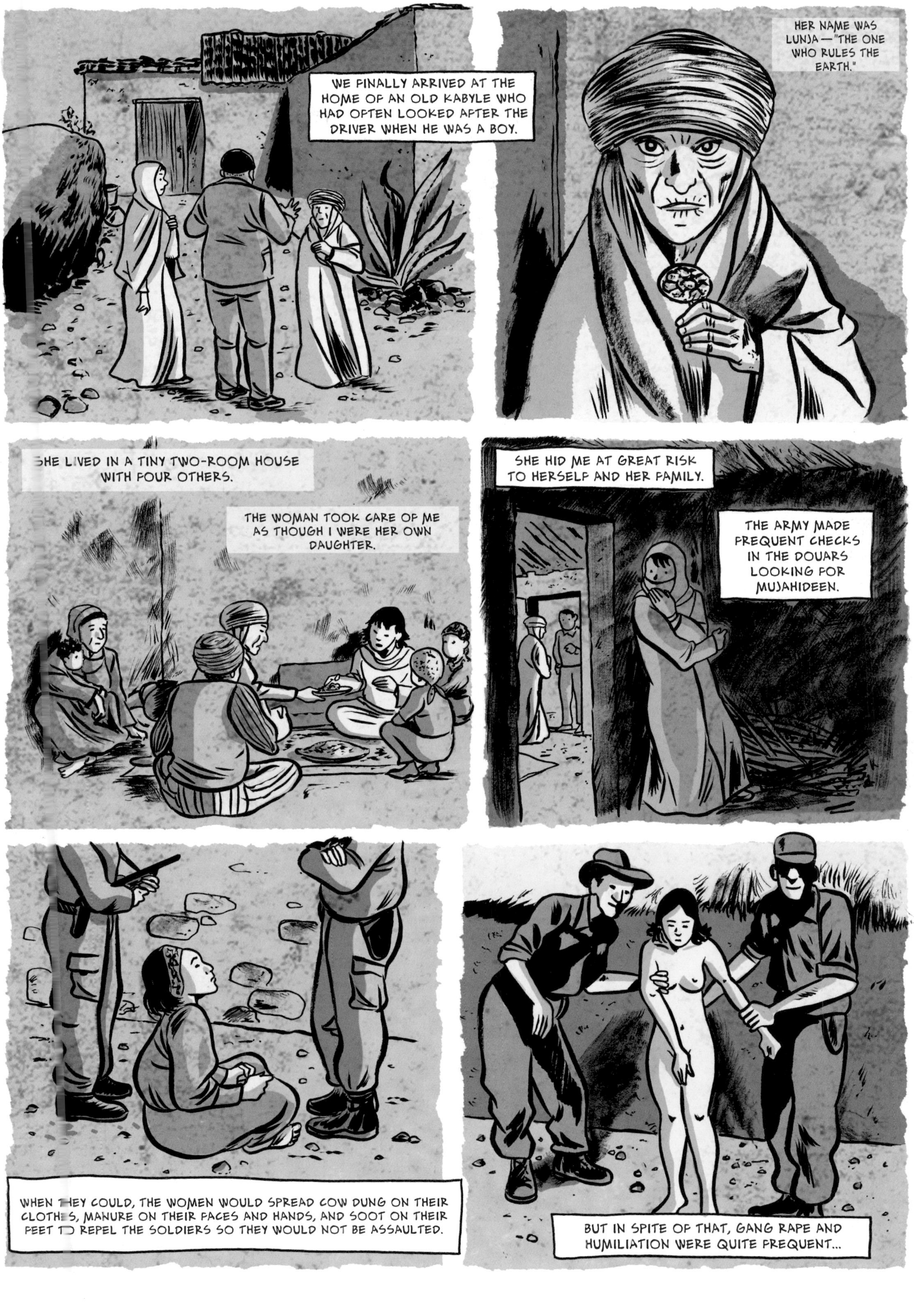
WE FINALLY ARRIVED AT THE HOME OF AN OLD KABYLE WHO HAD OFTEN LOOKED AFTER THE DRIVER WHEN HE WAS A BOY.
HER NAME WAS LUNJA — "THE ONE WHO RULES THE EARTH."
SHE LIVED IN A TINY TWO-ROOM HOUSE WITH FOUR OTHERS.
THE WOMAN TOOK CARE OF ME AS THOUGH I WERE HER OWN DAUGHTER.
SHE HID ME AT GREAT RISK TO HERSELF AND HER FAMILY.
THE ARMY MADE FREQUENT CHECKS IN THE DOUARS LOOKING FOR MUJAHIDEEN.
WHEN THEY COULD, THE WOMEN WOULD SPREAD COW DUNG ON THEIR CLOTHES, MANURE ON THEIR FACES AND HANDS, AND SOOT ON THEIR FEET TO REPEL THE SOLDIERS SO THEY WOULD NOT BE ASSAULTED.
BUT IN SPITE OF THAT, GANG RAPE AND HUMILIATION WERE QUITE FREQUENT...

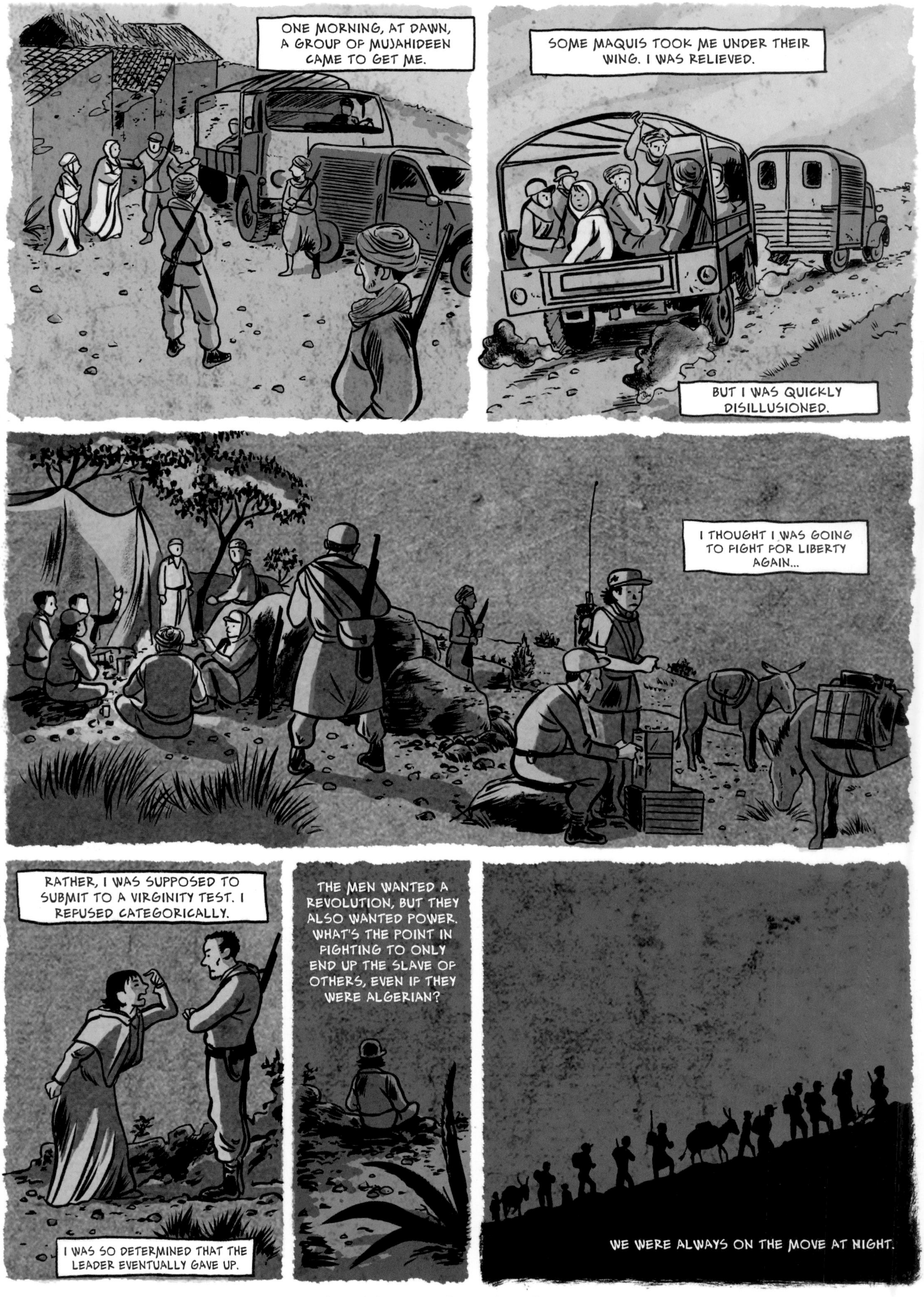

ONE MORNING, AT DAWN, A GROUP OF MUJAHIDEEN CAME TO GET ME.
SOME MAQUIS TOOK ME UNDER THEIR WING. I WAS RELIEVED.
BUT I WAS QUICKLY DISILLUSIONED.
I THOUGHT I WAS GOING TO FIGHT FOR LIBERTY AGAIN...
RATHER, I WAS SUPPOSED TO SUBMIT TO A VIRGINITY TEST. I REFUSED CATEGORICALLY.
I WAS SO DETERMINED THAT THE LEADER EVENTUALLY GAVE UP.
THE MEN WANTED A REVOLUTION, BUT THEY ALSO WANTED POWER. WHAT'S THE POINT IN FIGHTING TO ONLY END UP THE SLAVE OF OTHERS, EVEN IF THEY WERE ALGERIAN?
WE WERE ALWAYS ON THE MOVE AT NIGHT.

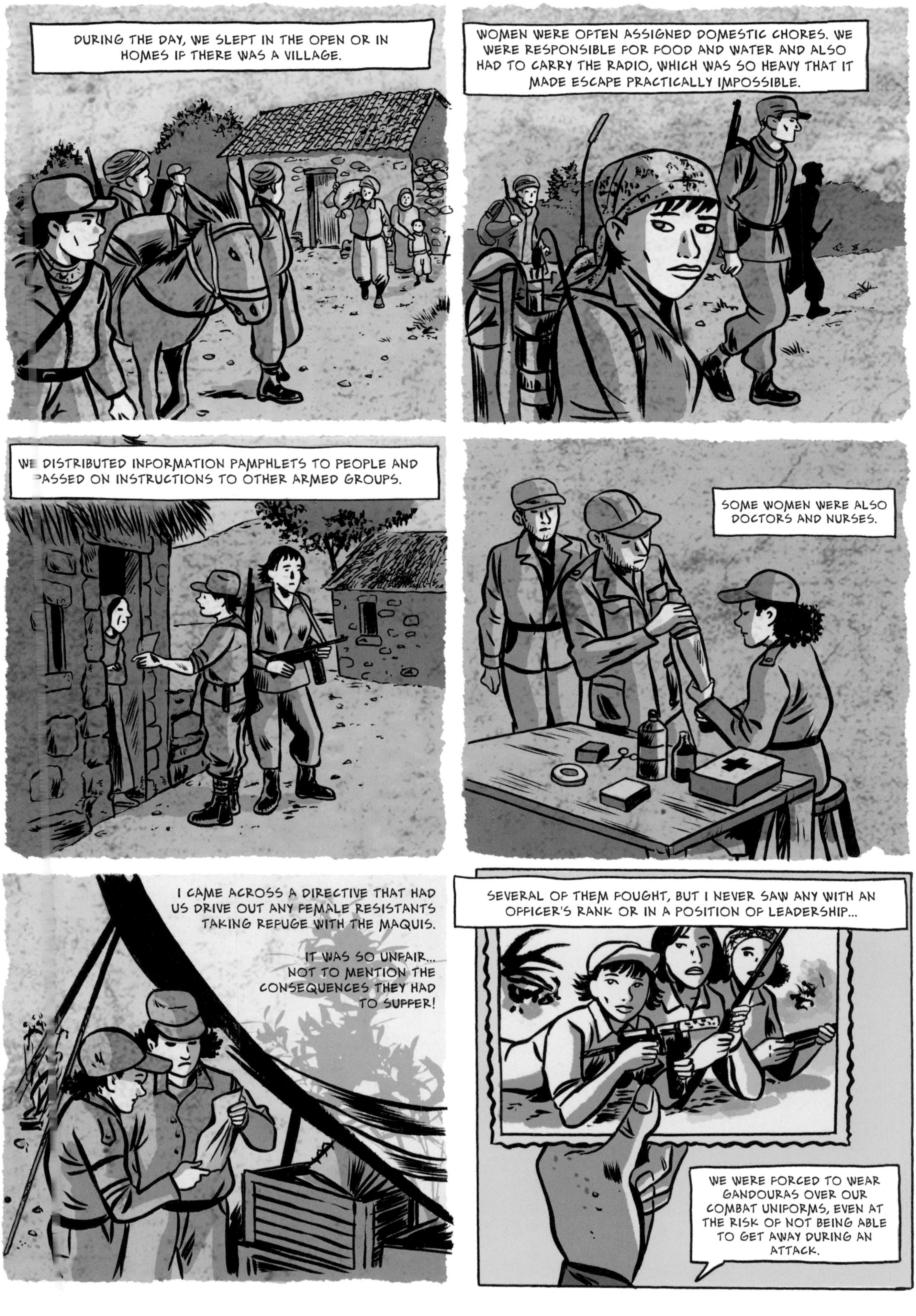

DURING THE DAY, WE SLEPT IN THE OPEN OR IN HOMES IF THERE WAS A VILLAGE.
WOMEN WERE OFTEN ASSIGNED DOMESTIC CHORES. WE WERE RESPONSIBLE FOR FOOD AND WATER AND ALSO HAD TO CARRY THE RADIO, WHICH WAS SO HEAVY THAT IT MADE ESCAPE PRACTICALLY IMPOSSIBLE.
WE DISTRIBUTED INFORMATION PAMPHLETS TO PEOPLE AND PASSED ON INSTRUCTIONS TO OTHER ARMED GROUPS.
SOME WOMEN WERE ALSO DOCTORS AND NURSES.
I CAME ACROSS A DIRECTIVE THAT HAD US DRIVE OUT ANY FEMALE RESISTANTS TAKING REFUGE WITH THE MAQUIS.
IT WAS SO UNFAIR... NOT TO MENTION THE CONSEQUENCES THEY HAD TO SUFFER!
SEVERAL OF THEM FOUGHT, BUT I NEVER SAW ANY WITH AN OFFICER'S RANK OR IN A POSITION OF LEADERSHIP...
WE WERE FORCED TO WEAR GANDOURAS OVER OUR COMBAT UNIFORMS, EVEN AT THE RISK OF NOT BEING ABLE TO GET AWAY DURING AN ATTACK.

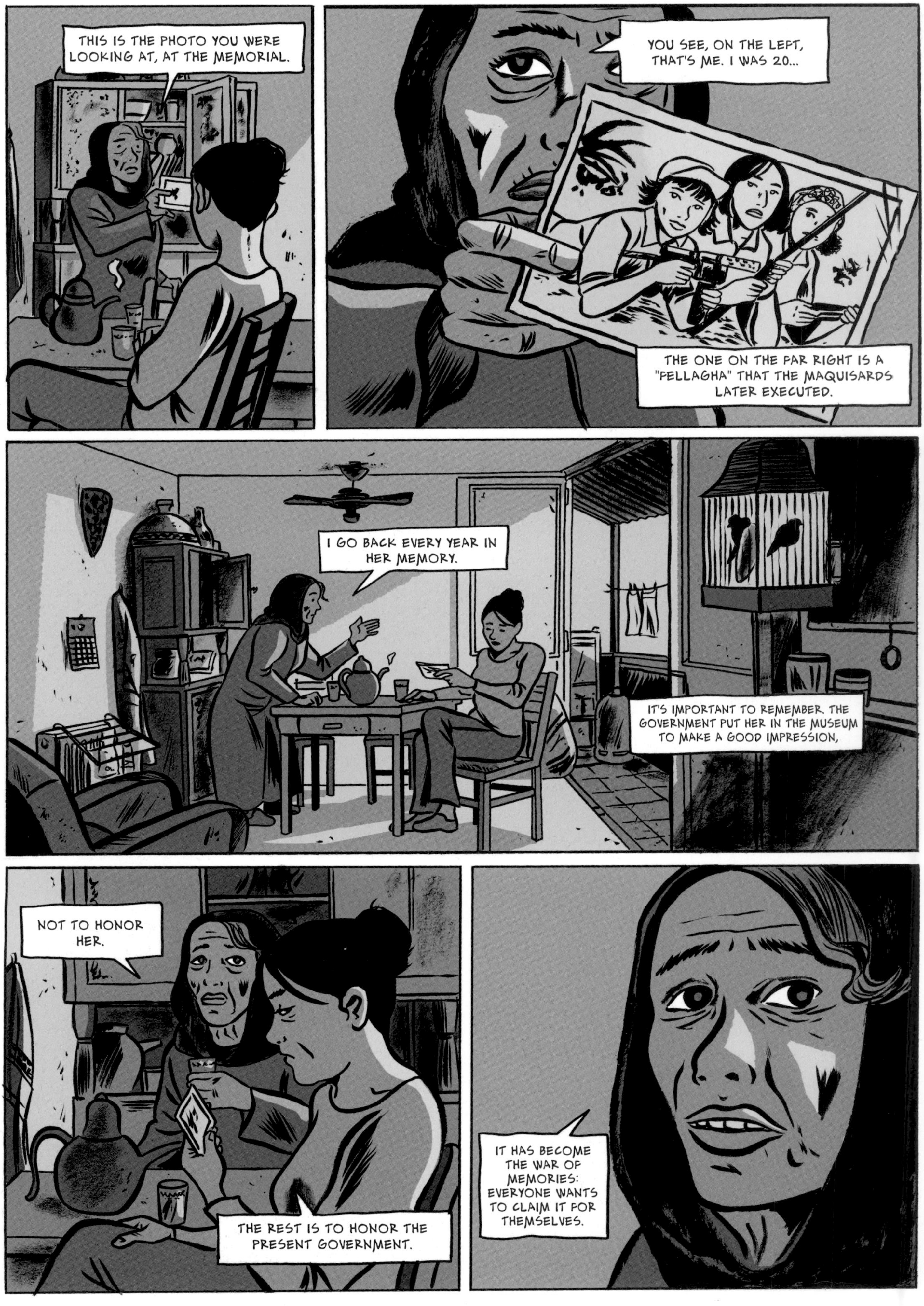
THIS IS THE PHOTO YOU WERE LOOKING AT, AT THE MEMORIAL.
YOU SEE, ON THE LEFT, THAT'S ME. I WAS 20...
THE ONE ON THE FAR RIGHT IS A "FELLAGHA" THAT THE MAQUISARDS LATER EXECUTED.
I GO BACK EVERY YEAR IN HER MEMORY.
IT'S IMPORTANT TO REMEMBER. THE GOVERNMENT PUT HER IN THE MUSEUM TO MAKE A GOOD IMPRESSION,
NOT TO HONOR HER.
THE REST IS TO HONOR THE PRESENT GOVERNMENT.
IT HAS BECOME THE WAR OF MEMORIES: EVERYONE WANTS TO CLAIM IT FOR THEMSELVES.

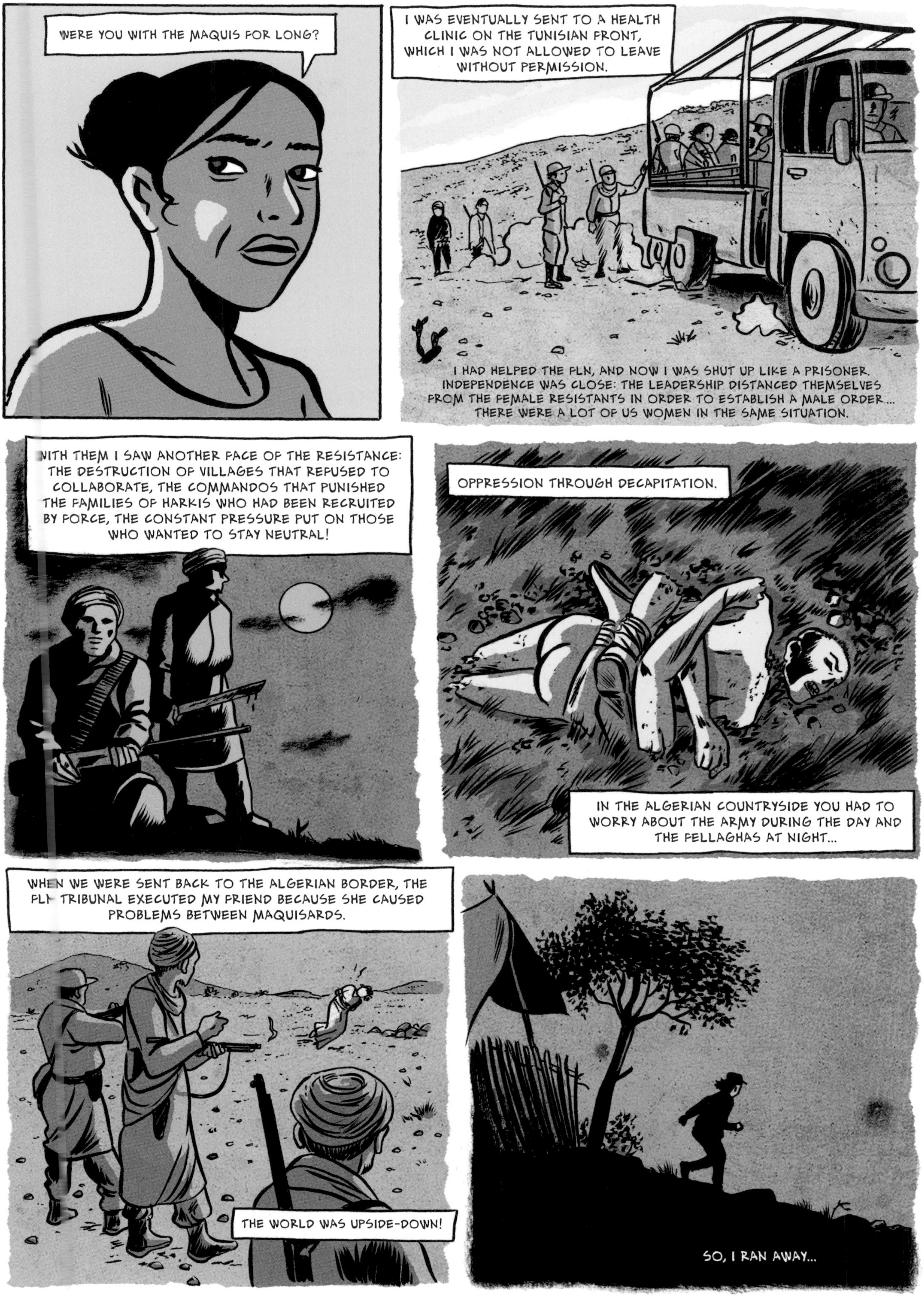
WERE YOU WITH THE MAQUIS FOR LONG?
I WAS EVENTUALLY SENT TO A HEALTH CLINIC ON THE TUNISIAN FRONT, WHICH I WAS NOT ALLOWED TO LEAVE WITHOUT PERMISSION.
I HAD HELPED THE FLN, AND NOW I WAS SHUT UP LIKE A PRISONER. INDEPENDENCE WAS CLOSE: THE LEADERSHIP DISTANCED THEMSELVES FROM THE FEMALE RESISTANTS IN ORDER TO ESTABLISH A MALE ORDER... THERE WERE A LOT OF US WOMEN IN THE SAME SITUATION.
WITH THEM I SAW ANOTHER FACE OF THE RESISTANCE: THE DESTRUCTION OF VILLAGES THAT REFUSED TO COLLABORATE, THE COMMANDOS THAT PUNISHED THE FAMILIES OF HARKIS WHO HAD BEEN RECRUITED BY FORCE, THE CONSTANT PRESSURE PUT ON THOSE WHO WANTED TO STAY NEUTRAL!
OPPRESSION THROUGH DECAPITATION.
IN THE ALGERIAN COUNTRYSIDE YOU HAD TO WORRY ABOUT THE ARMY DURING THE DAY AND THE FELLAGHAS AT NIGHT...
WHEN WE WERE SENT BACK TO THE ALGERIAN BORDER, THE FLN TRIBUNAL EXECUTED MY FRIEND BECAUSE SHE CAUSED PROBLEMS BETWEEN MAQUISARDS.
THE WORLD WAS UPSIDE-DOWN!
SO, I RAN AWAY...

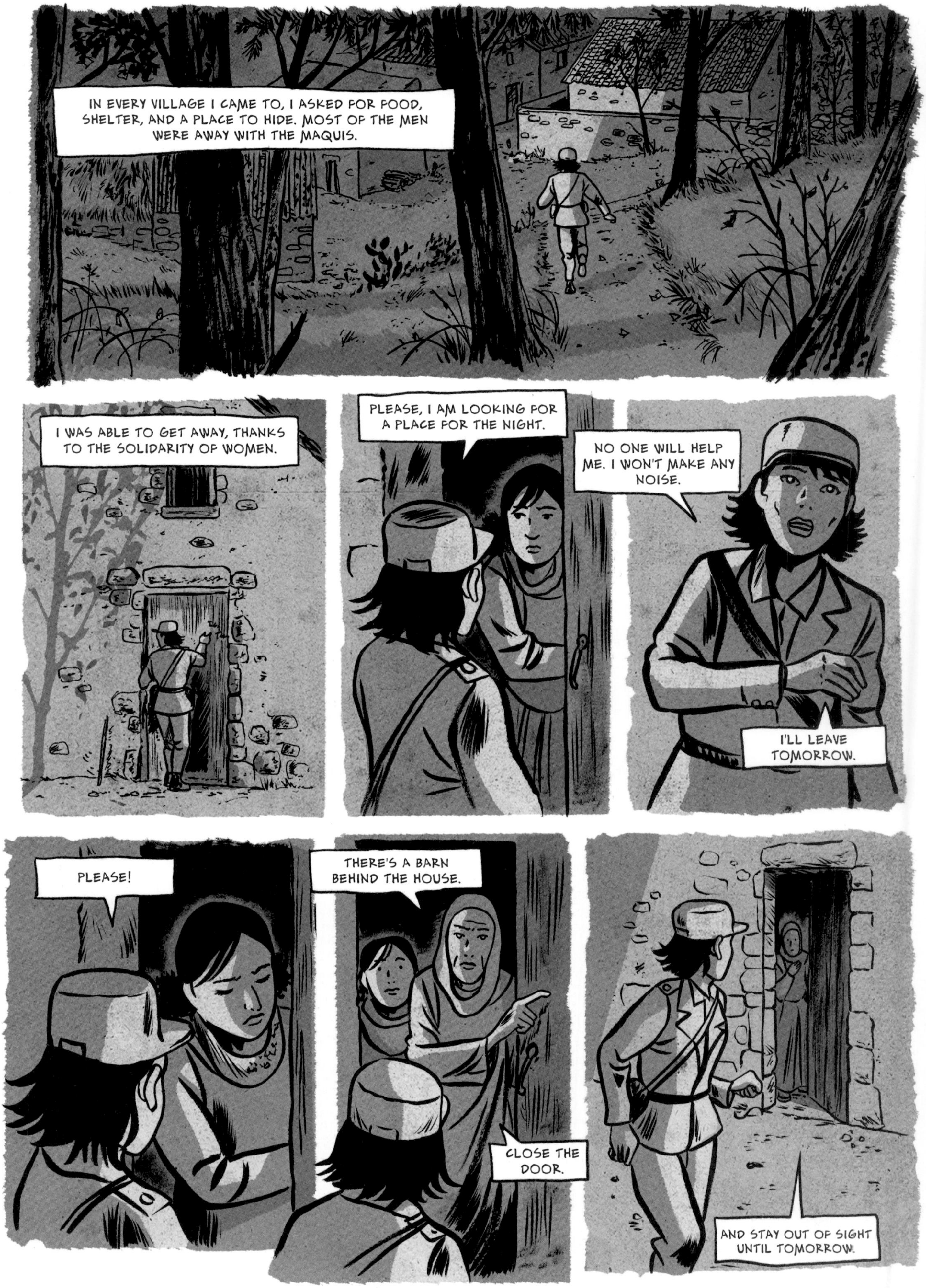
IN EVERY VILLAGE I CAME TO, I ASKED FOR FOOD, SHELTER, AND A PLACE TO HIDE. MOST OF THE MEN WERE AWAY WITH THE MAQUIS.
I WAS ABLE TO GET AWAY, THANKS TO THE SOLIDARITY OF WOMEN.
PLEASE, I AM LOOKING FOR A PLACE FOR THE NIGHT.
NO ONE WILL HELP ME. I WON'T MAKE ANY NOISE.
I'LL LEAVE TOMORROW.
PLEASE!
THERE'S A BARN BEHIND THE HOUSE.
CLOSE THE DOOR.
AND STAY OUT OF SIGHT UNTIL TOMORROW.

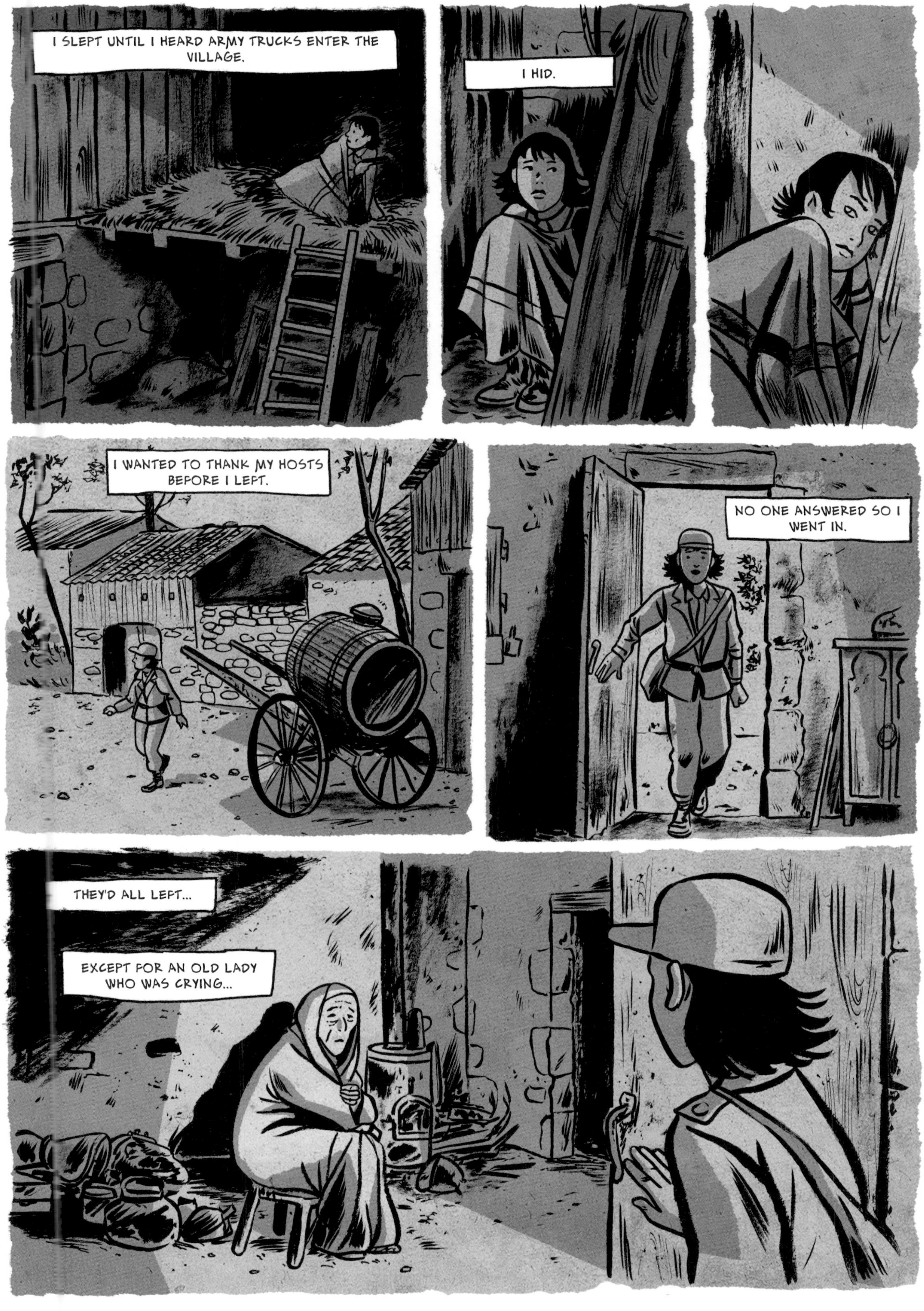
I SLEPT UNTIL I HEARD ARMY TRUCKS ENTER THE VILLAGE.
I HID.
I WANTED TO THANK MY HOSTS BEFORE I LEFT.
NO ONE ANSWERED SO I WENT IN.
THEY'D ALL LEFT...
EXCEPT FOR AN OLD LADY WHO WAS CRYING...

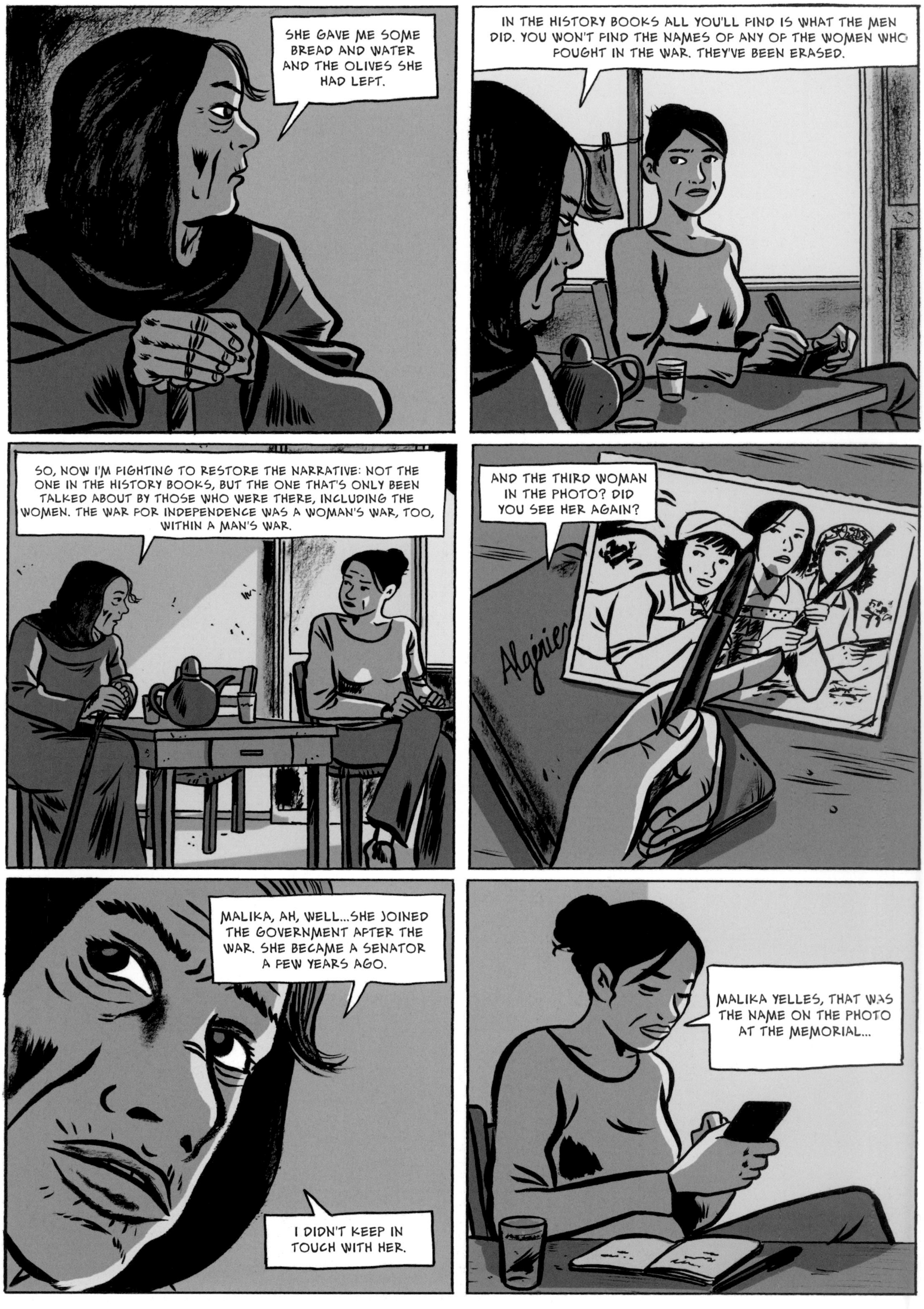
SHE GAVE ME SOME BREAD AND WATER AND THE OLIVES SHE HAD LEFT.
IN THE HISTORY BOOKS ALL YOU'LL FIND IS WHAT THE MEN DID. YOU WON'T FIND THE NAMES OF ANY OF THE WOMEN WHO FOUGHT IN THE WAR. THEY'VE BEEN ERASED.
SO, NOW I'M FIGHTING TO RESTORE THE NARRATIVE: NOT THE ONE IN THE HISTORY BOOKS, BUT THE ONE THAT'S ONLY BEEN TALKED ABOUT BY THOSE WHO WERE THERE, INCLUDING THE WOMEN. THE WAR FOR INDEPENDENCE WAS A WOMAN'S WAR, TOO, WITHIN A MAN'S WAR.
AND THE THIRD WOMAN IN THE PHOTO? DID YOU SEE HER AGAIN?
Algérie
MALIKA, AH, WELL...SHE JOINED THE GOVERNMENT AFTER THE WAR. SHE BECAME A SENATOR A FEW YEARS AGO.
I DIDN'T KEEP IN TOUCH WITH HER.
MALIKA YELLES, THAT WAS THE NAME ON THE PHOTO AT THE MEMORIAL...

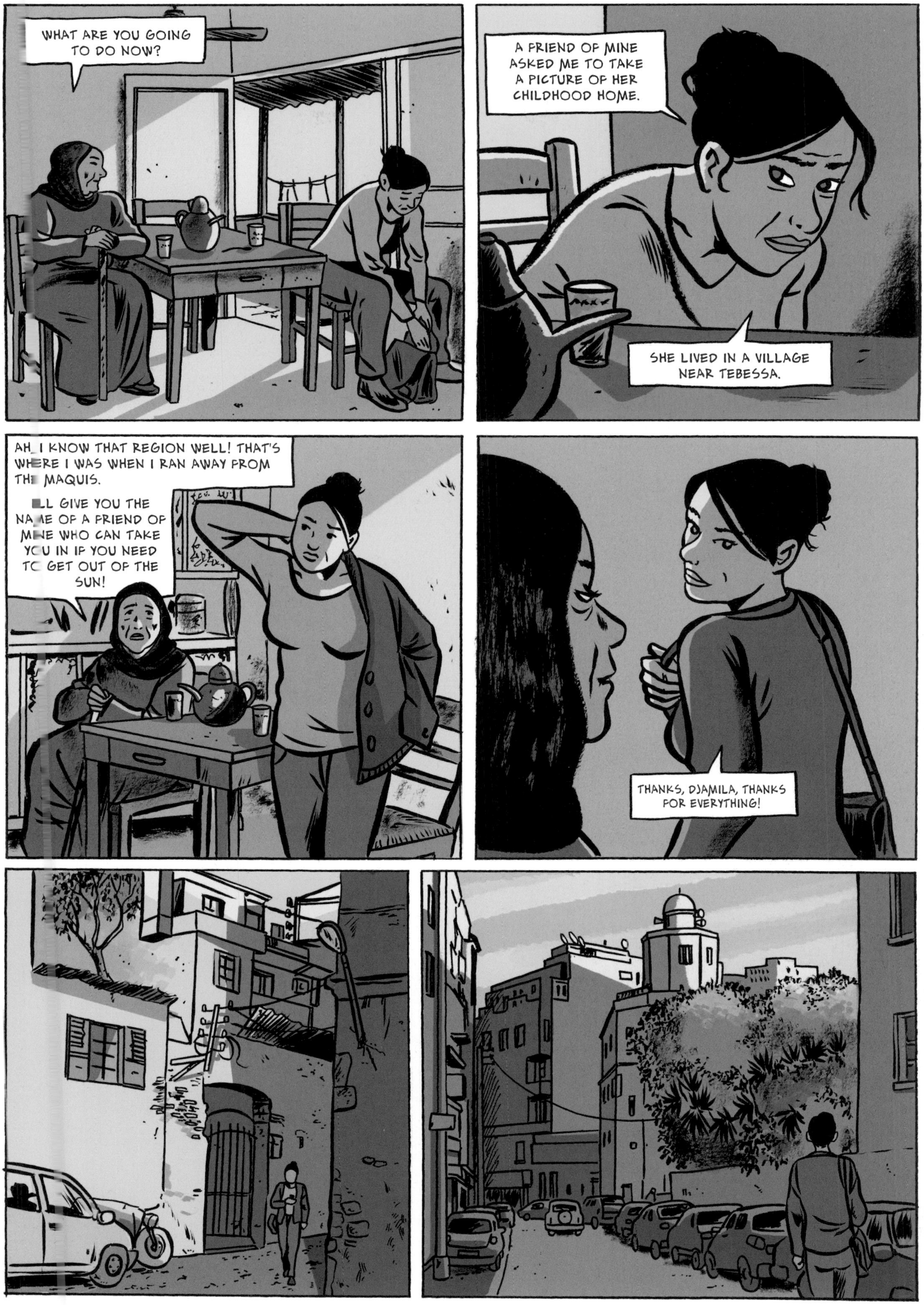
WHAT ARE YOU GOING TO DO NOW?
A FRIEND OF MINE ASKED ME TO TAKE A PICTURE OF HER CHILDHOOD HOME.
SHE LIVED IN A VILLAGE NEAR TEBESSA.
AH, I KNOW THAT REGION WELL! THAT'S WHERE I WAS WHEN I RAN AWAY FROM THE MAQUIS.
I'LL GIVE YOU THE NAME OF A FRIEND OF MINE WHO CAN TAKE YOU IN IF YOU NEED TO GET OUT OF THE SUN!
THANKS, DJAMILA, THANKS FOR EVERYTHING!

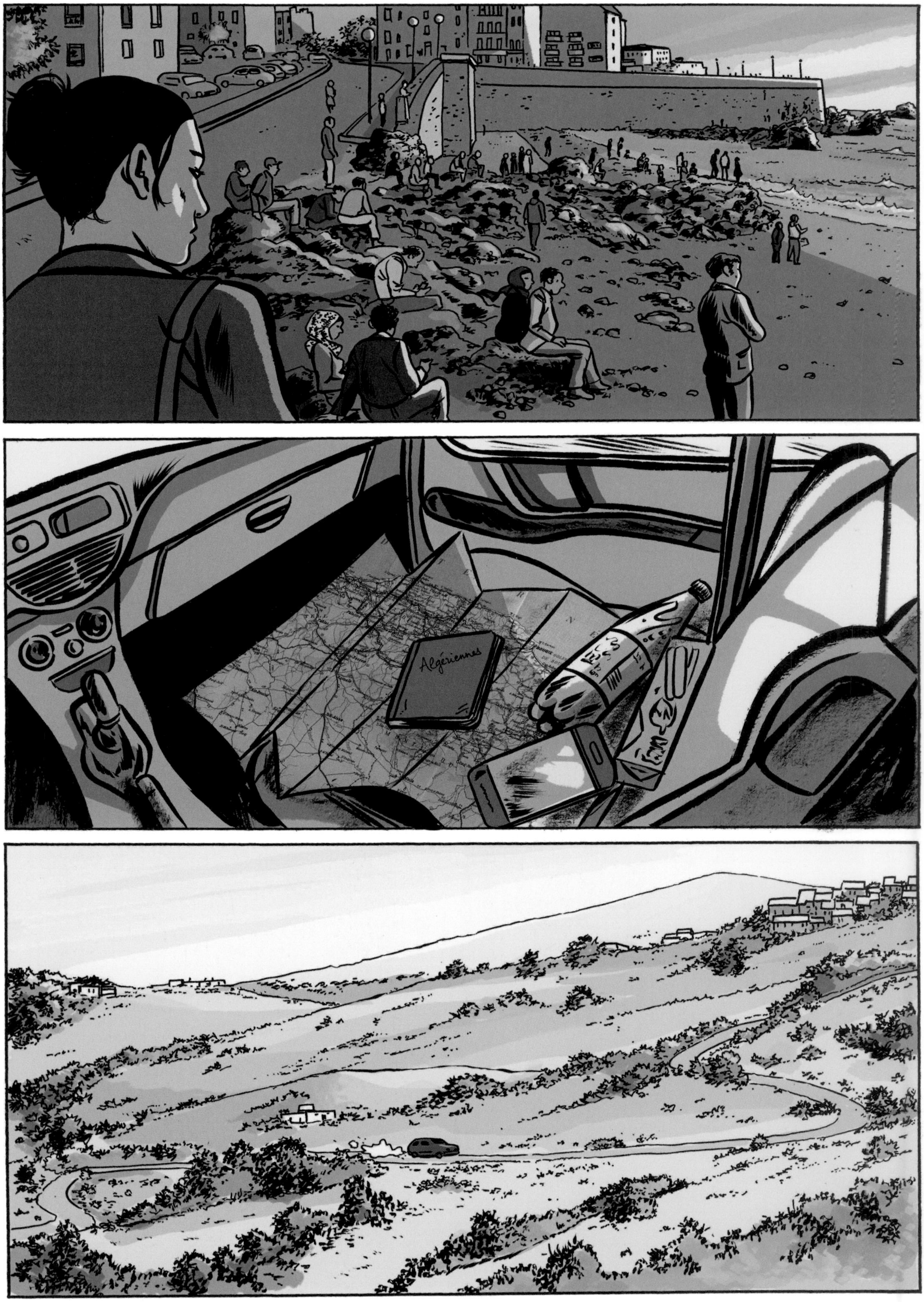
Algériennes

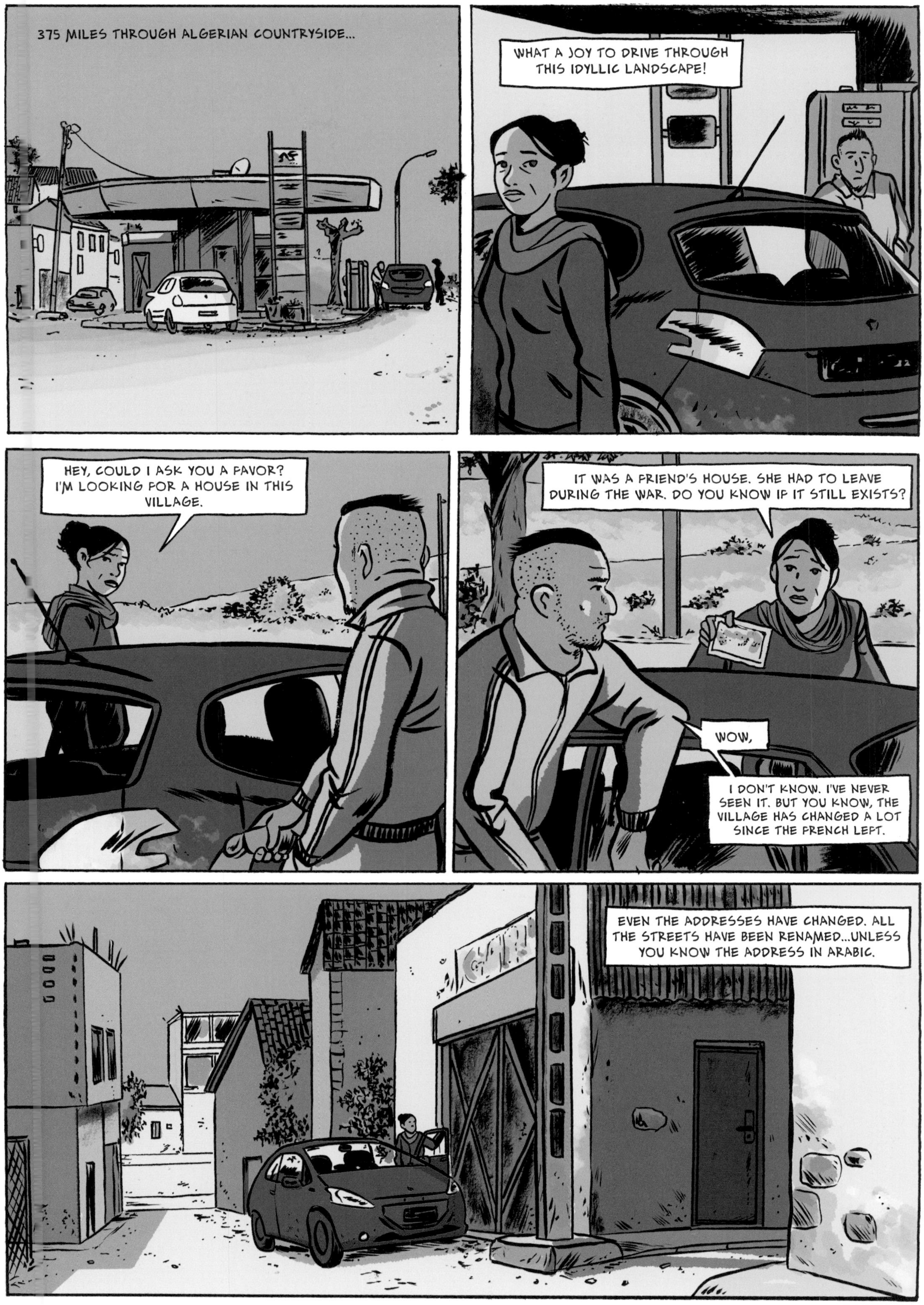
375 MILES THROUGH ALGERIAN COUNTRYSIDE...
WHAT A JOY TO DRIVE THROUGH THIS IDYLLIC LANDSCAPE!
HEY, COULD I ASK YOU A FAVOR? I'M LOOKING FOR A HOUSE IN THIS VILLAGE.
IT WAS A FRIEND'S HOUSE. SHE HAD TO LEAVE DURING THE WAR. DO YOU KNOW IF IT STILL EXISTS?
WOW,
I DON'T KNOW. I'VE NEVER SEEN IT. BUT YOU KNOW, THE VILLAGE HAS CHANGED A LOT SINCE THE FRENCH LEFT.
EVEN THE ADDRESSES HAVE CHANGED. ALL THE STREETS HAVE BEEN RENAMED...UNLESS YOU KNOW THE ADDRESS IN ARABIC.

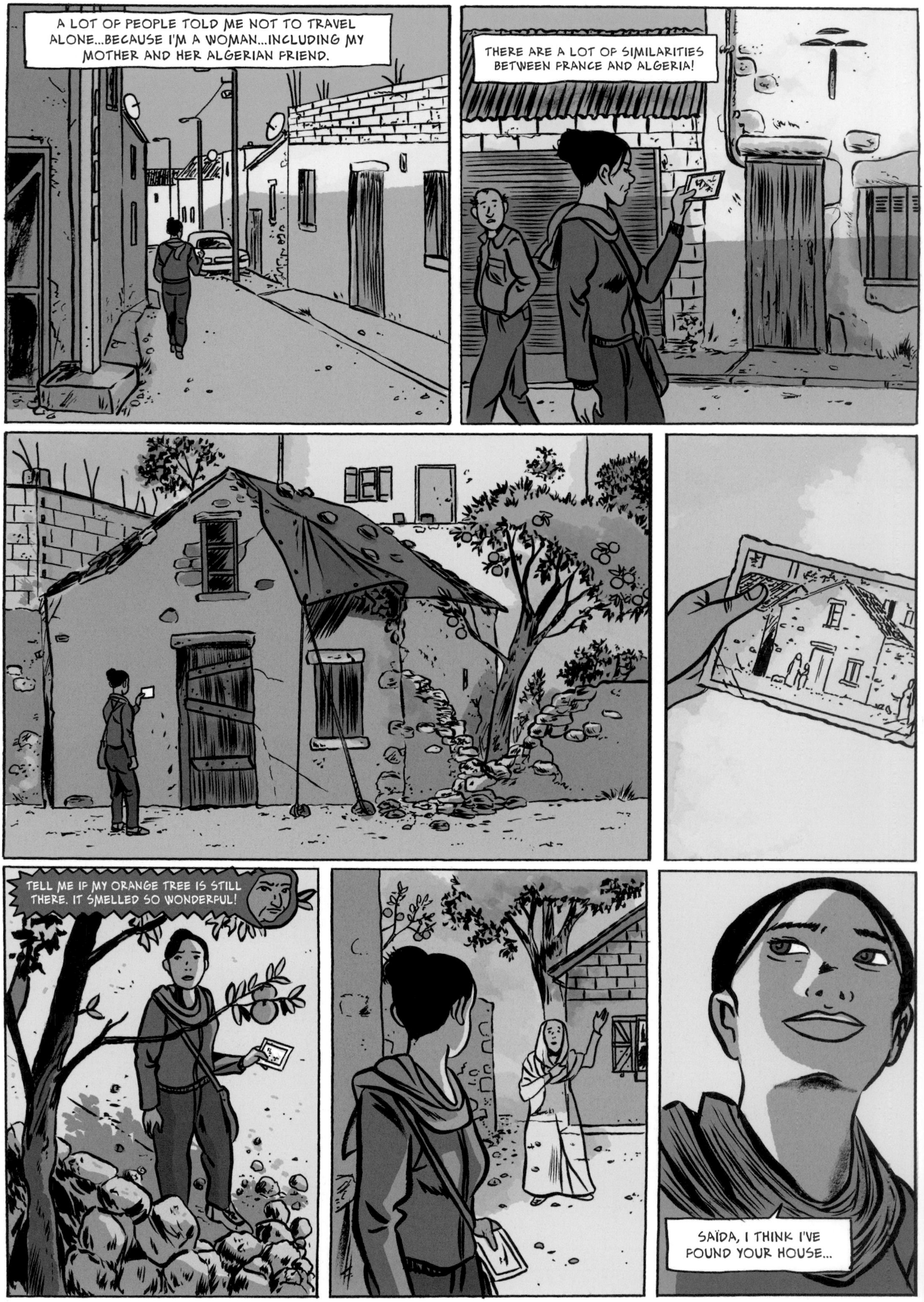

A LOT OF PEOPLE TOLD ME NOT TO TRAVEL ALONE...BECAUSE I'M A WOMAN...INCLUDING MY MOTHER AND HER ALGERIAN FRIEND.
THERE ARE A LOT OF SIMILARITIES BETWEEN FRANCE AND ALGERIA!
TELL ME IF MY ORANGE TREE IS STILL THERE. IT SMELLED SO WONDERFUL!
SAÏDA, I THINK I'VE FOUND YOUR HOUSE...

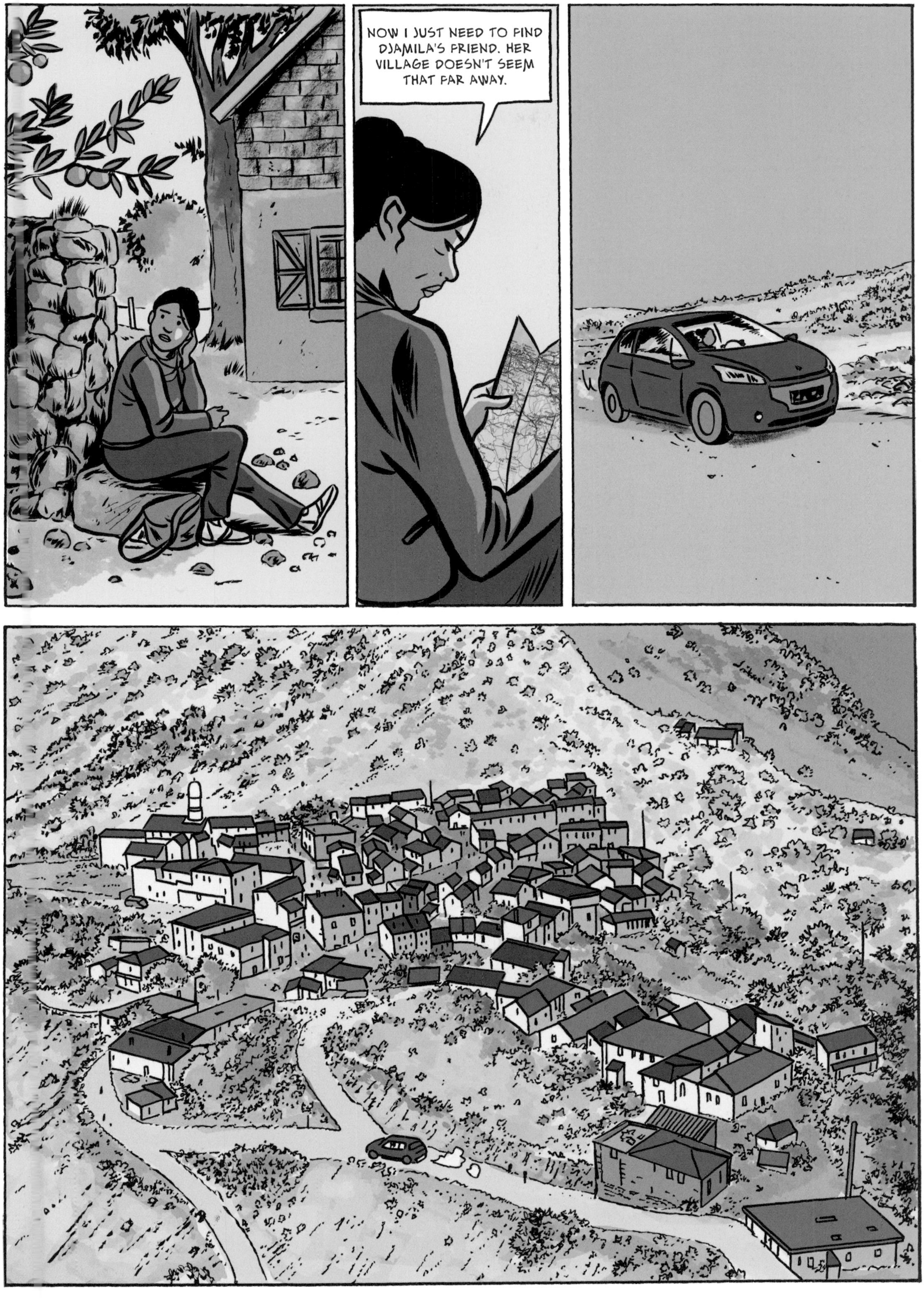
NOW I JUST NEED TO FIND DJAMILA'S FRIEND. HER VILLAGE DOESN'T SEEM THAT FAR AWAY.

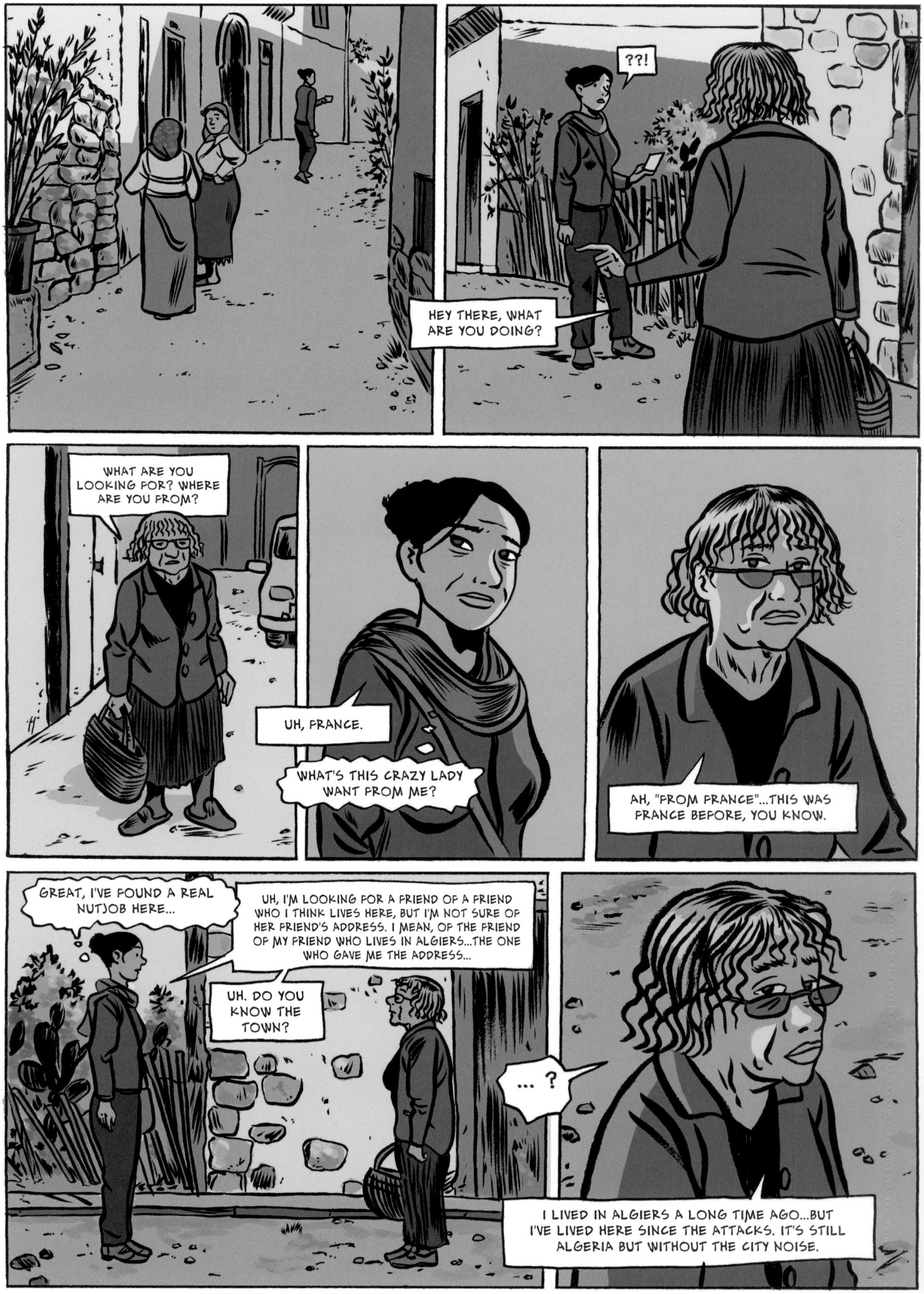
??!
HEY THERE, WHAT ARE YOU DOING?
WHAT ARE YOU LOOKING FOR? WHERE ARE YOU FROM?
UH, FRANCE.
WHAT'S THIS CRAZY LADY WANT FROM ME?
AH, "FROM FRANCE"...THIS WAS FRANCE BEFORE, YOU KNOW.
GREAT, I'VE FOUND A REAL NUTJOB HERE...
UH, I'M LOOKING FOR A FRIEND OF A FRIEND WHO I THINK LIVES HERE, BUT I'M NOT SURE OF HER FRIEND'S ADDRESS. I MEAN, OF THE FRIEND OF MY FRIEND WHO LIVES IN ALGIERS...THE ONE WHO GAVE ME THE ADDRESS...
UH. DO YOU KNOW THE TOWN?
... ?
I LIVED IN ALGIERS A LONG TIME AGO...BUT I'VE LIVED HERE SINCE THE ATTACKS. IT'S STILL ALGERIA BUT WITHOUT THE CITY NOISE.

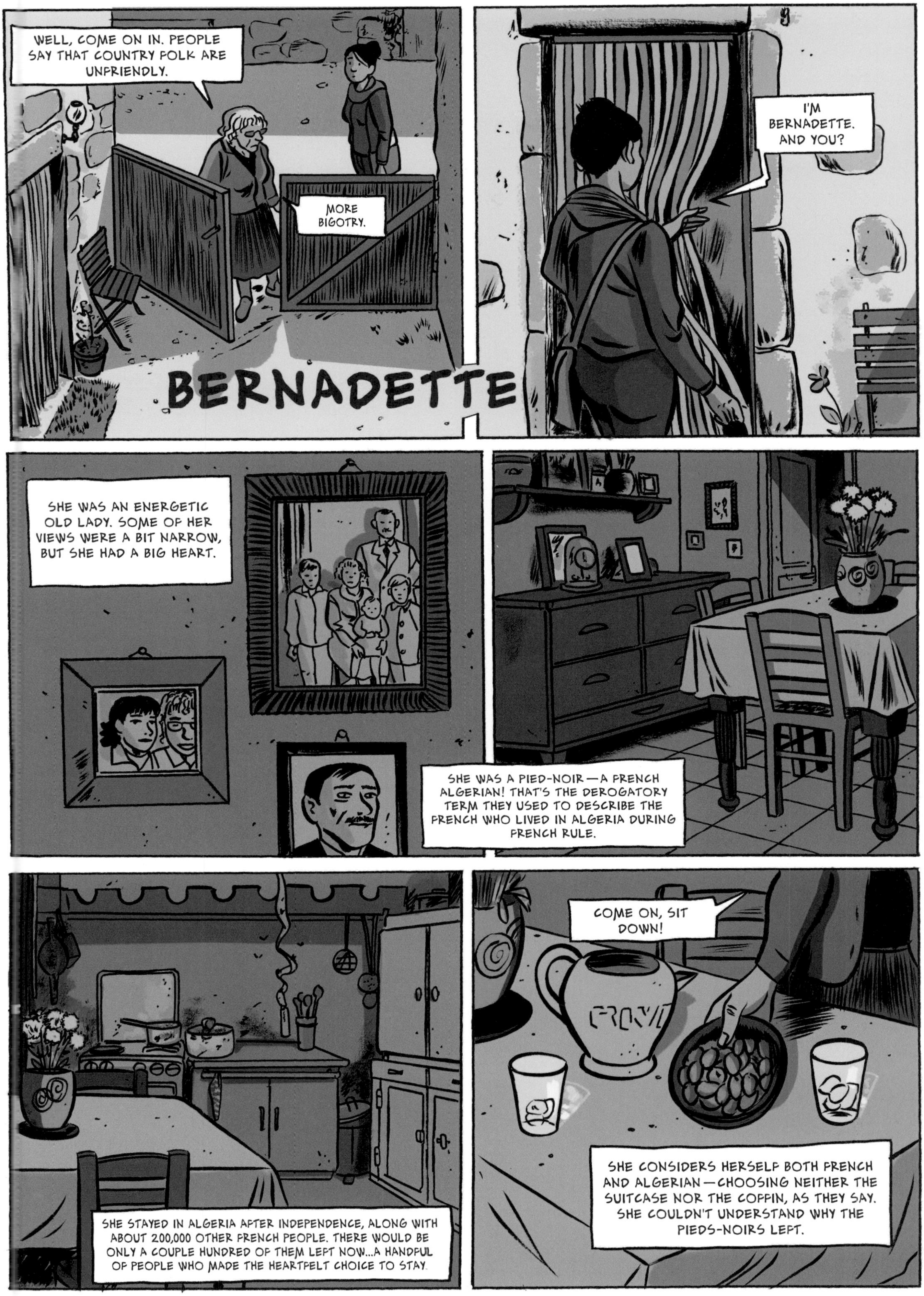
WELL, COME ON IN. PEOPLE SAY THAT COUNTRY FOLK ARE UNFRIENDLY.
MORE BIGOTRY.
BERNADETTE
I'M BERNADETTE. AND YOU?
SHE WAS AN ENERGETIC OLD LADY. SOME OF HER VIEWS WERE A BIT NARROW, BUT SHE HAD A BIG HEART.
SHE WAS A PIED-NOIR—A FRENCH ALGERIAN! THAT'S THE DEROGATORY TERM THEY USED TO DESCRIBE THE FRENCH WHO LIVED IN ALGERIA DURING FRENCH RULE.
SHE STAYED IN ALGERIA AFTER INDEPENDENCE, ALONG WITH ABOUT 200,000 OTHER FRENCH PEOPLE. THERE WOULD BE ONLY A COUPLE HUNDRED OF THEM LEFT NOW...A HANDFUL OF PEOPLE WHO MADE THE HEARTFELT CHOICE TO STAY.
COME ON, SIT DOWN!
SHE CONSIDERS HERSELF BOTH FRENCH AND ALGERIAN—CHOOSING NEITHER THE SUITCASE NOR THE COFFIN, AS THEY SAY. SHE COULDN'T UNDERSTAND WHY THE PIEDS-NOIRS LEFT.

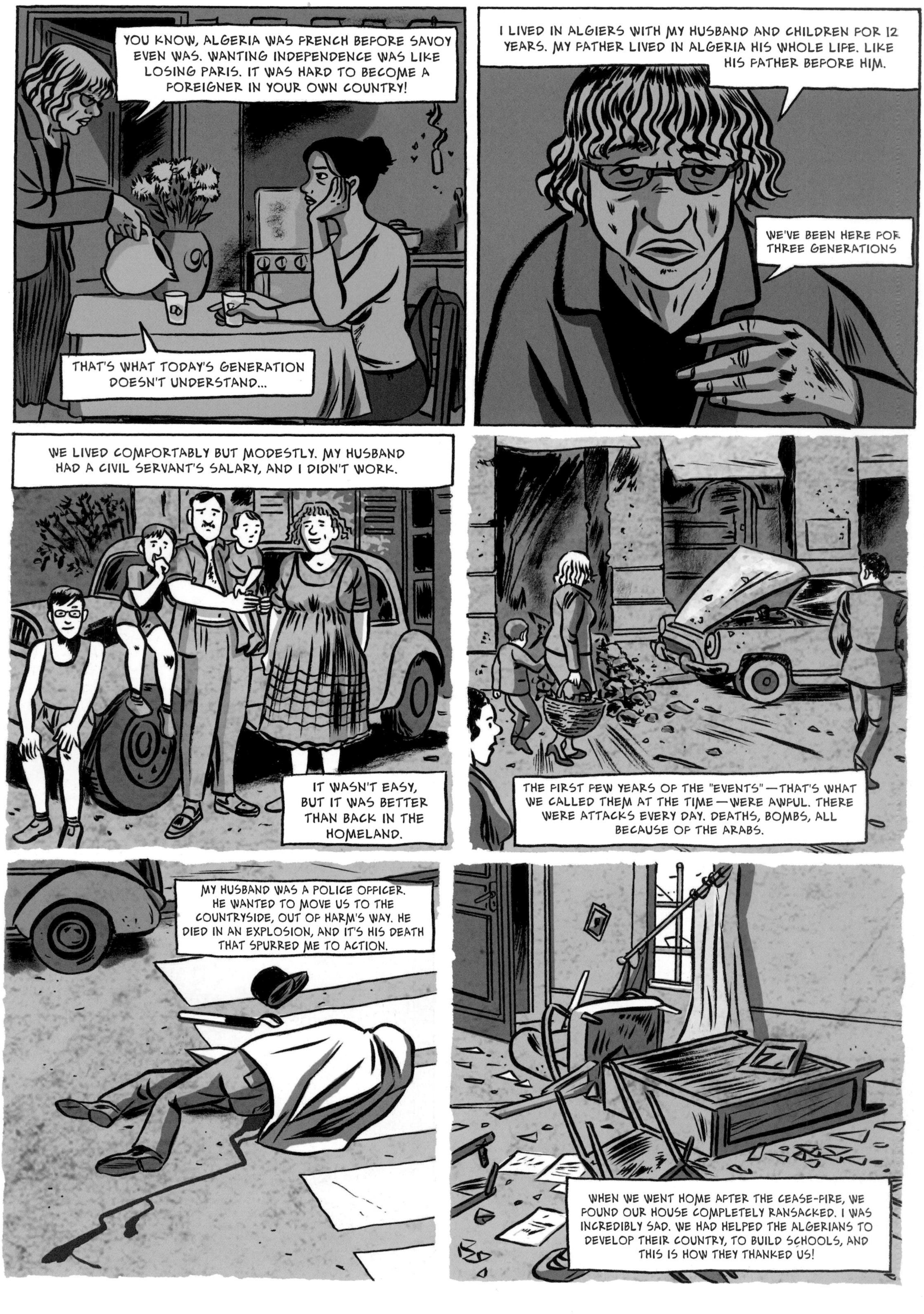

YOU KNOW, ALGERIA WAS FRENCH BEFORE SAVOY EVEN WAS. WANTING INDEPENDENCE WAS LIKE LOSING PARIS. IT WAS HARD TO BECOME A FOREIGNER IN YOUR OWN COUNTRY!
THAT'S WHAT TODAY'S GENERATION DOESN'T UNDERSTAND...
I LIVED IN ALGIERS WITH MY HUSBAND AND CHILDREN FOR 12 YEARS. MY FATHER LIVED IN ALGERIA HIS WHOLE LIFE. LIKE HIS FATHER BEFORE HIM.
WE'VE BEEN HERE FOR THREE GENERATIONS
WE LIVED COMFORTABLY BUT MODESTLY. MY HUSBAND HAD A CIVIL SERVANT'S SALARY, AND I DIDN'T WORK.
IT WASN'T EASY, BUT IT WAS BETTER THAN BACK IN THE HOMELAND.
THE FIRST FEW YEARS OF THE "EVENTS"—THAT'S WHAT WE CALLED THEM AT THE TIME—WERE AWFUL. THERE WERE ATTACKS EVERY DAY. DEATHS, BOMBS, ALL BECAUSE OF THE ARABS.
MY HUSBAND WAS A POLICE OFFICER. HE WANTED TO MOVE US TO THE COUNTRYSIDE, OUT OF HARM'S WAY. HE DIED IN AN EXPLOSION, AND IT'S HIS DEATH THAT SPURRED ME TO ACTION.
WHEN WE WENT HOME AFTER THE CEASE-FIRE, WE FOUND OUR HOUSE COMPLETELY RANSACKED. I WAS INCREDIBLY SAD. WE HAD HELPED THE ALGERIANS TO DEVELOP THEIR COUNTRY, TO BUILD SCHOOLS, AND THIS IS HOW THEY THANKED US!

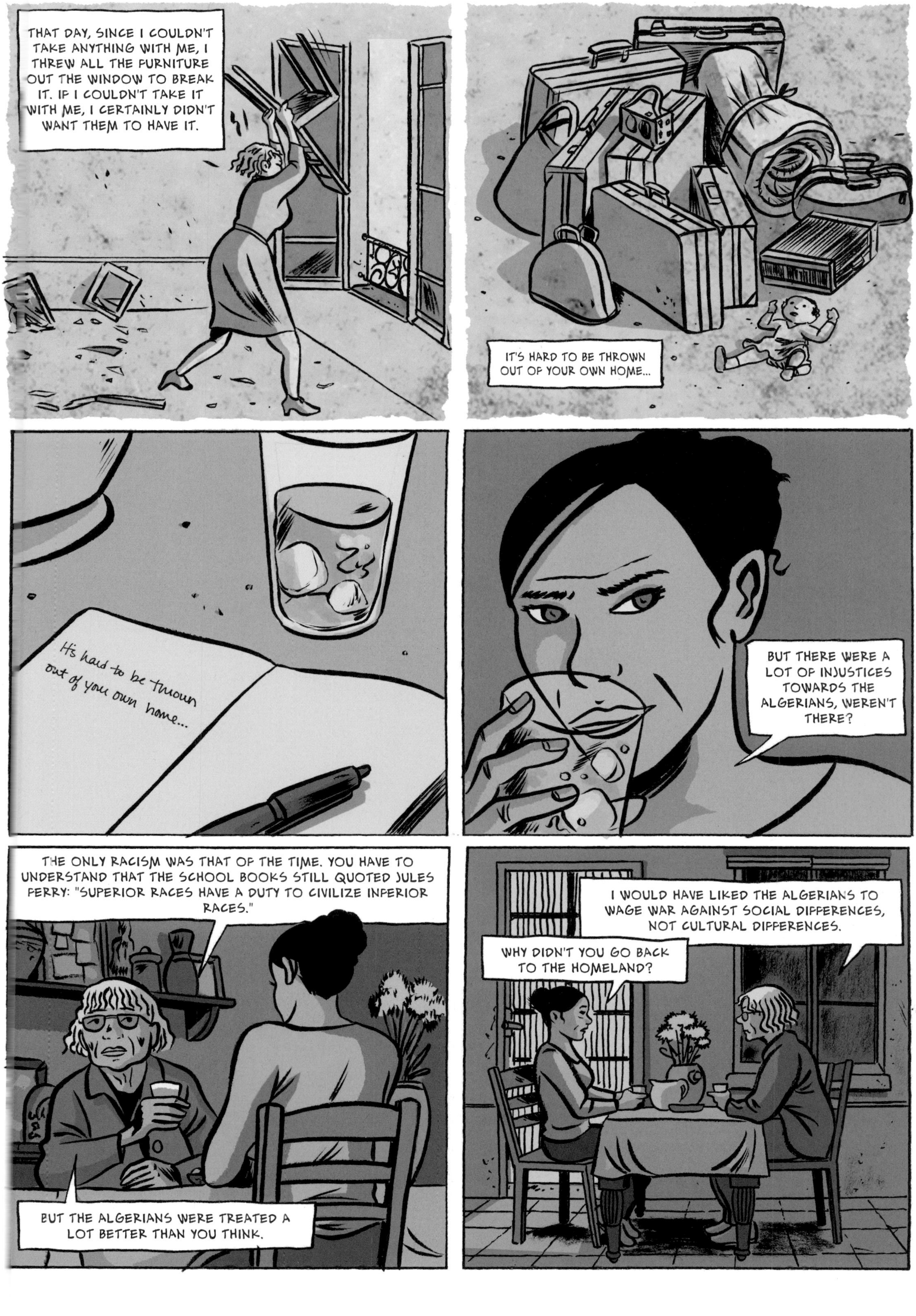
THAT DAY, SINCE I COULDN'T TAKE ANYTHING WITH ME, I THREW ALL THE FURNITURE OUT THE WINDOW TO BREAK IT. IF I COULDN'T TAKE IT WITH ME, I CERTAINLY DIDN'T WANT THEM TO HAVE IT.
IT'S HARD TO BE THROWN OUT OF YOUR OWN HOME...
It's hard to be thrown out of you own home...
BUT THERE WERE A LOT OF INJUSTICES TOWARDS THE ALGERIANS, WEREN'T THERE?
THE ONLY RACISM WAS THAT OF THE TIME. YOU HAVE TO UNDERSTAND THAT THE SCHOOL BOOKS STILL QUOTED JULES FERRY: "SUPERIOR RACES HAVE A DUTY TO CIVILIZE INFERIOR RACES."
BUT THE ALGERIANS WERE TREATED A LOT BETTER THAN YOU THINK.
WHY DIDN'T YOU GO BACK TO THE HOMELAND?
I WOULD HAVE LIKED THE ALGERIANS TO WAGE WAR AGAINST SOCIAL DIFFERENCES, NOT CULTURAL DIFFERENCES.

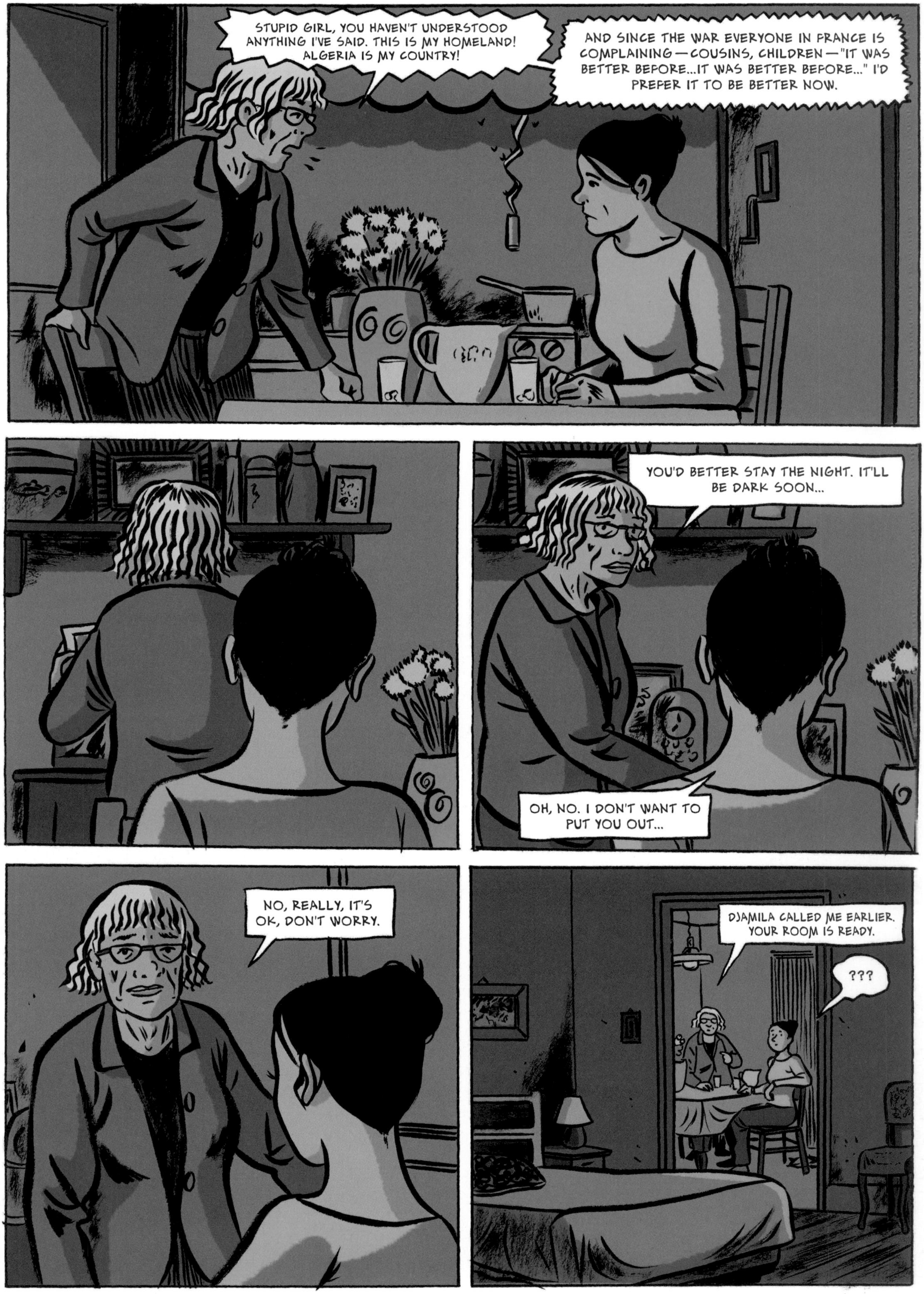
STUPID GIRL, YOU HAVEN'T UNDERSTOOD ANYTHING I'VE SAID. THIS IS MY HOMELAND! ALGERIA IS MY COUNTRY!
AND SINCE THE WAR EVERYONE IN FRANCE IS COMPLAINING—COUSINS, CHILDREN—"IT WAS BETTER BEFORE...IT WAS BETTER BEFORE..." I'D PREFER IT TO BE BETTER NOW.
YOU'D BETTER STAY THE NIGHT. IT'LL BE DARK SOON...
OH, NO. I DON'T WANT TO PUT YOU OUT...
NO, REALLY, IT'S OK, DON'T WORRY.
DJAMILA CALLED ME EARLIER. YOUR ROOM IS READY.
???

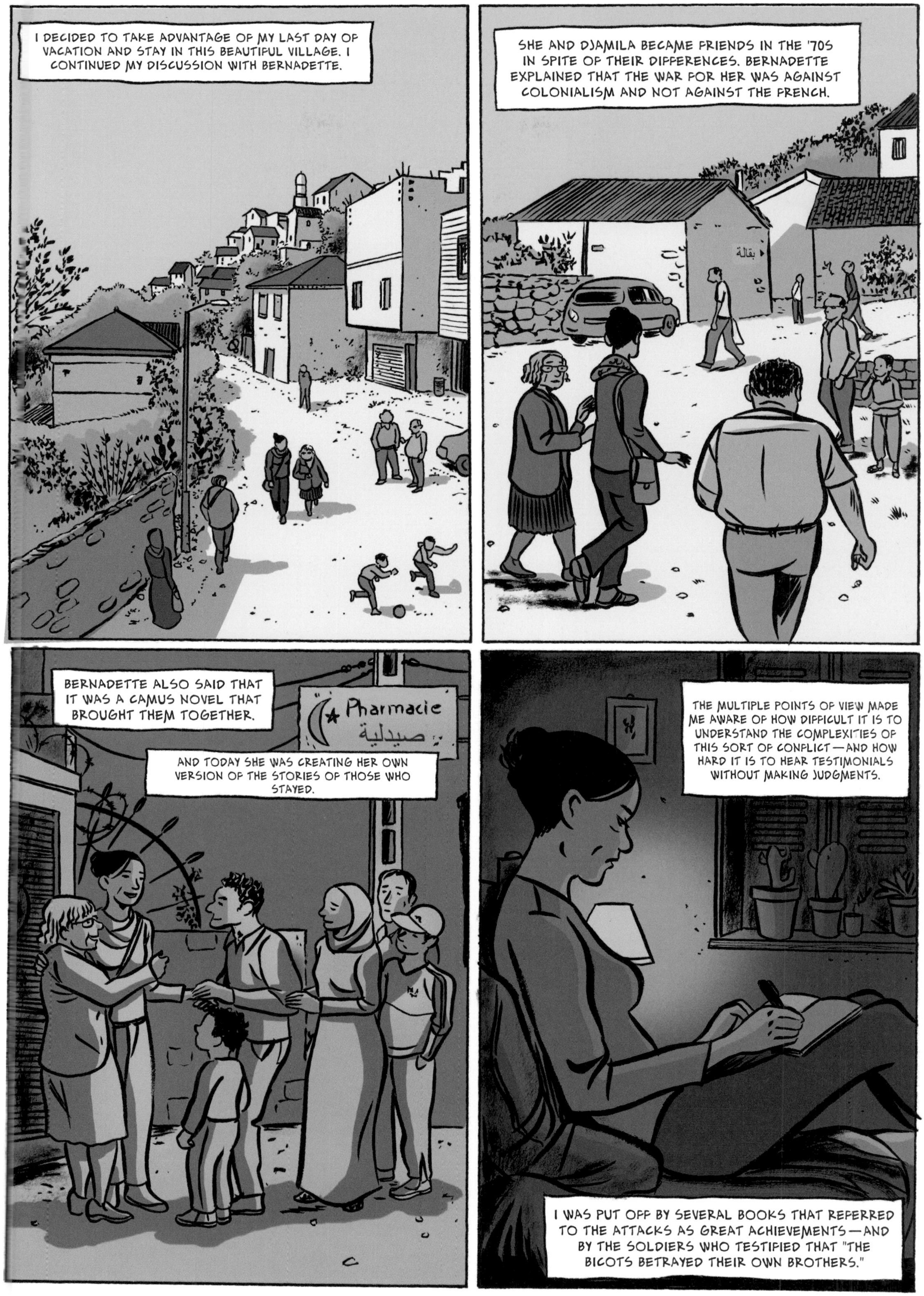
I DECIDED TO TAKE ADVANTAGE OF MY LAST DAY OF VACATION AND STAY IN THIS BEAUTIFUL VILLAGE. I CONTINUED MY DISCUSSION WITH BERNADETTE.
SHE AND DJAMILA BECAME FRIENDS IN THE '70S IN SPITE OF THEIR DIFFERENCES. BERNADETTE EXPLAINED THAT THE WAR FOR HER WAS AGAINST COLONIALISM AND NOT AGAINST THE FRENCH.
بقالة
BERNADETTE ALSO SAID THAT IT WAS A CAMUS NOVEL THAT BROUGHT THEM TOGETHER.
Pharmacie
صيدلية
AND TODAY SHE WAS CREATING HER OWN VERSION OF THE STORIES OF THOSE WHO STAYED.
THE MULTIPLE POINTS OF VIEW MADE ME AWARE OF HOW DIFFICULT IT IS TO UNDERSTAND THE COMPLEXITIES OF THIS SORT OF CONFLICT—AND HOW HARD IT IS TO HEAR TESTIMONIALS WITHOUT MAKING JUDGMENTS.
I WAS PUT OFF BY SEVERAL BOOKS THAT REFERRED TO THE ATTACKS AS GREAT ACHIEVEMENTS—AND BY THE SOLDIERS WHO TESTIFIED THAT "THE BICOTS BETRAYED THEIR OWN BROTHERS."

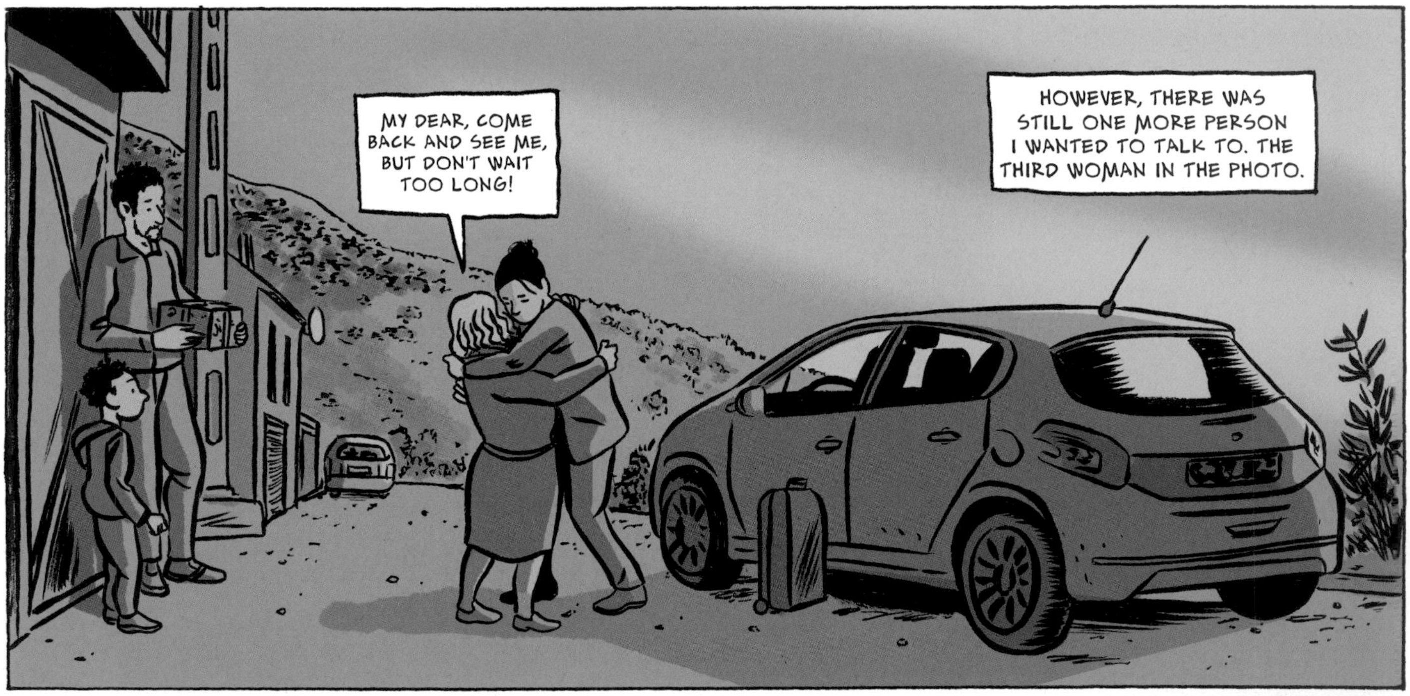
MY DEAR, COME BACK AND SEE ME, BUT DON'T WAIT TOO LONG!
HOWEVER, THERE WAS STILL ONE MORE PERSON I WANTED TO TALK TO. THE THIRD WOMAN IN THE PHOTO.

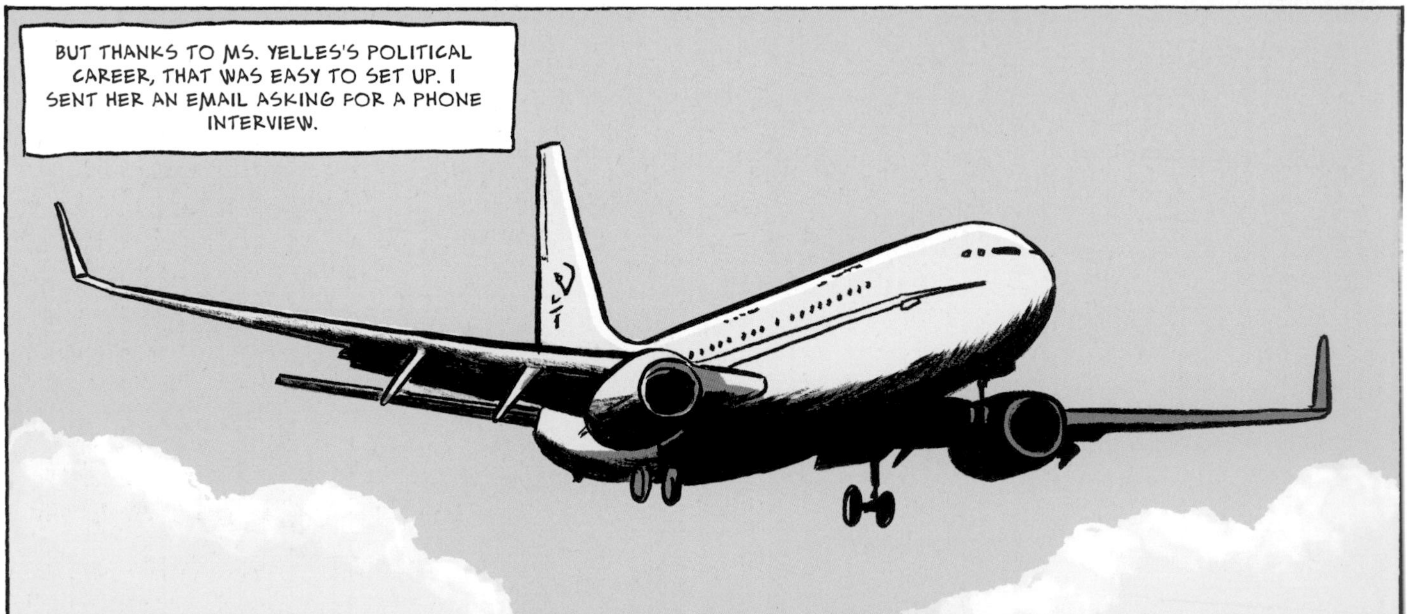
BUT THANKS TO MS. YELLES'S POLITICAL CAREER, THAT WAS EASY TO SET UP. I SENT HER AN EMAIL ASKING FOR A PHONE INTERVIEW.

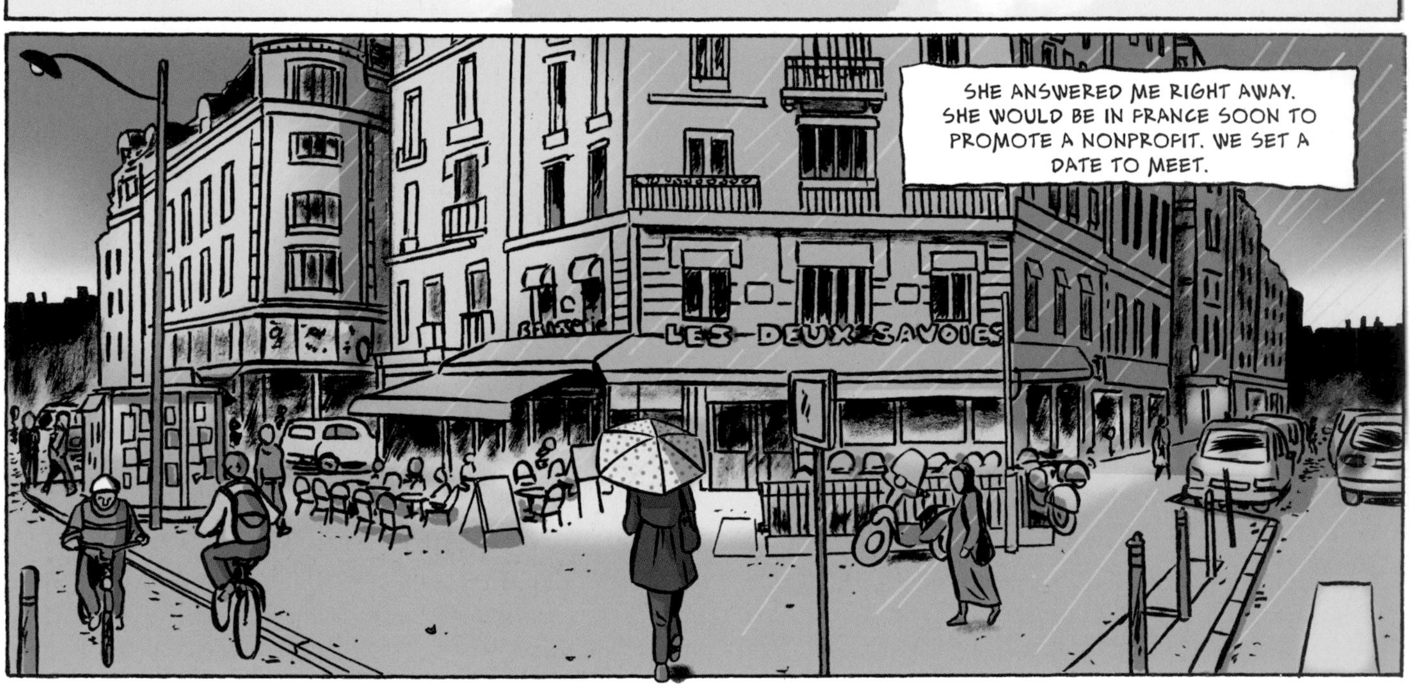
SHE ANSWERED ME RIGHT AWAY. SHE WOULD BE IN FRANCE SOON TO PROMOTE A NONPROFIT. WE SET A DATE TO MEET.
LES DEUX SAVOIES

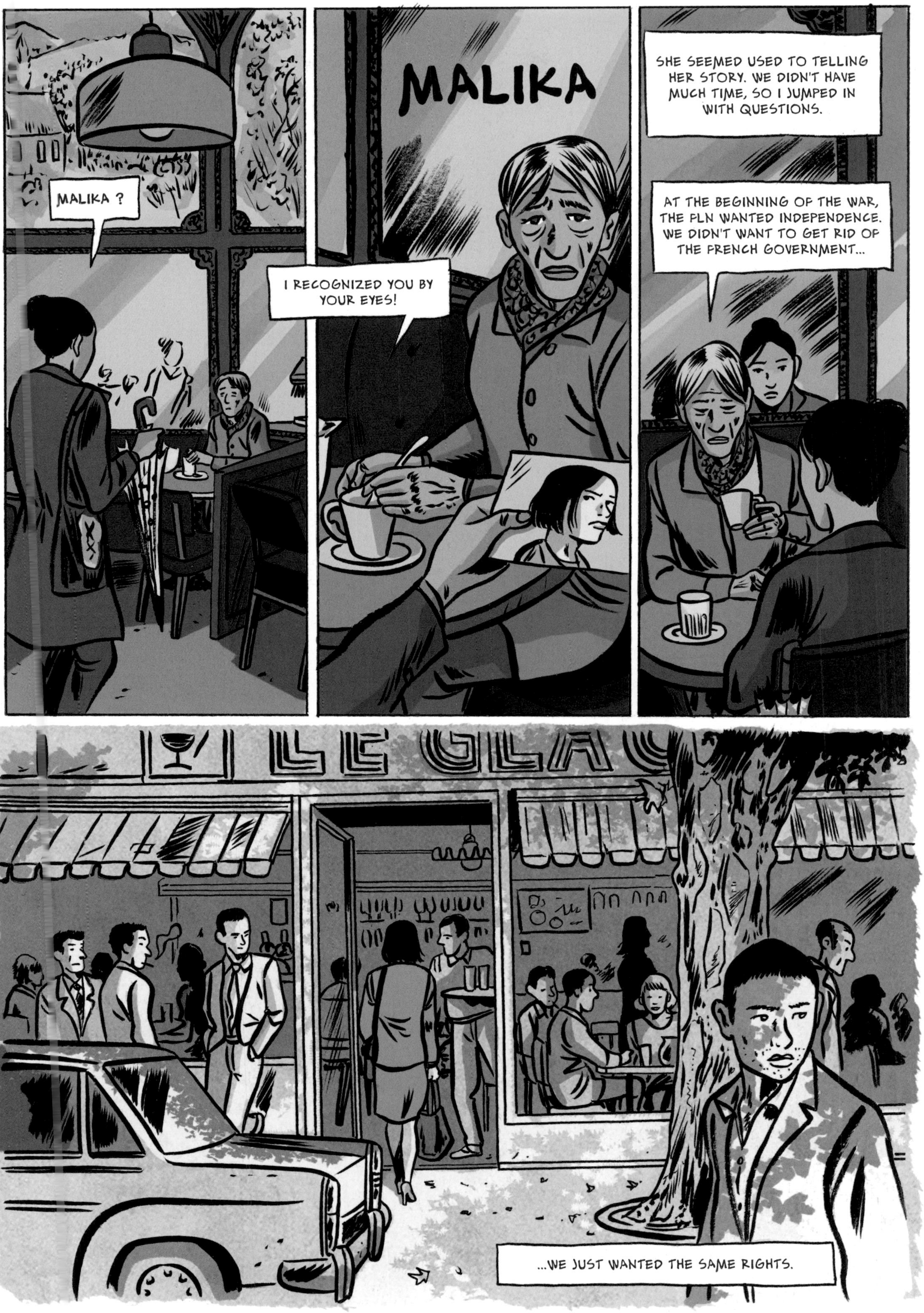
MALIKA ?
MALIKA
I RECOGNIZED YOU BY YOUR EYES!
SHE SEEMED USED TO TELLING HER STORY. WE DIDN'T HAVE MUCH TIME, SO I JUMPED IN WITH QUESTIONS.
AT THE BEGINNING OF THE WAR, THE FLN WANTED INDEPENDENCE. WE DIDN'T WANT TO GET RID OF THE FRENCH GOVERNMENT...
...WE JUST WANTED THE SAME RIGHTS.

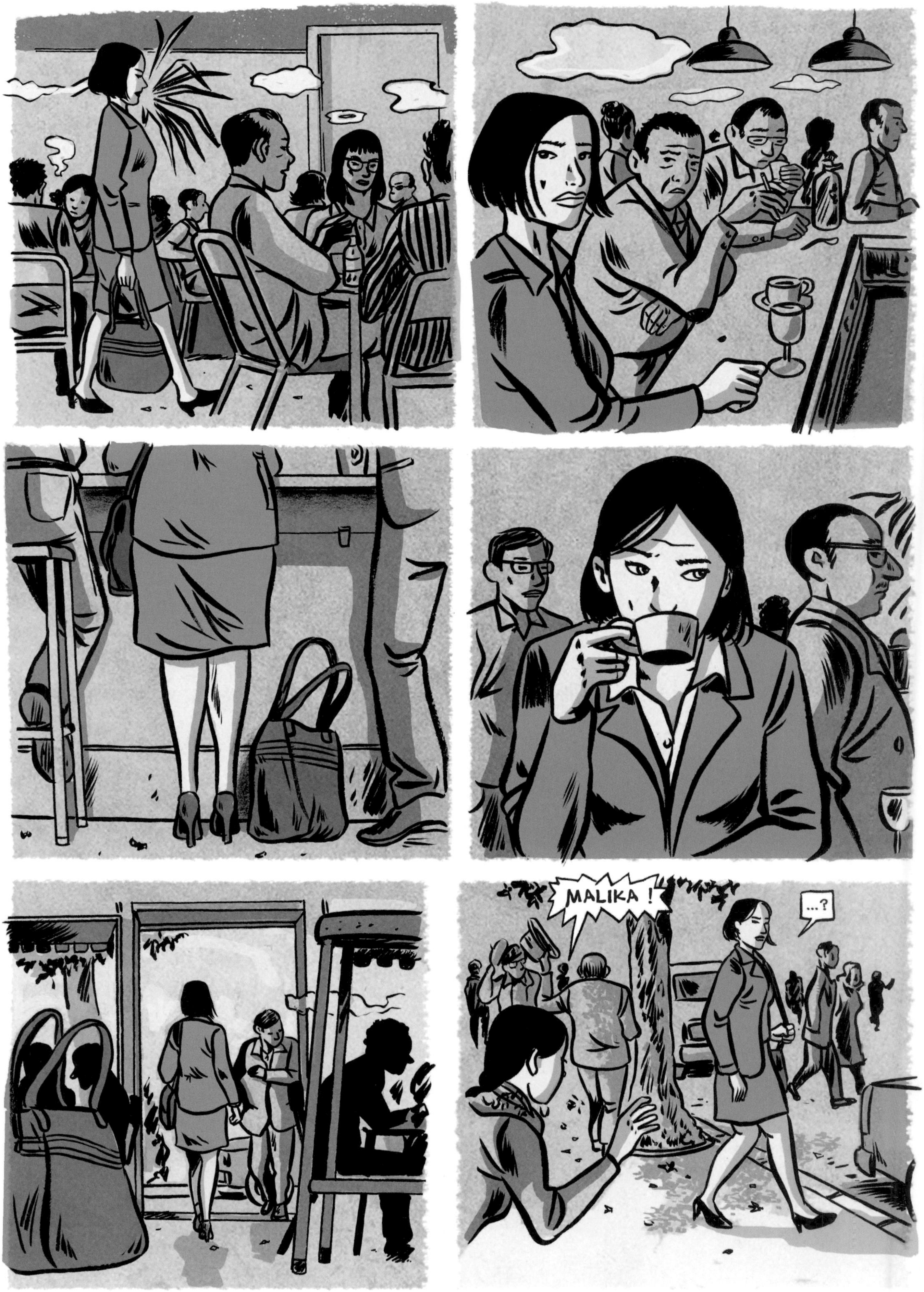
MALIKA !
...?

78

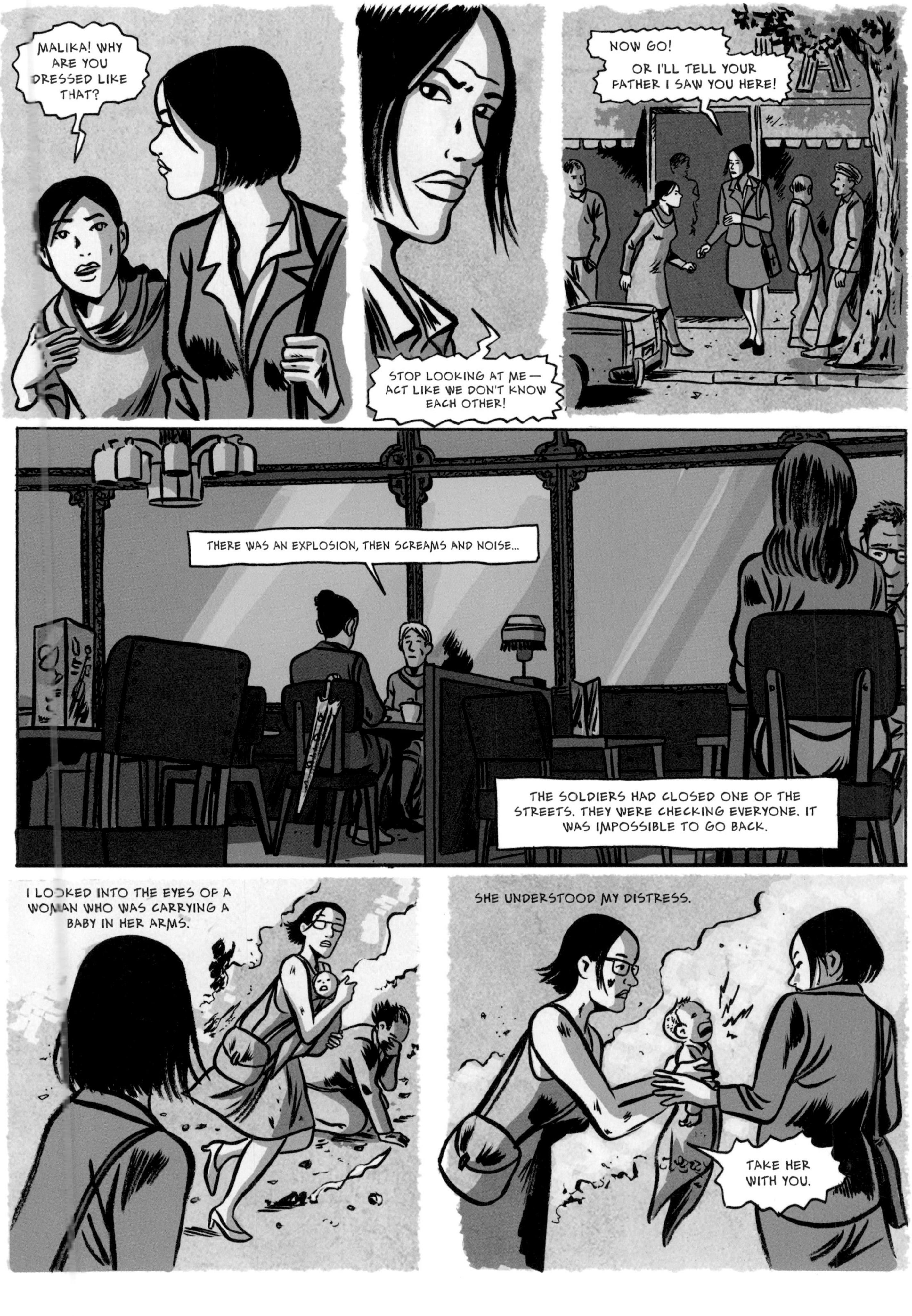
MALIKA! WHY ARE YOU DRESSED LIKE THAT?
STOP LOOKING AT ME— ACT LIKE WE DON'T KNOW EACH OTHER!
NOW GO!
OR I'LL TELL YOUR FATHER I SAW YOU HERE!
THERE WAS AN EXPLOSION, THEN SCREAMS AND NOISE...
THE SOLDIERS HAD CLOSED ONE OF THE STREETS. THEY WERE CHECKING EVERYONE. IT WAS IMPOSSIBLE TO GO BACK.
I LOOKED INTO THE EYES OF A WOMAN WHO WAS CARRYING A BABY IN HER ARMS.
SHE UNDERSTOOD MY DISTRESS.
TAKE HER WITH YOU.

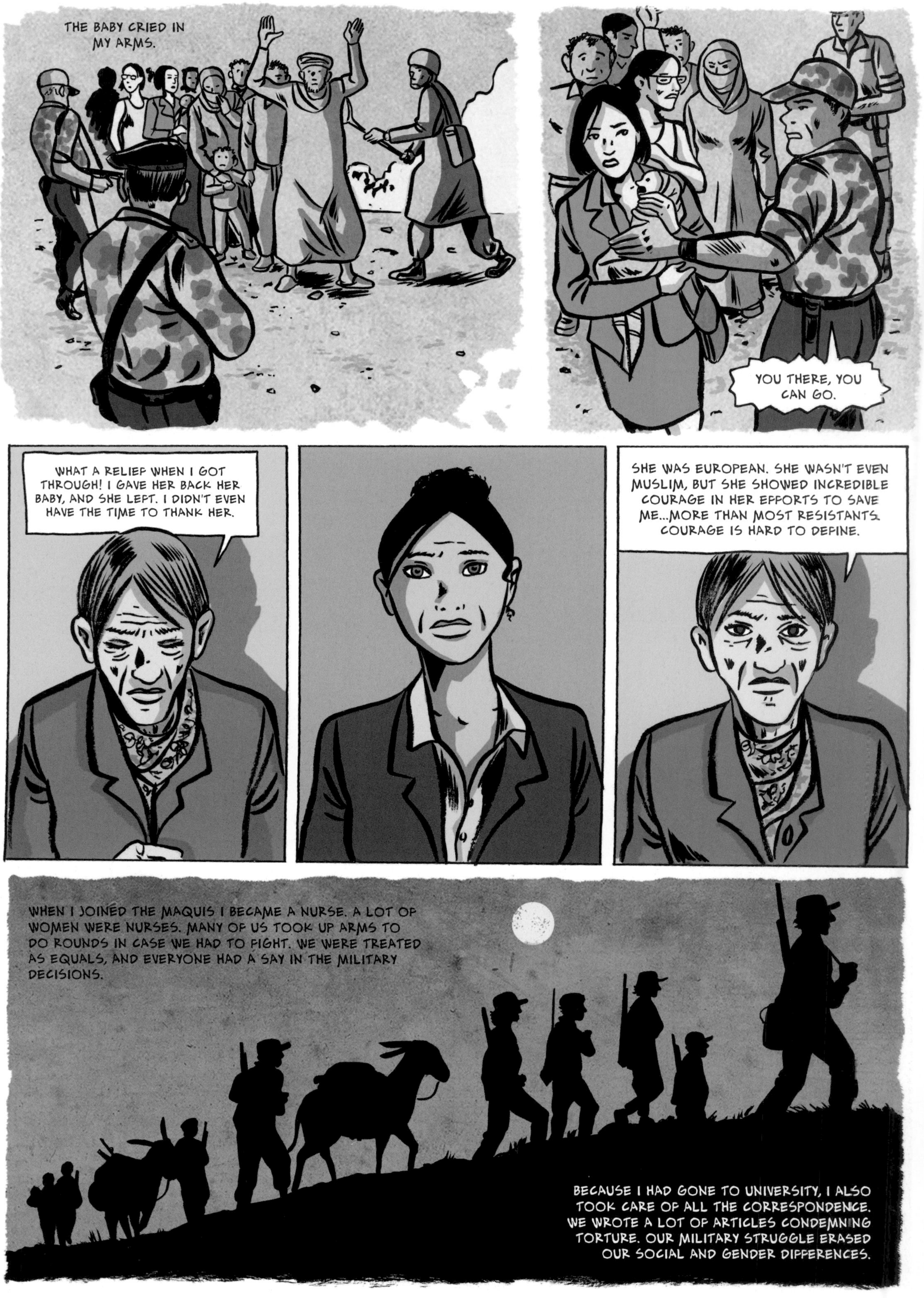

THE BABY CRIED IN MY ARMS.
YOU THERE, YOU CAN GO.
WHAT A RELIEF WHEN I GOT THROUGH! I GAVE HER BACK HER BABY, AND SHE LEFT. I DIDN'T EVEN HAVE THE TIME TO THANK HER.
SHE WAS EUROPEAN. SHE WASN'T EVEN MUSLIM, BUT SHE SHOWED INCREDIBLE COURAGE IN HER EFFORTS TO SAVE ME...MORE THAN MOST RESISTANTS. COURAGE IS HARD TO DEFINE.
WHEN I JOINED THE MAQUIS I BECAME A NURSE. A LOT OF WOMEN WERE NURSES. MANY OF US TOOK UP ARMS TO DO ROUNDS IN CASE WE HAD TO FIGHT. WE WERE TREATED AS EQUALS, AND EVERYONE HAD A SAY IN THE MILITARY DECISIONS.
BECAUSE I HAD GONE TO UNIVERSITY, I ALSO TOOK CARE OF ALL THE CORRESPONDENCE. WE WROTE A LOT OF ARTICLES CONDEMNING TORTURE. OUR MILITARY STRUGGLE ERASED OUR SOCIAL AND GENDER DIFFERENCES.

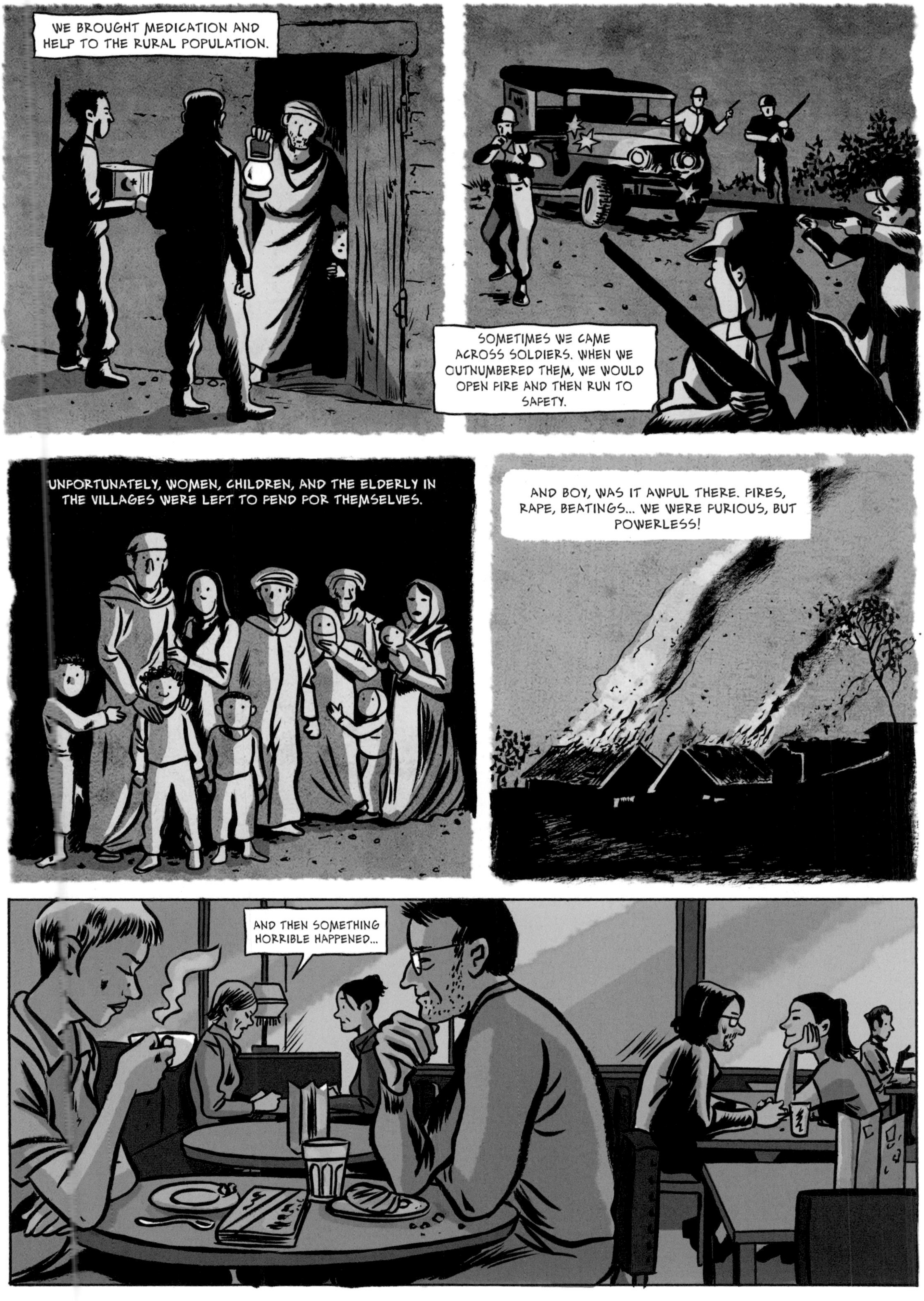
WE BROUGHT MEDICATION AND HELP TO THE RURAL POPULATION.
SOMETIMES WE CAME ACROSS SOLDIERS. WHEN WE OUTNUMBERED THEM, WE WOULD OPEN FIRE AND THEN RUN TO SAFETY.
UNFORTUNATELY, WOMEN, CHILDREN, AND THE ELDERLY IN THE VILLAGES WERE LEFT TO FEND FOR THEMSELVES.
AND BOY, WAS IT AWFUL THERE. FIRES, RAPE, BEATINGS... WE WERE FURIOUS, BUT POWERLESS!
AND THEN SOMETHING HORRIBLE HAPPENED...

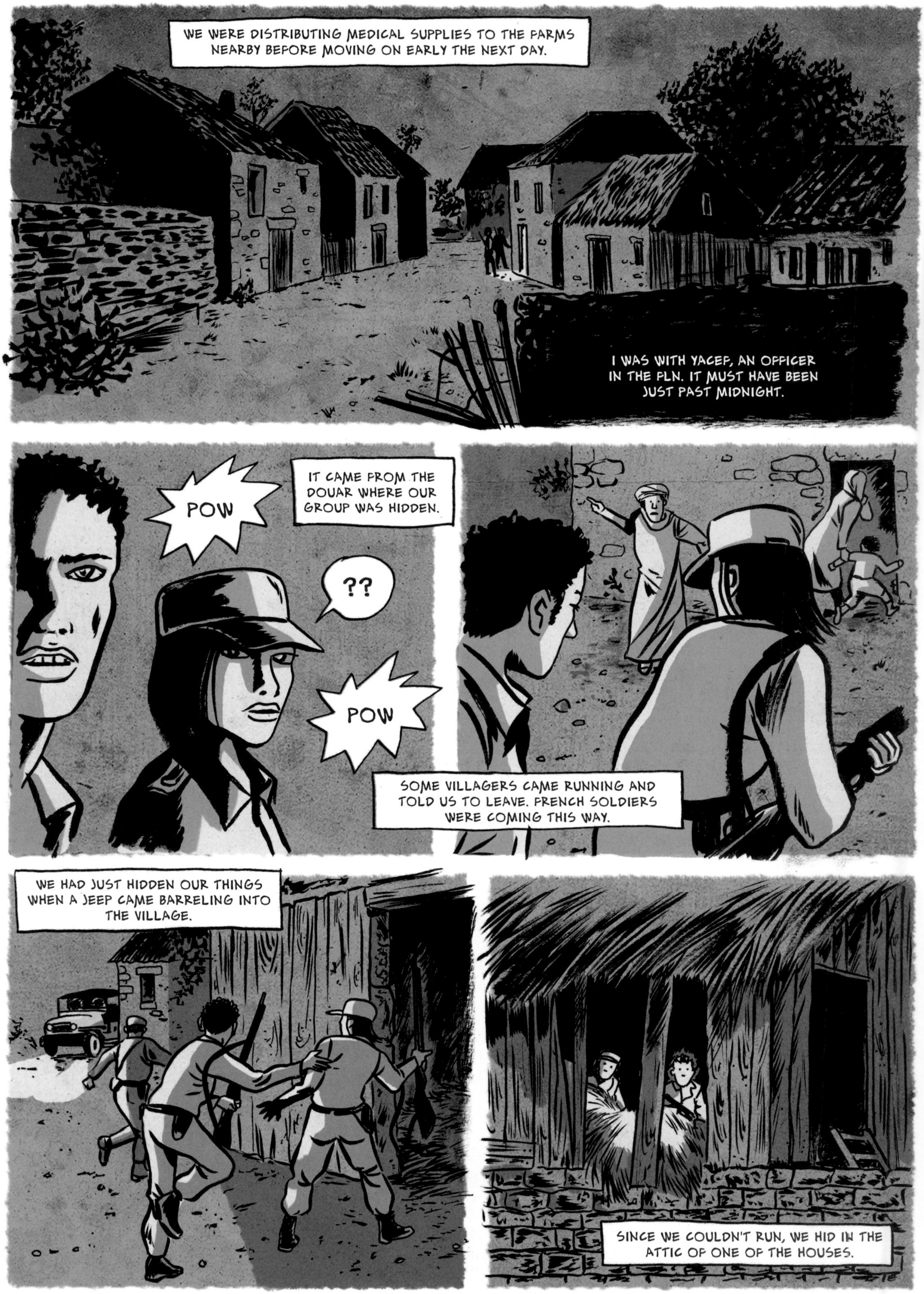
WE WERE DISTRIBUTING MEDICAL SUPPLIES TO THE FARMS NEARBY BEFORE MOVING ON EARLY THE NEXT DAY.
I WAS WITH YACEF, AN OFFICER IN THE FLN. IT MUST HAVE BEEN JUST PAST MIDNIGHT.
POW
IT CAME FROM THE DOUAR WHERE OUR GROUP WAS HIDDEN.
??
POW
SOME VILLAGERS CAME RUNNING AND TOLD US TO LEAVE. FRENCH SOLDIERS WERE COMING THIS WAY.
WE HAD JUST HIDDEN OUR THINGS WHEN A JEEP CAME BARRELING INTO THE VILLAGE.
SINCE WE COULDN'T RUN, WE HID IN THE ATTIC OF ONE OF THE HOUSES.

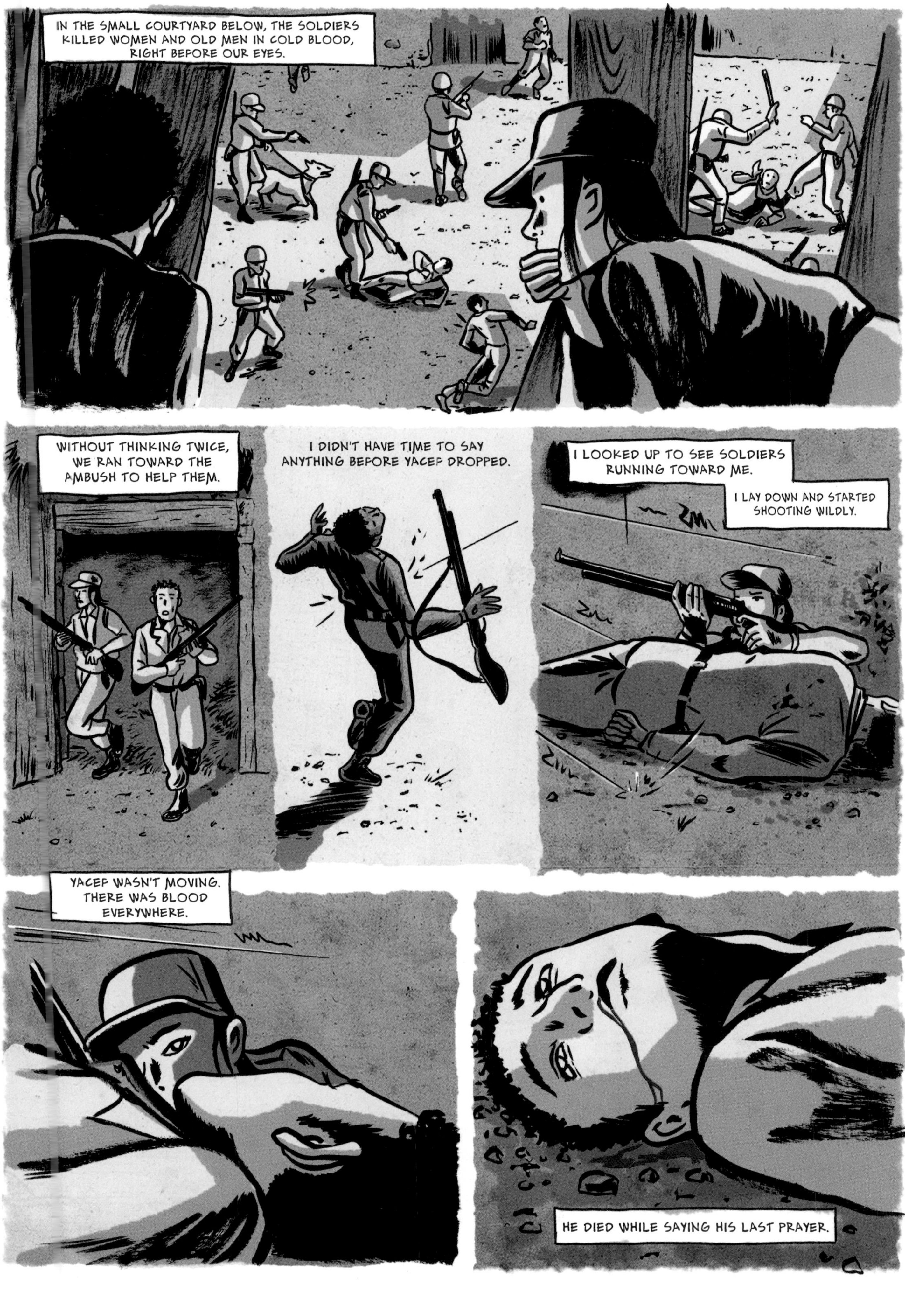
IN THE SMALL COURTYARD BELOW, THE SOLDIERS KILLED WOMEN AND OLD MEN IN COLD BLOOD, RIGHT BEFORE OUR EYES.
WITHOUT THINKING TWICE, WE RAN TOWARD THE AMBUSH TO HELP THEM.
I DIDN'T HAVE TIME TO SAY ANYTHING BEFORE YACEF DROPPED.
I LOOKED UP TO SEE SOLDIERS RUNNING TOWARD ME.
I LAY DOWN AND STARTED SHOOTING WILDLY.
YACEF WASN'T MOVING. THERE WAS BLOOD EVERYWHERE.
HE DIED WHILE SAYING HIS LAST PRAYER.

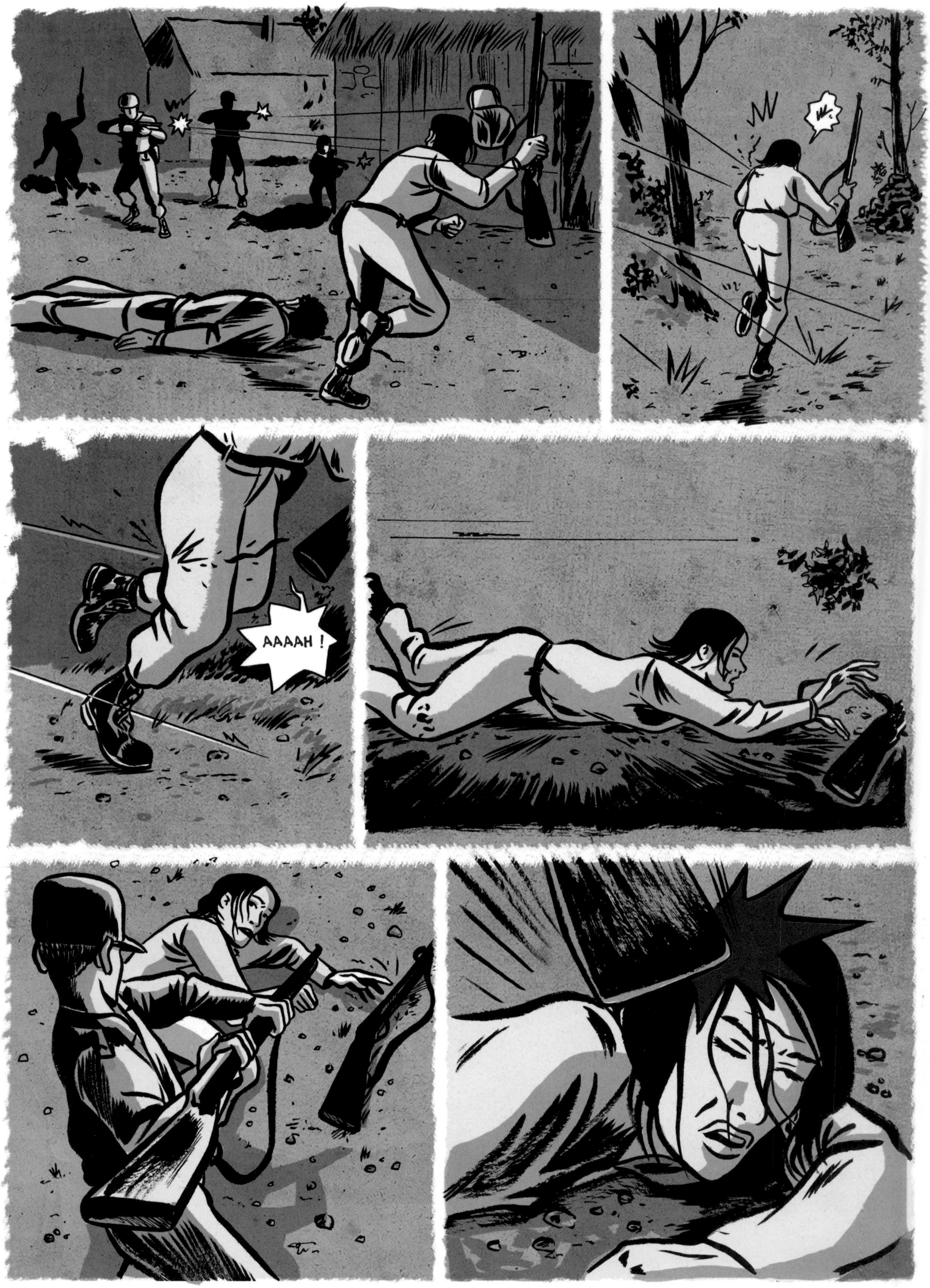
AAAAH !

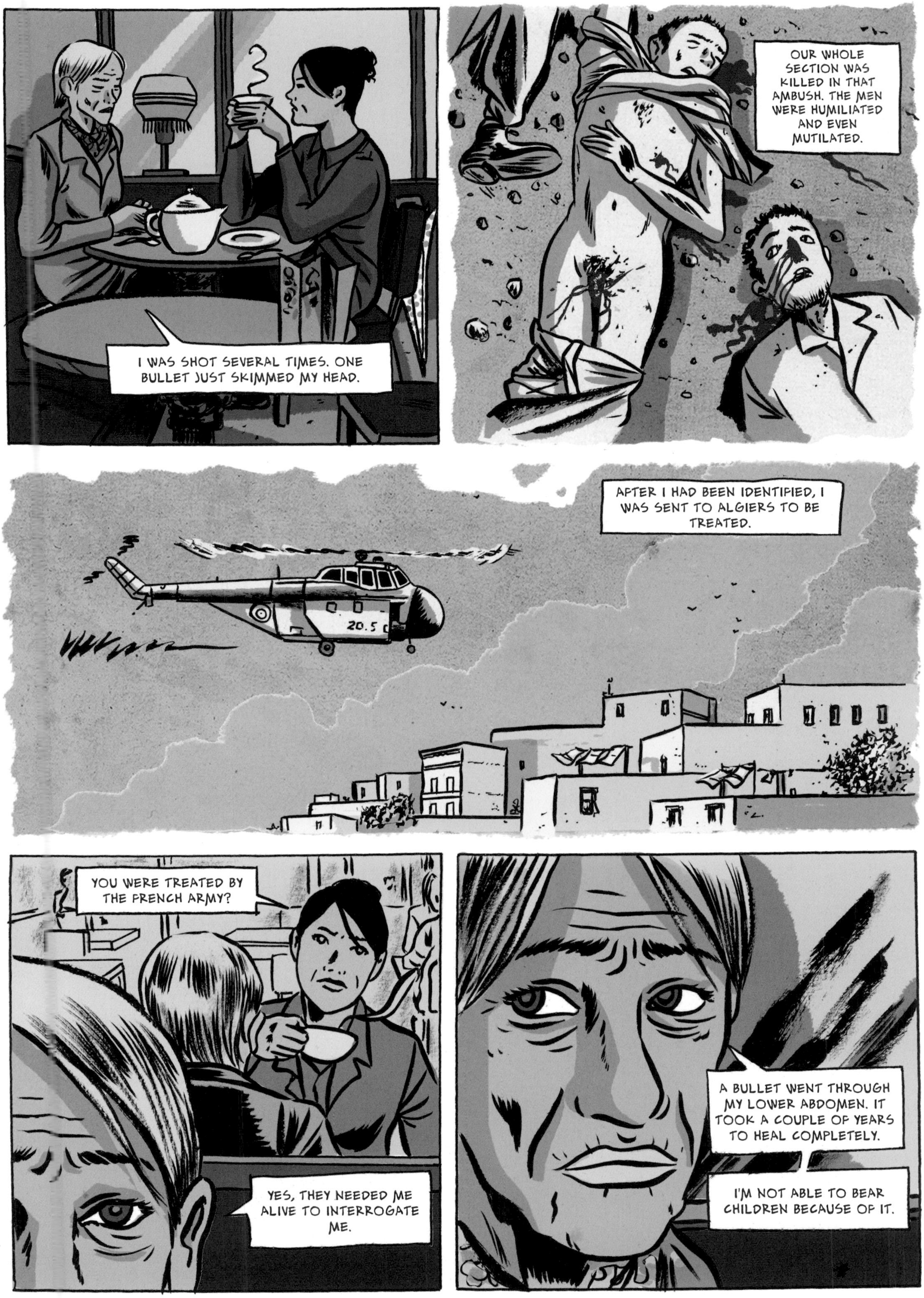
I WAS SHOT SEVERAL TIMES. ONE BULLET JUST SKIMMED MY HEAD.
OUR WHOLE SECTION WAS KILLED IN THAT AMBUSH. THE MEN WERE HUMILIATED AND EVEN MUTILATED.
AFTER I HAD BEEN IDENTIFIED, I WAS SENT TO ALGIERS TO BE TREATED.
20.5
YOU WERE TREATED BY THE FRENCH ARMY?
YES, THEY NEEDED ME ALIVE TO INTERROGATE ME.
A BULLET WENT THROUGH MY LOWER ABDOMEN. IT TOOK A COUPLE OF YEARS TO HEAL COMPLETELY.
I'M NOT ABLE TO BEAR CHILDREN BECAUSE OF IT.

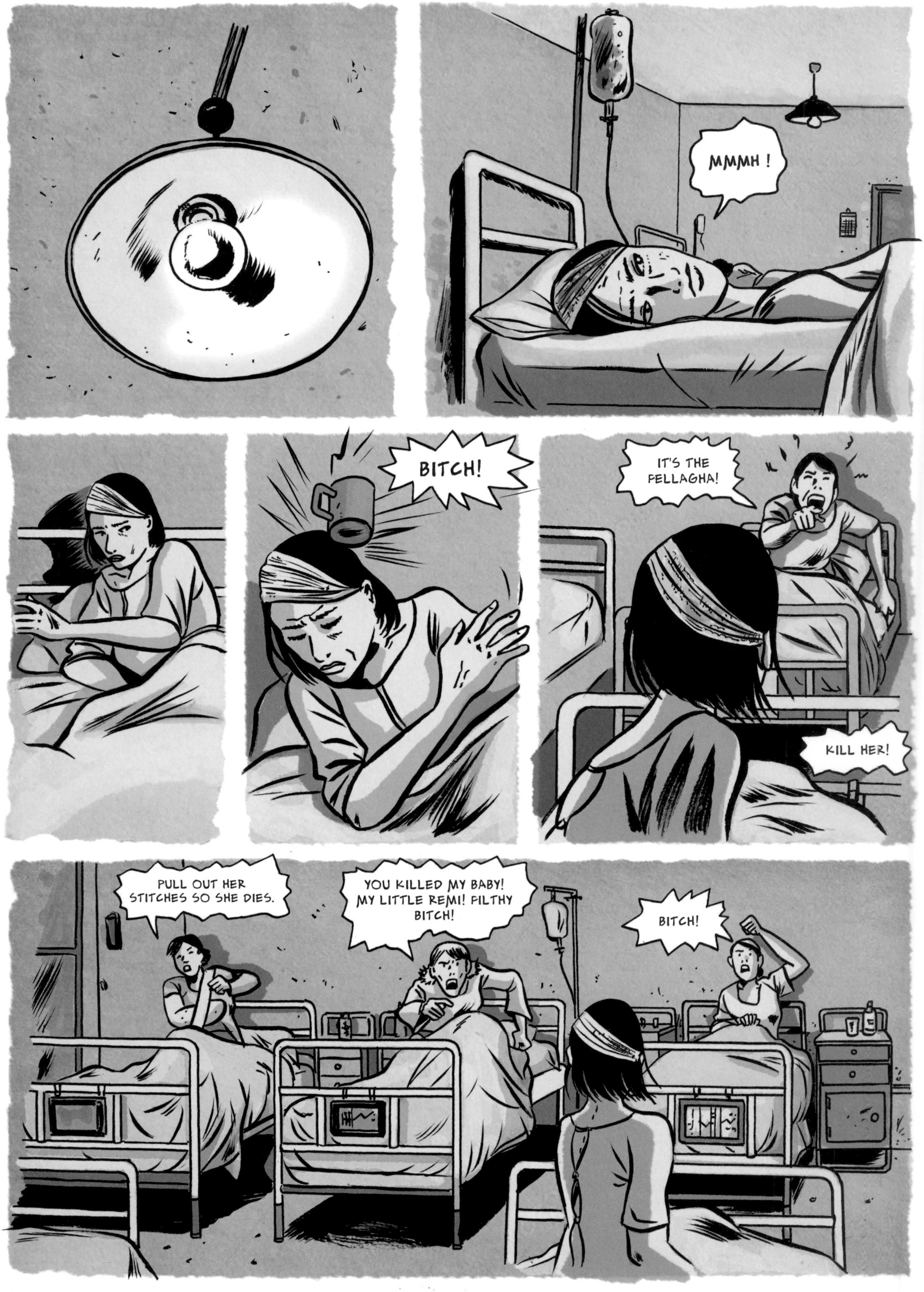
MMMH !
BITCH!
IT'S THE FELLAGHA!
KILL HER!
PULL OUT HER STITCHES SO SHE DIES.
YOU KILLED MY BABY! MY LITTLE REMI! FILTHY BITCH!
BITCH!

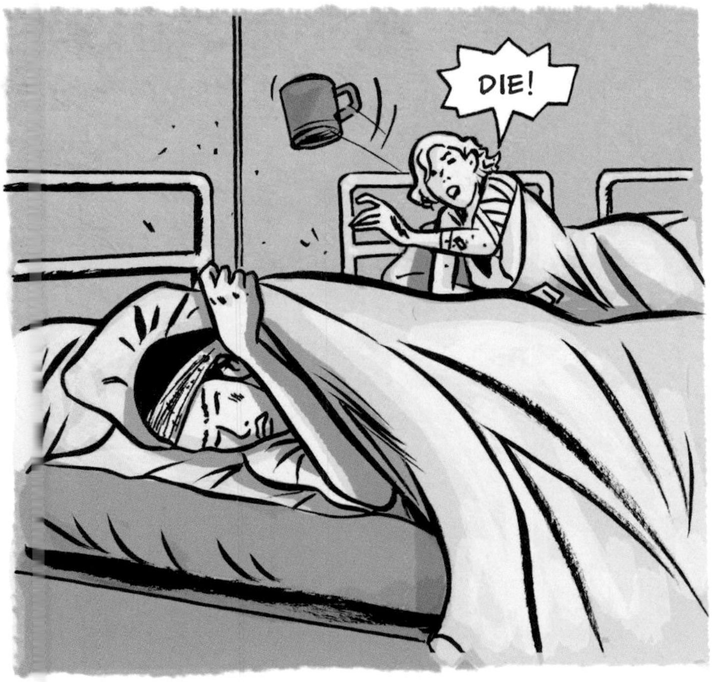
DIE!

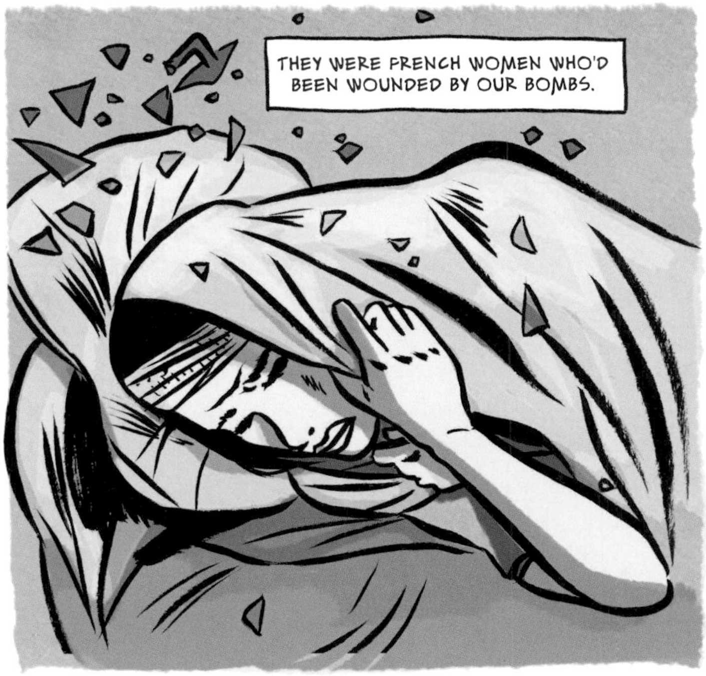
THEY WERE FRENCH WOMEN WHO'D BEEN WOUNDED BY OUR BOMBS.

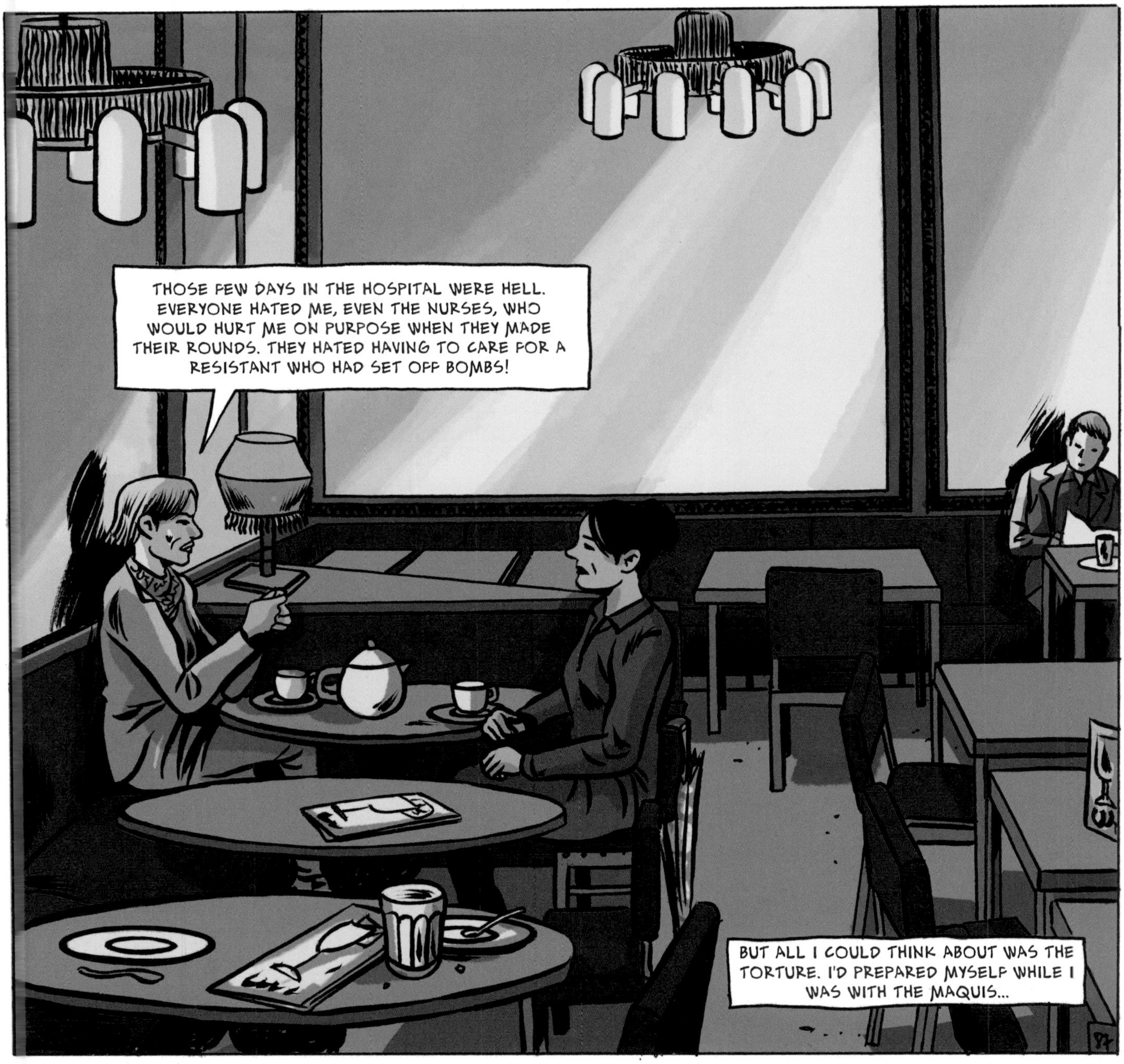
THOSE FEW DAYS IN THE HOSPITAL WERE HELL. EVERYONE HATED ME, EVEN THE NURSES, WHO WOULD HURT ME ON PURPOSE WHEN THEY MADE THEIR ROUNDS. THEY HATED HAVING TO CARE FOR A RESISTANT WHO HAD SET OFF BOMBS!
BUT ALL I COULD THINK ABOUT WAS THE TORTURE. I'D PREPARED MYSELF WHILE I WAS WITH THE MAQUIS...

I HOPED I WAS READY.

OW!

WHAT I WAS MOST AFRAID OF WAS WHAT THEY WOULD DO TO MY FAMILY.

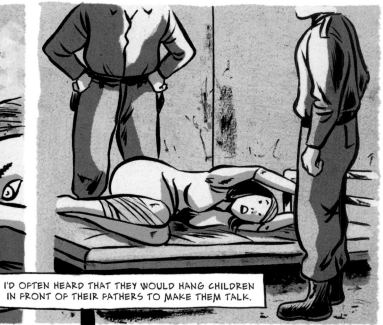

I'D OFTEN HEARD THAT THEY WOULD HANG CHILDREN IN FRONT OF THEIR FATHERS TO MAKE THEM TALK.

88

YOU'LL SEE, THOSE LITTLE FELLAGHAS ARE TOUGH.

PLEASE...

NO!

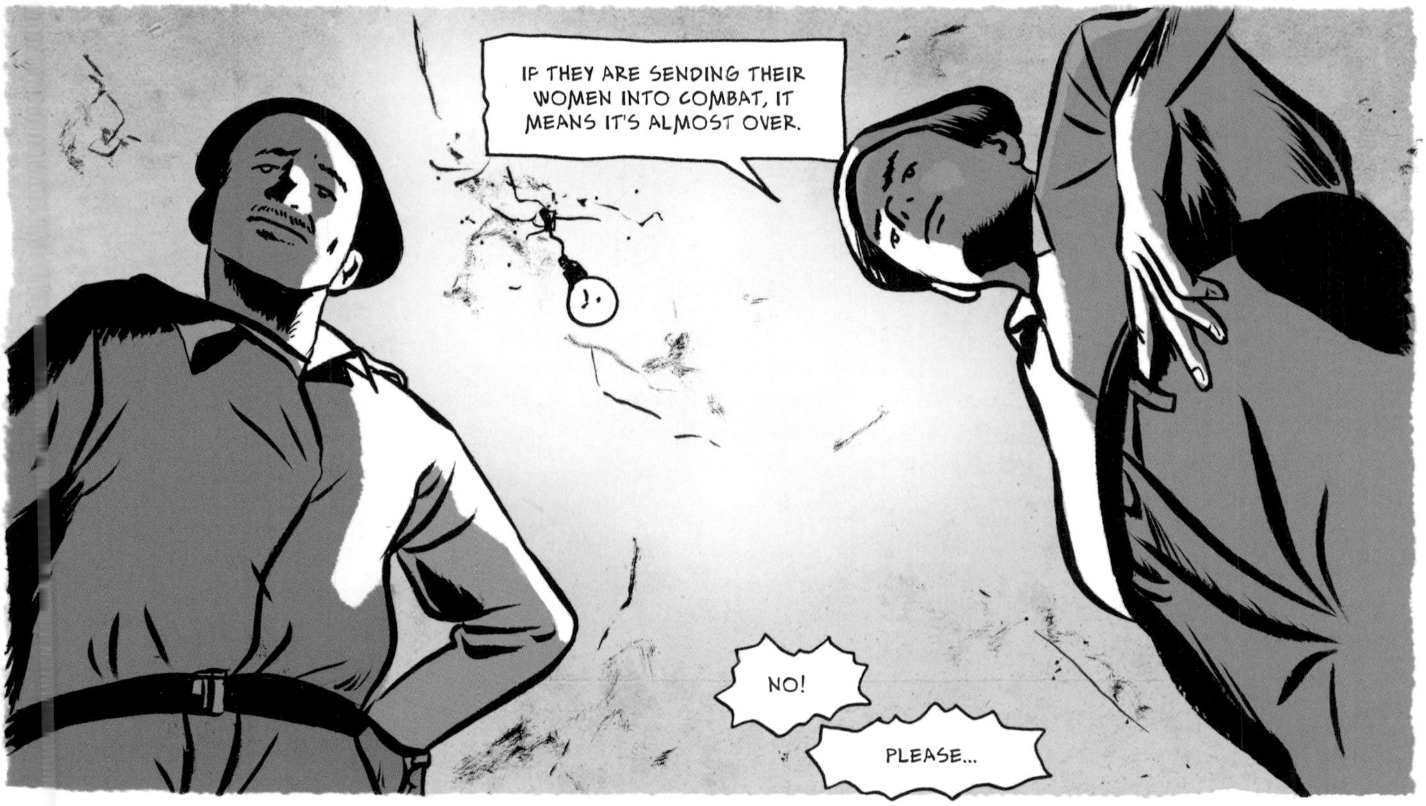
IF THEY ARE SENDING THEIR WOMEN INTO COMBAT, IT MEANS IT'S ALMOST OVER.
NO!
PLEASE...

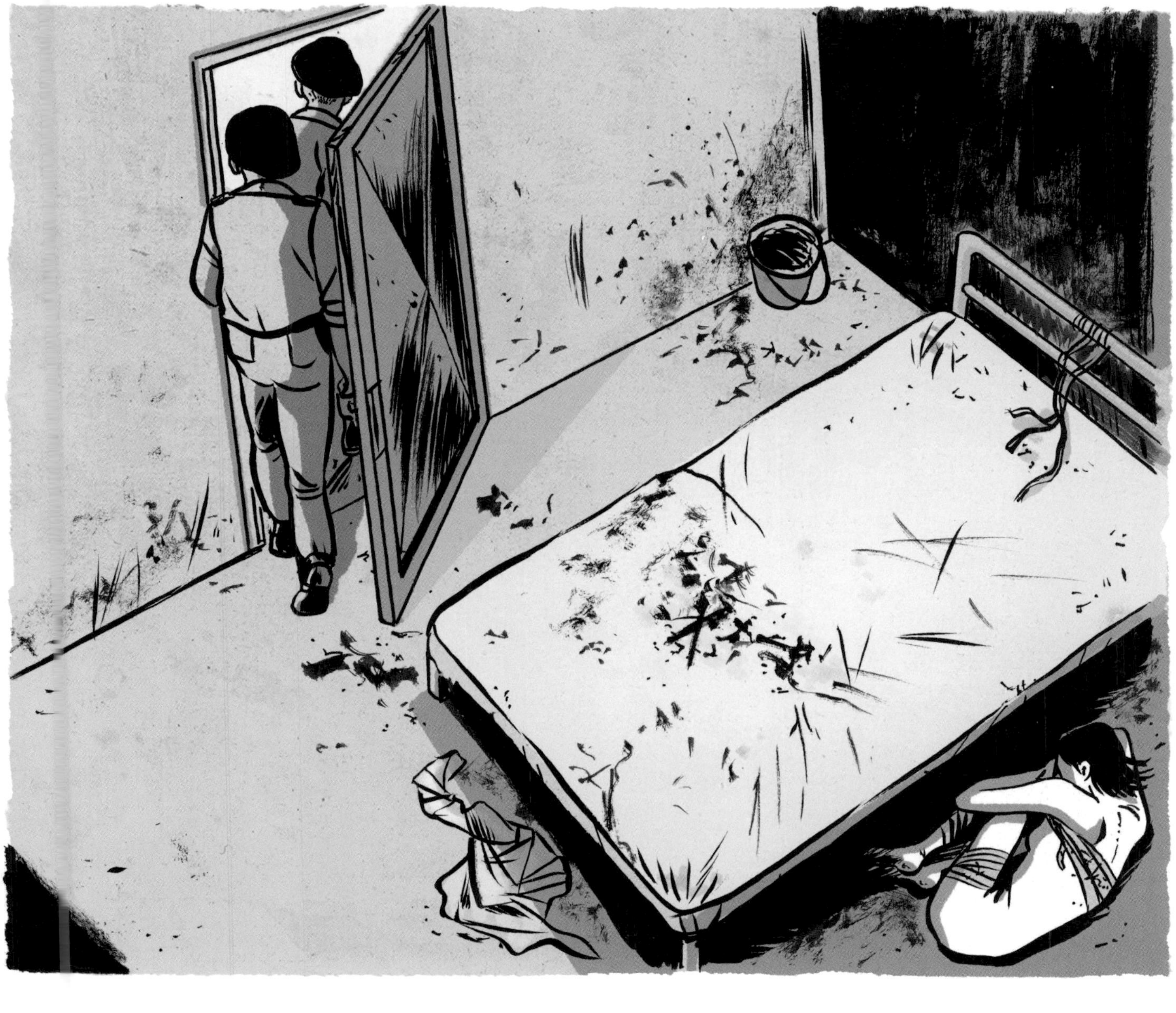

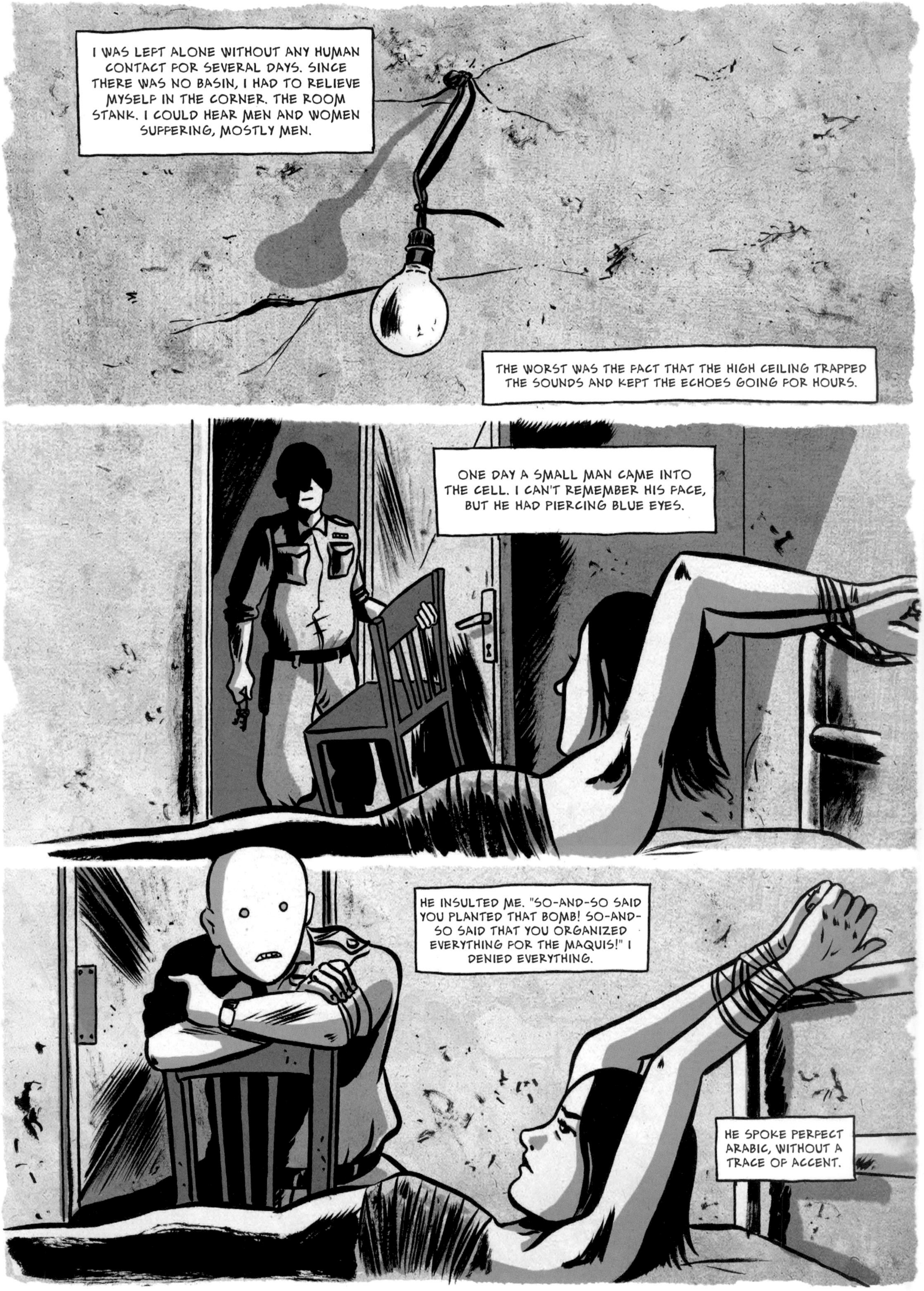
I WAS LEFT ALONE WITHOUT ANY HUMAN CONTACT FOR SEVERAL DAYS. SINCE THERE WAS NO BASIN, I HAD TO RELIEVE MYSELF IN THE CORNER. THE ROOM STANK. I COULD HEAR MEN AND WOMEN SUFFERING, MOSTLY MEN.
THE WORST WAS THE FACT THAT THE HIGH CEILING TRAPPED THE SOUNDS AND KEPT THE ECHOES GOING FOR HOURS.
ONE DAY A SMALL MAN CAME INTO THE CELL. I CAN'T REMEMBER HIS FACE, BUT HE HAD PIERCING BLUE EYES.
HE INSULTED ME. "SO-AND-SO SAID YOU PLANTED THAT BOMB! SO-AND-SO SAID THAT YOU ORGANIZED EVERYTHING FOR THE MAQUIS!" I DENIED EVERYTHING.
HE SPOKE PERFECT ARABIC, WITHOUT A TRACE OF ACCENT.

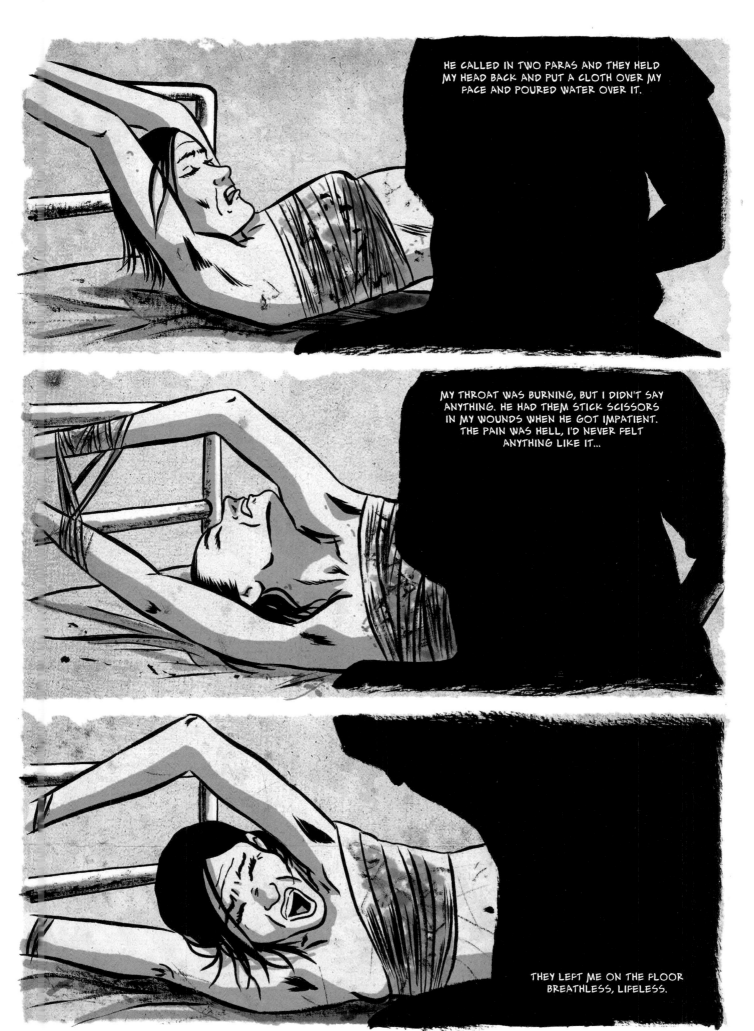

HE CALLED IN TWO PARAS AND THEY HELD MY HEAD BACK AND PUT A CLOTH OVER MY FACE AND POURED WATER OVER IT.

MY THROAT WAS BURNING, BUT I DIDN'T SAY ANYTHING. HE HAD THEM STICK SCISSORS IN MY WOUNDS WHEN HE GOT IMPATIENT. THE PAIN WAS HELL, I'D NEVER FELT ANYTHING LIKE IT...

THEY LEFT ME ON THE FLOOR BREATHLESS, LIFELESS.

THIS WAS REPEATED EACH DAY, INCESSANTLY. THE WORST WAS THAT YOU NEVER KNEW WHEN THEY WOULD BE BACK.

DAY...

...OR NIGHT. ALWAYS QUIETLY.

THEY OFTEN BROUGHT FELLAGHAS WHO WERE COVERED WITH BURNS AND BRUISES.

ONE OF THE FORMS OF TORTURE WAS TO BURN GENITALS WITH A BLOWTORCH. THE PARAS WANTED ME TO IDENTIFY THEM. THEY WOULD SAY, "SO-AND-SO HAS TOLD US ALL ABOUT YOU."

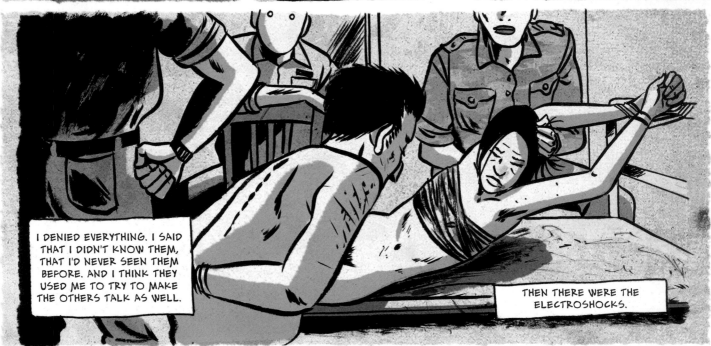

I DENIED EVERYTHING. I SAID THAT I DIDN'T KNOW THEM, THAT I'D NEVER SEEN THEM BEFORE. AND I THINK THEY USED ME TO TRY TO MAKE THE OTHERS TALK AS WELL.

THEN THERE WERE THE ELECTROSHOCKS.

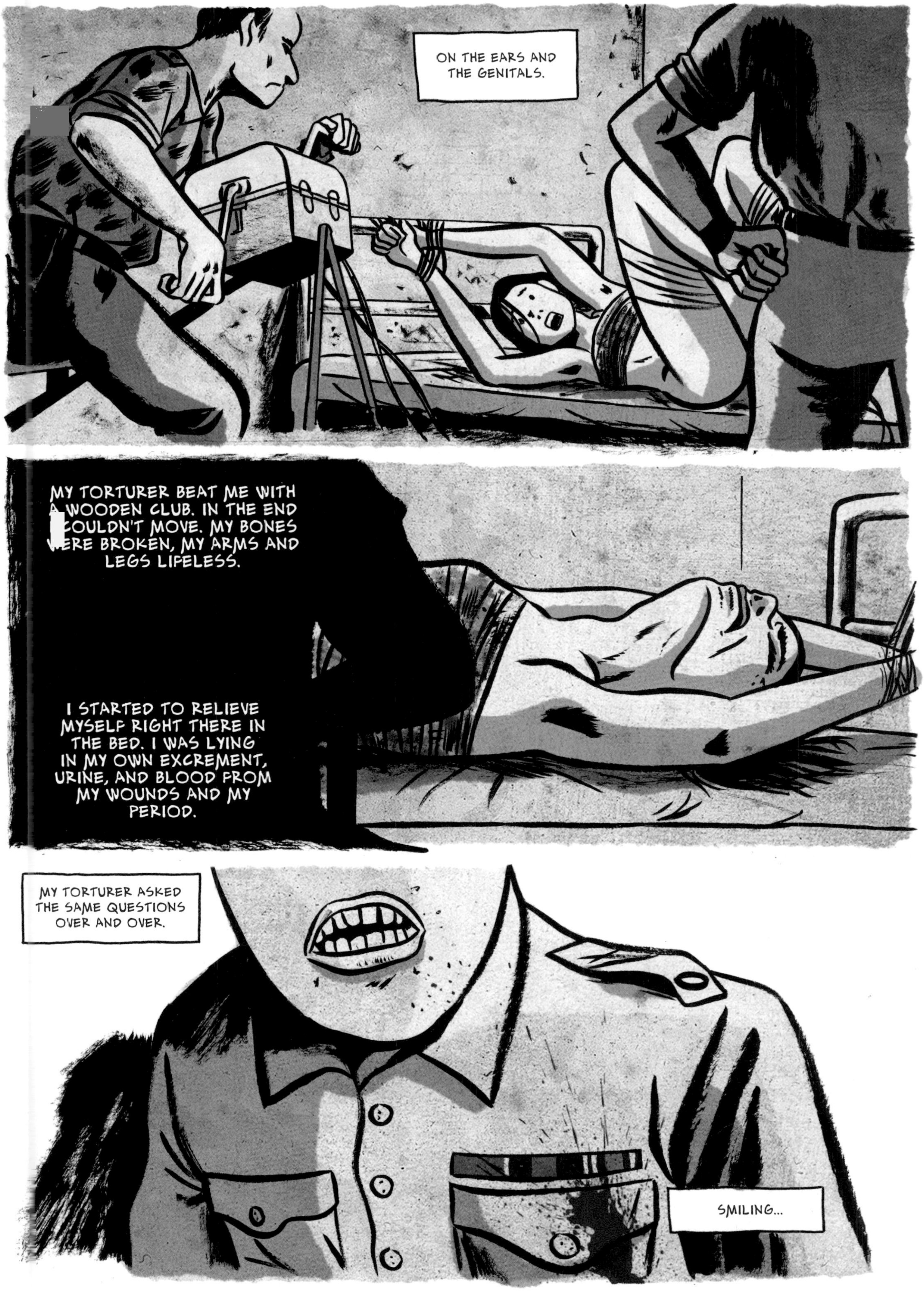
ON THE EARS AND THE GENITALS.
MY TORTURER BEAT ME WITH A WOODEN CLUB. IN THE END COULDN'T MOVE. MY BONES WERE BROKEN, MY ARMS AND LEGS LIFELESS.
I STARTED TO RELIEVE MYSELF RIGHT THERE IN THE BED. I WAS LYING IN MY OWN EXCREMENT, URINE, AND BLOOD FROM MY WOUNDS AND MY PERIOD.
MY TORTURER ASKED THE SAME QUESTIONS OVER AND OVER.
SMILING...

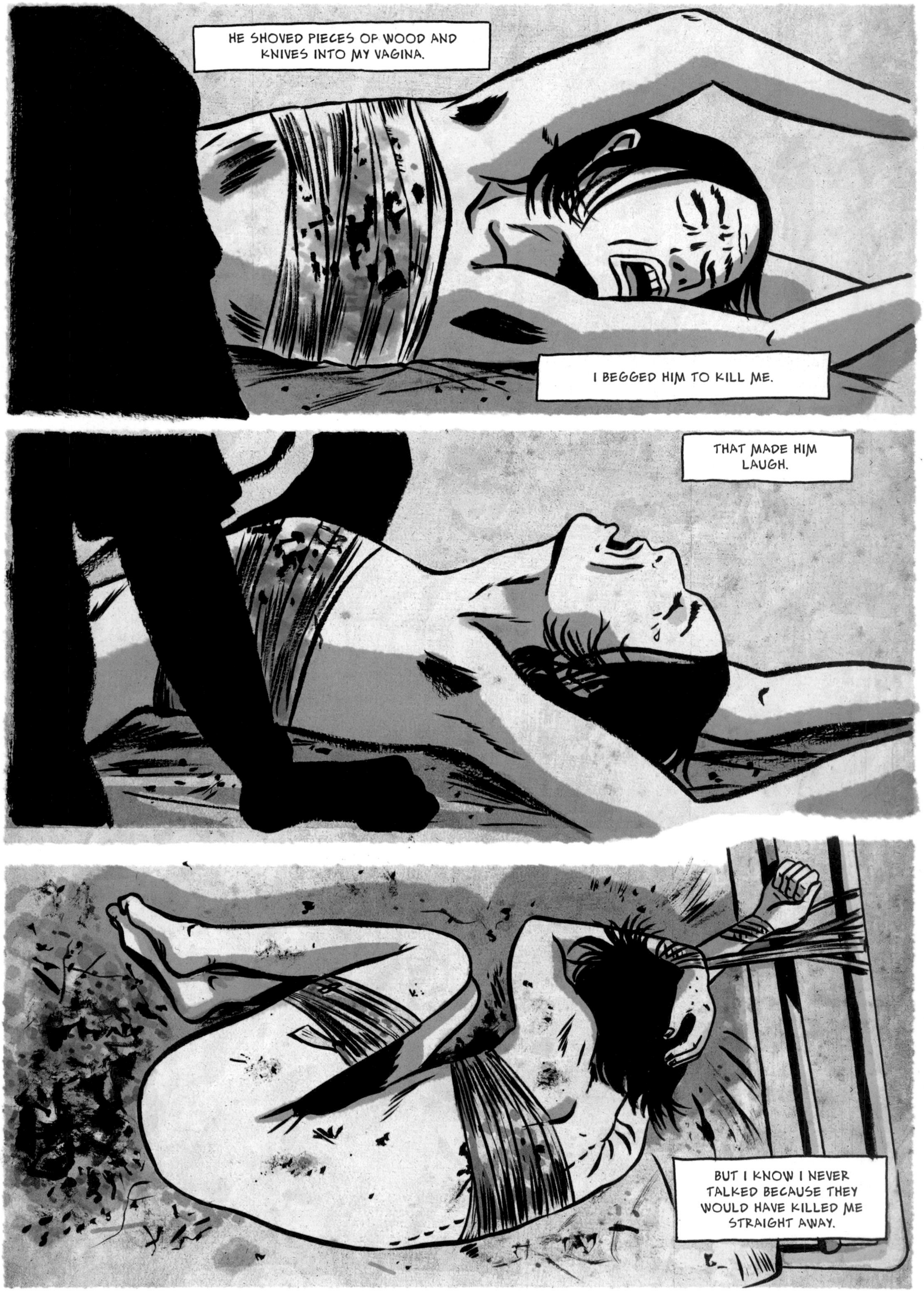
HE SHOVED PIECES OF WOOD AND KNIVES INTO MY VAGINA.
I BEGGED HIM TO KILL ME.
THAT MADE HIM LAUGH.
BUT I KNOW I NEVER TALKED BECAUSE THEY WOULD HAVE KILLED ME STRAIGHT AWAY.

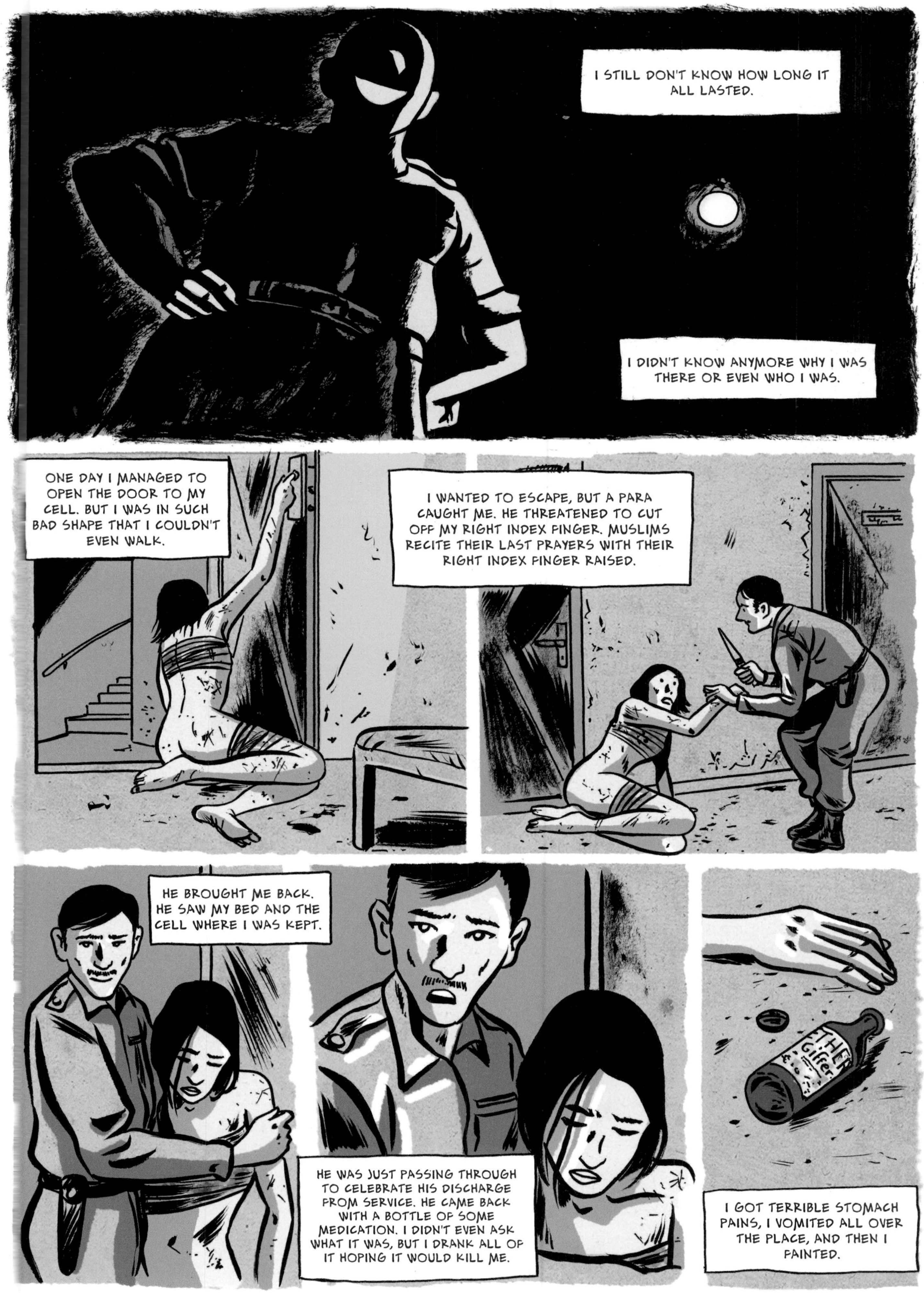
I STILL DON'T KNOW HOW LONG IT ALL LASTED.
I DIDN'T KNOW ANYMORE WHY I WAS THERE OR EVEN WHO I WAS.
ONE DAY I MANAGED TO OPEN THE DOOR TO MY CELL. BUT I WAS IN SUCH BAD SHAPE THAT I COULDN'T EVEN WALK.
I WANTED TO ESCAPE, BUT A PARA CAUGHT ME. HE THREATENED TO CUT OFF MY RIGHT INDEX FINGER. MUSLIMS RECITE THEIR LAST PRAYERS WITH THEIR RIGHT INDEX FINGER RAISED.
HE BROUGHT ME BACK. HE SAW MY BED AND THE CELL WHERE I WAS KEPT.
HE WAS JUST PASSING THROUGH TO CELEBRATE HIS DISCHARGE FROM SERVICE. HE CAME BACK WITH A BOTTLE OF SOME MEDICATION. I DIDN'T EVEN ASK WHAT IT WAS, BUT I DRANK ALL OF IT HOPING IT WOULD KILL ME.
I GOT TERRIBLE STOMACH PAINS, I VOMITED ALL OVER THE PLACE, AND THEN I FAINTED.

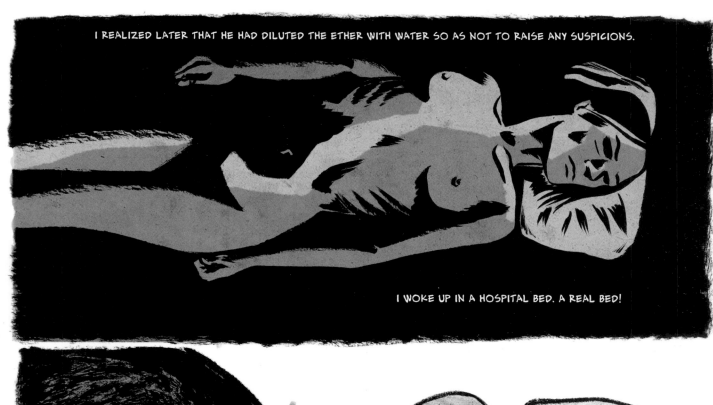

I REALIZED LATER THAT HE HAD DILUTED THE ETHER WITH WATER SO AS NOT TO RAISE ANY SUSPICIONS.

I WOKE UP IN A HOSPITAL BED. A REAL BED!

UNDER THE LIGHT, MY BODY LOOKED TERRIBLE. I WAS SKIN AND BONES AND COVERED IN BRUISES.

THE PARA CAME BACK BUT DIDN'T COME INTO THE CELL. I HEARD HIM BEHIND THE DOOR. HE TOLD THE DOCTOR TO SAY I WAS DYING. THAT I HAD HEPATITIS AND WAS CONTAGIOUS AND COULD NOT GO BACK TO THE CENTER. IT WASN'T TRUE, OBVIOUSLY. THE DOCTOR REFUSED.

THE PARA GAVE HIM MONEY TO DO IT. THEN HE LEFT, AND I NEVER SAW HIM AGAIN.

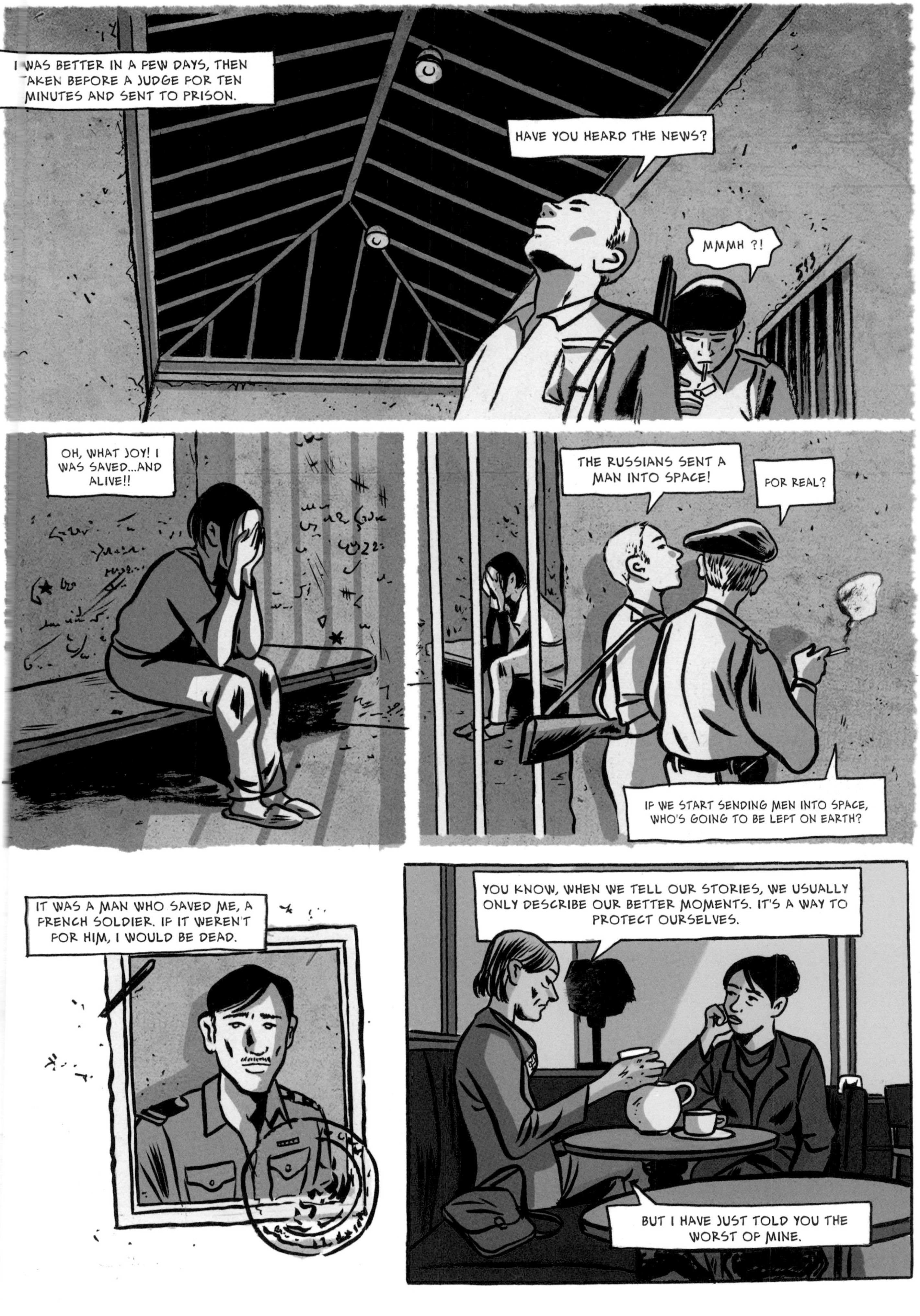

I WAS BETTER IN A FEW DAYS, THEN TAKEN BEFORE A JUDGE FOR TEN MINUTES AND SENT TO PRISON.
HAVE YOU HEARD THE NEWS?
MMMH ?!
OH, WHAT JOY! I WAS SAVED...AND ALIVE!!
THE RUSSIANS SENT A MAN INTO SPACE!
FOR REAL?
IF WE START SENDING MEN INTO SPACE, WHO'S GOING TO BE LEFT ON EARTH?
IT WAS A MAN WHO SAVED ME, A FRENCH SOLDIER. IF IT WEREN'T FOR HIM, I WOULD BE DEAD.
YOU KNOW, WHEN WE TELL OUR STORIES, WE USUALLY ONLY DESCRIBE OUR BETTER MOMENTS. IT'S A WAY TO PROTECT OURSELVES.
BUT I HAVE JUST TOLD YOU THE WORST OF MINE.

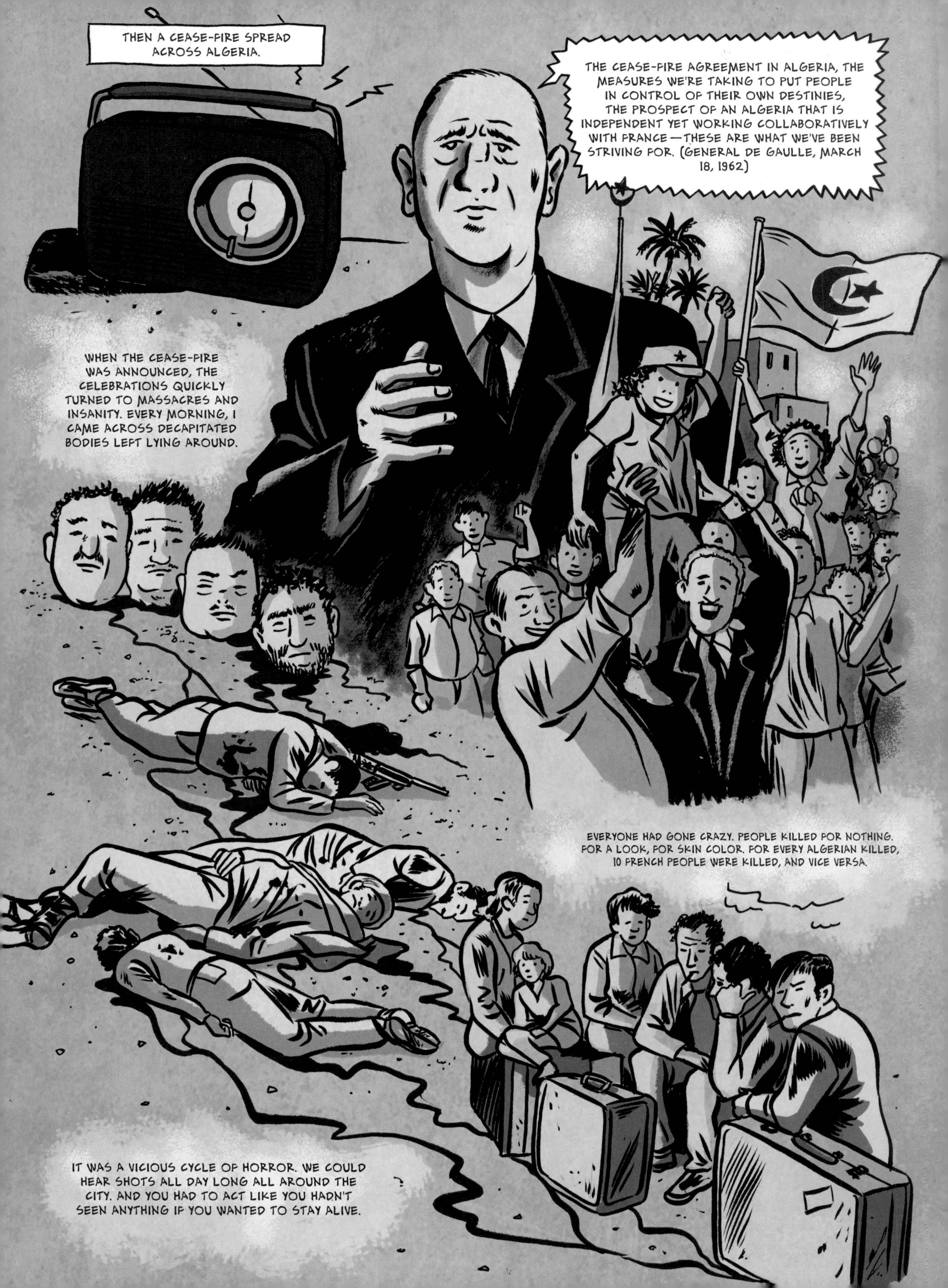
THEN A CEASE-FIRE SPREAD ACROSS ALGERIA.
THE CEASE-FIRE AGREEMENT IN ALGERIA, THE MEASURES WE'RE TAKING TO PUT PEOPLE IN CONTROL OF THEIR OWN DESTINIES, THE PROSPECT OF AN ALGERIA THAT IS INDEPENDENT YET WORKING COLLABORATIVELY WITH FRANCE—THESE ARE WHAT WE'VE BEEN STRIVING FOR. (GENERAL DE GAULLE, MARCH 18, 1962)
WHEN THE CEASE-FIRE WAS ANNOUNCED, THE CELEBRATIONS QUICKLY TURNED TO MASSACRES AND INSANITY. EVERY MORNING, I CAME ACROSS DECAPITATED BODIES LEFT LYING AROUND.
EVERYONE HAD GONE CRAZY. PEOPLE KILLED FOR NOTHING. FOR A LOOK, FOR SKIN COLOR. FOR EVERY ALGERIAN KILLED, 10 FRENCH PEOPLE WERE KILLED, AND VICE VERSA.
IT WAS A VICIOUS CYCLE OF HORROR. WE COULD HEAR SHOTS ALL DAY LONG ALL AROUND THE CITY. AND YOU HAD TO ACT LIKE YOU HADN'T SEEN ANYTHING IF YOU WANTED TO STAY ALIVE.

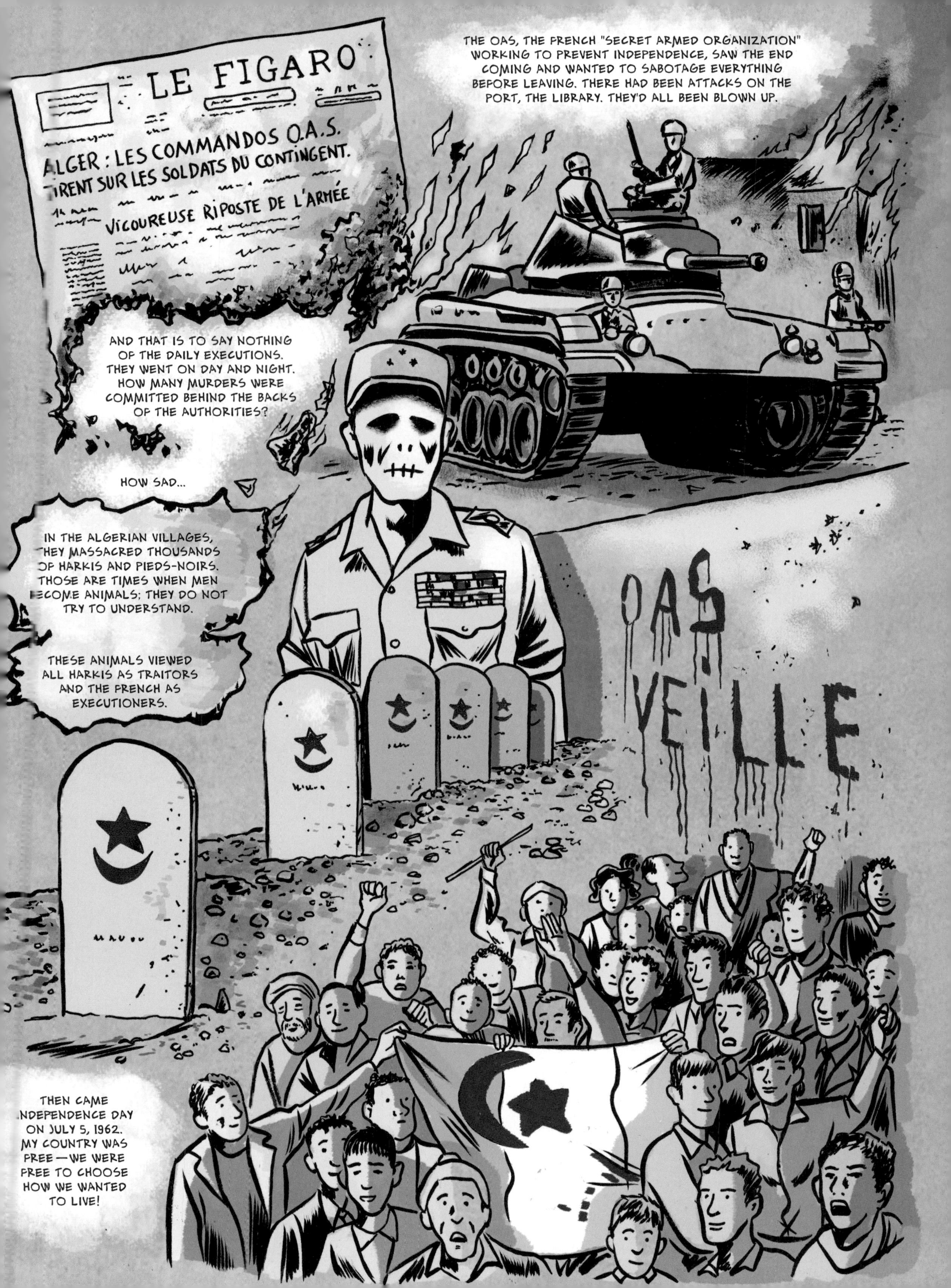
LE FIGARO
ALGER : LES COMMANDOS O.A.S. TIRENT SUR LES SOLDATS DU CONTINGENT.
VIGOUREUSE RIPOSTE DE L'ARMÉE
THE OAS, THE FRENCH "SECRET ARMED ORGANIZATION" WORKING TO PREVENT INDEPENDENCE, SAW THE END COMING AND WANTED TO SABOTAGE EVERYTHING BEFORE LEAVING. THERE HAD BEEN ATTACKS ON THE PORT, THE LIBRARY. THEY'D ALL BEEN BLOWN UP.
AND THAT IS TO SAY NOTHING OF THE DAILY EXECUTIONS. THEY WENT ON DAY AND NIGHT. HOW MANY MURDERS WERE COMMITTED BEHIND THE BACKS OF THE AUTHORITIES?
HOW SAD...
IN THE ALGERIAN VILLAGES, THEY MASSACRED THOUSANDS OF HARKIS AND PIEDS-NOIRS. THOSE ARE TIMES WHEN MEN BECOME ANIMALS; THEY DO NOT TRY TO UNDERSTAND.
THESE ANIMALS VIEWED ALL HARKIS AS TRAITORS AND THE FRENCH AS EXECUTIONERS.
OAS VEILLE
THEN CAME INDEPENDENCE DAY ON JULY 5, 1962. MY COUNTRY WAS FREE—WE WERE FREE TO CHOOSE HOW WE WANTED TO LIVE!

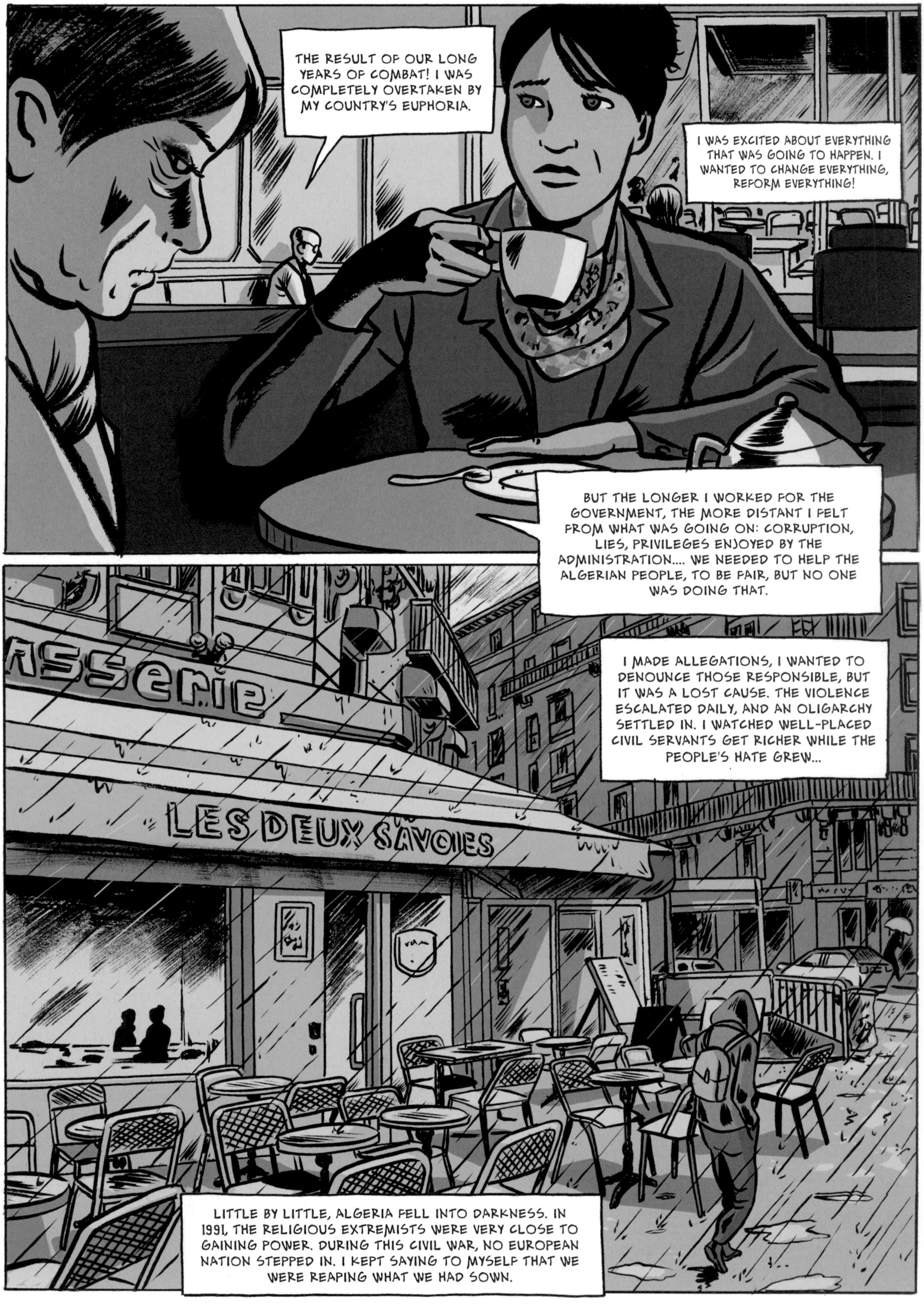

THE RESULT OF OUR LONG YEARS OF COMBAT! I WAS COMPLETELY OVERTAKEN BY MY COUNTRY'S EUPHORIA.
I WAS EXCITED ABOUT EVERYTHING THAT WAS GOING TO HAPPEN. I WANTED TO CHANGE EVERYTHING, REFORM EVERYTHING!
BUT THE LONGER I WORKED FOR THE GOVERNMENT, THE MORE DISTANT I FELT FROM WHAT WAS GOING ON: CORRUPTION, LIES, PRIVILEGES ENJOYED BY THE ADMINISTRATION.... WE NEEDED TO HELP THE ALGERIAN PEOPLE, TO BE FAIR, BUT NO ONE WAS DOING THAT.
ASSERIE
LES DEUX SAVOIES
I MADE ALLEGATIONS, I WANTED TO DENOUNCE THOSE RESPONSIBLE, BUT IT WAS A LOST CAUSE. THE VIOLENCE ESCALATED DAILY, AND AN OLIGARCHY SETTLED IN. I WATCHED WELL-PLACED CIVIL SERVANTS GET RICHER WHILE THE PEOPLE'S HATE GREW...
LITTLE BY LITTLE, ALGERIA FELL INTO DARKNESS. IN 1991, THE RELIGIOUS EXTREMISTS WERE VERY CLOSE TO GAINING POWER. DURING THIS CIVIL WAR, NO EUROPEAN NATION STEPPED IN. I KEPT SAYING TO MYSELF THAT WE WERE REAPING WHAT WE HAD SOWN.

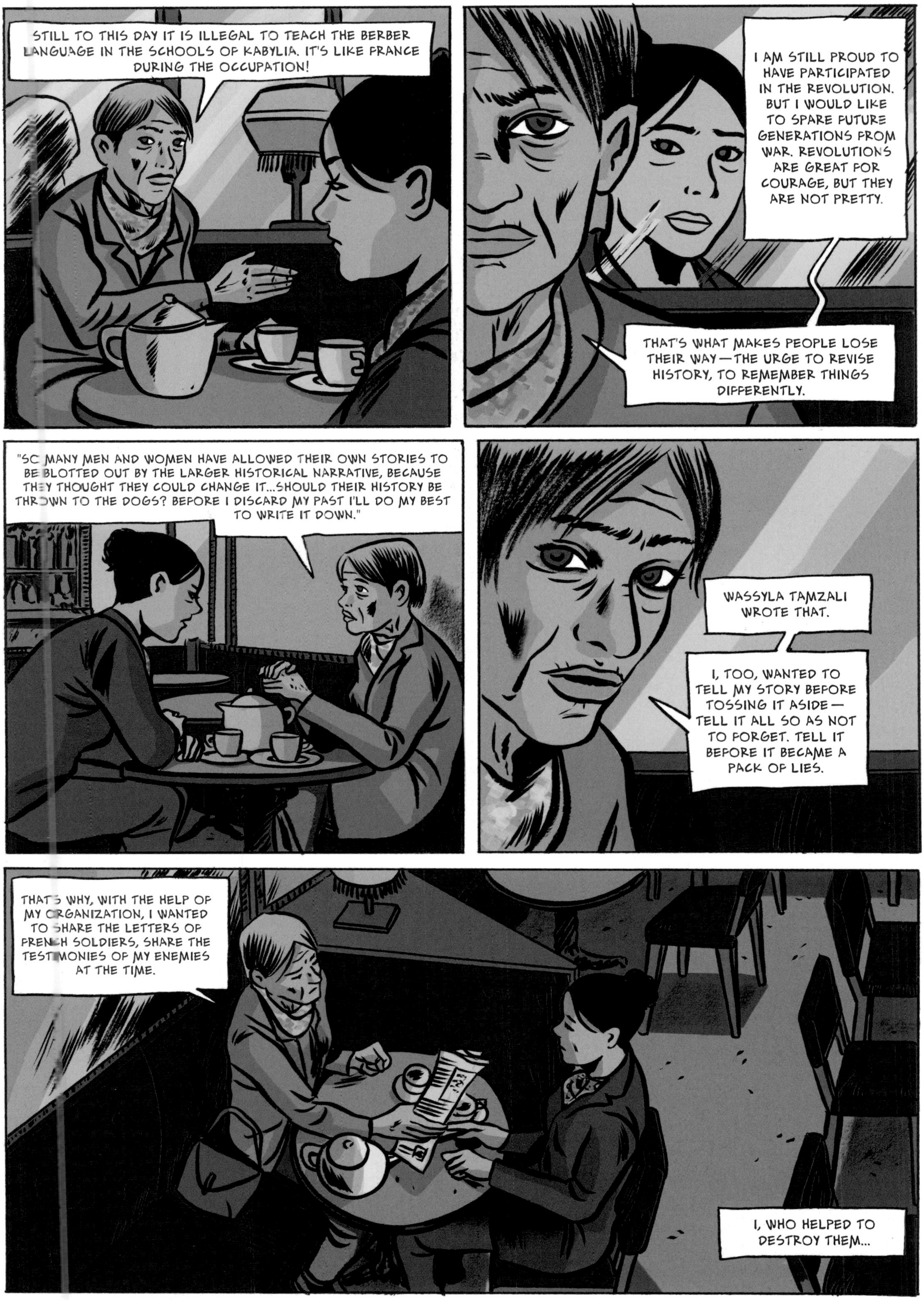
STILL TO THIS DAY IT IS ILLEGAL TO TEACH THE BERBER LANGUAGE IN THE SCHOOLS OF KABYLIA. IT'S LIKE FRANCE DURING THE OCCUPATION!
I AM STILL PROUD TO HAVE PARTICIPATED IN THE REVOLUTION. BUT I WOULD LIKE TO SPARE FUTURE GENERATIONS FROM WAR. REVOLUTIONS ARE GREAT FOR COURAGE, BUT THEY ARE NOT PRETTY.
THAT'S WHAT MAKES PEOPLE LOSE THEIR WAY—THE URGE TO REVISE HISTORY, TO REMEMBER THINGS DIFFERENTLY.
"SO MANY MEN AND WOMEN HAVE ALLOWED THEIR OWN STORIES TO BE BLOTTED OUT BY THE LARGER HISTORICAL NARRATIVE, BECAUSE THEY THOUGHT THEY COULD CHANGE IT...SHOULD THEIR HISTORY BE THROWN TO THE DOGS? BEFORE I DISCARD MY PAST I'LL DO MY BEST TO WRITE IT DOWN."
WASSYLA TAMZALI WROTE THAT.
I, TOO, WANTED TO TELL MY STORY BEFORE TOSSING IT ASIDE—TELL IT ALL SO AS NOT TO FORGET. TELL IT BEFORE IT BECAME A PACK OF LIES.
THAT'S WHY, WITH THE HELP OF MY ORGANIZATION, I WANTED TO SHARE THE LETTERS OF FRENCH SOLDIERS, SHARE THE TESTIMONIES OF MY ENEMIES AT THE TIME.
I, WHO HELPED TO DESTROY THEM...

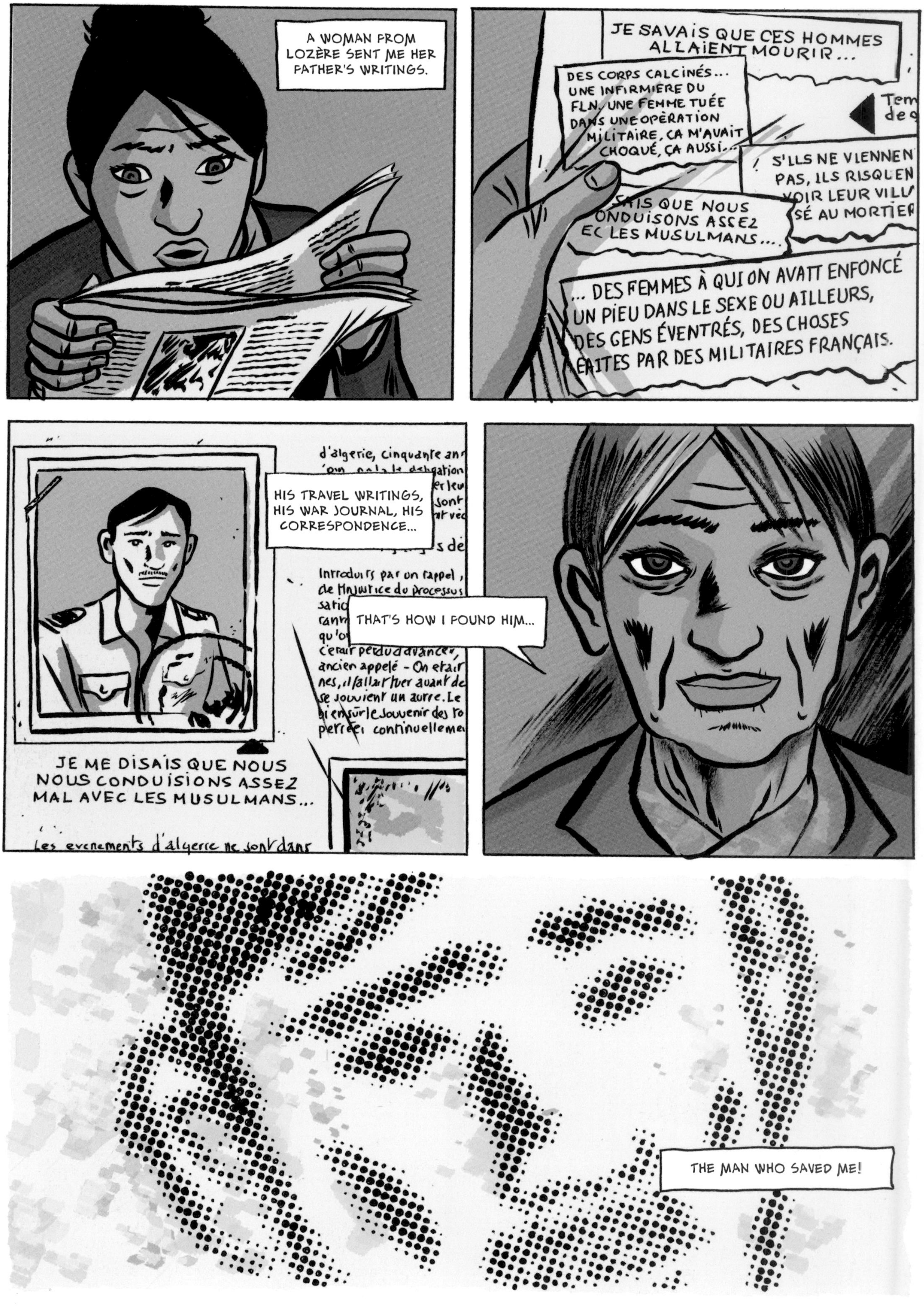
A WOMAN FROM LOZÈRE SENT ME HER FATHER'S WRITINGS.
JE SAVAIS QUE CES HOMMES ALLAIENT MOURIR…
DES CORPS CALCINÉS… UNE INFIRMIERE DU FLN, UNE FEMME TUÉE DANS UNE OPÉRATION MILITAIRE, ÇA M'AVAIT CHOQUÉ, ÇA AUSSI…
… DES FEMMES À QUI ON AVAIT ENFONCÉ UN PIEU DANS LE SEXE OU AILLEURS, DES GENS ÉVENTRÉS, DES CHOSES FAITES PAR DES MILITAIRES FRANÇAIS.
HIS TRAVEL WRITINGS, HIS WAR JOURNAL, HIS CORRESPONDENCE…
JE ME DISAIS QUE NOUS NOUS CONDUISIONS ASSEZ MAL AVEC LES MUSULMANS…
THAT'S HOW I FOUND HIM…
THE MAN WHO SAVED ME!

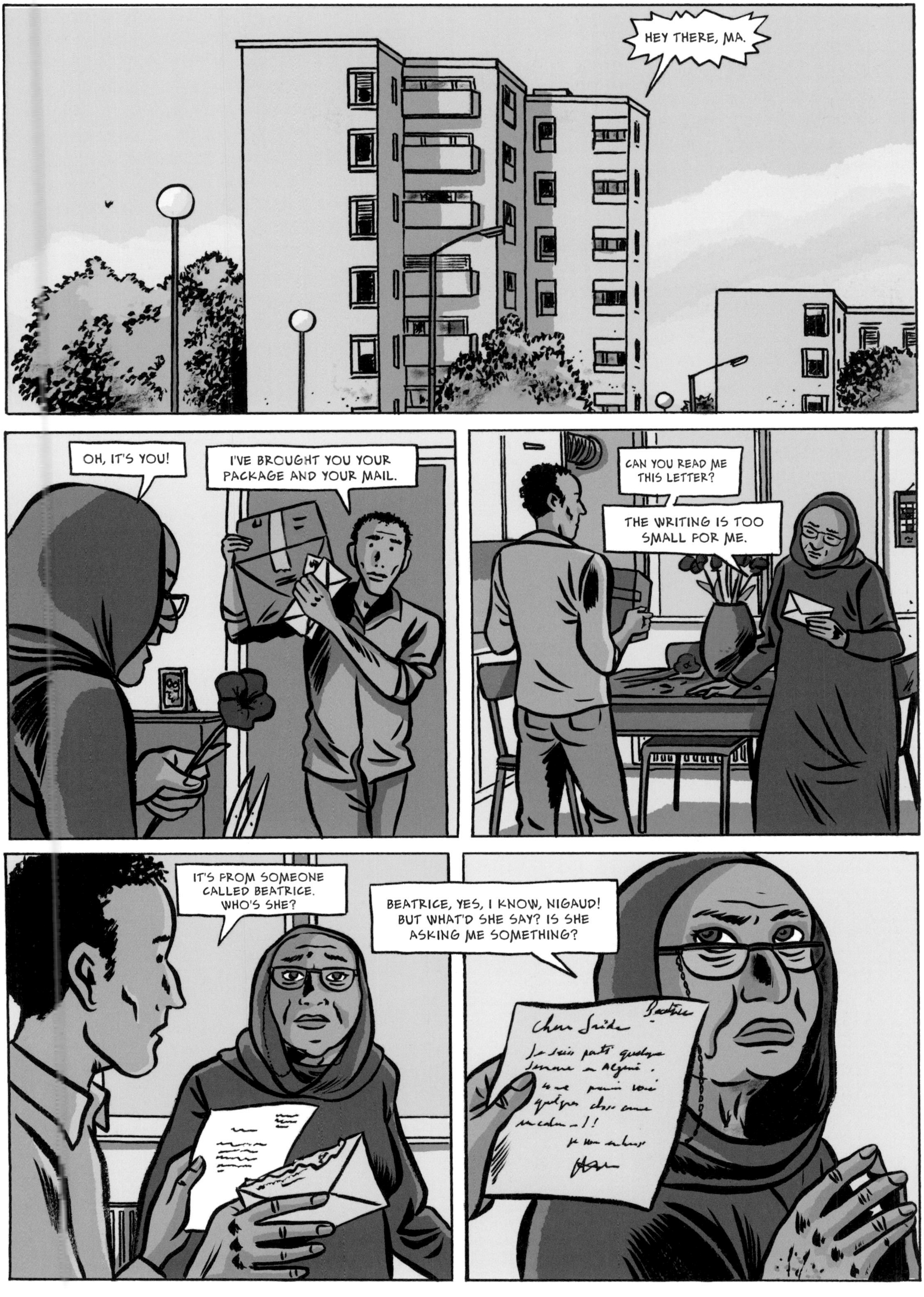
HEY THERE, MA.
OH, IT'S YOU!
I'VE BROUGHT YOU YOUR PACKAGE AND YOUR MAIL.
CAN YOU READ ME THIS LETTER?
THE WRITING IS TOO SMALL FOR ME.
IT'S FROM SOMEONE CALLED BEATRICE. WHO'S SHE?
BEATRICE, YES, I KNOW, NIGAUD! BUT WHAT'D SHE SAY? IS SHE ASKING ME SOMETHING?

SHE'S SENT YOU A PHOTO OF YOUR HOUSE.
MY HOUSE!
THERE'S SOMETHING IN THE ENVELOPE!
???
???
My dearest Saïda,
A "photo" of scents from home. A breath of joy from your old house...
Warm regards,
Beatrice

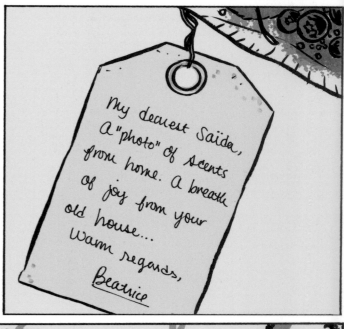

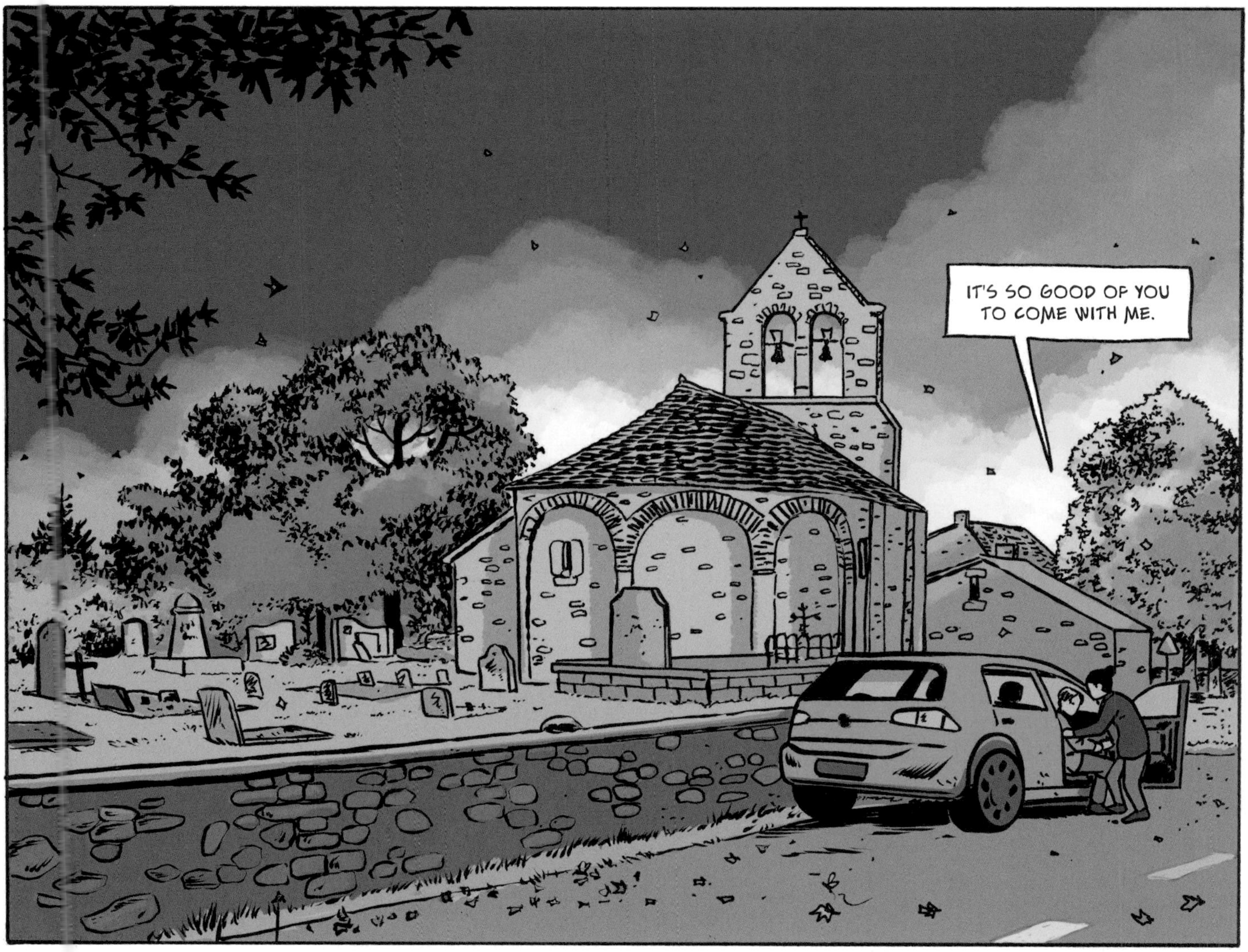
IT'S SO GOOD OF YOU TO COME WITH ME.

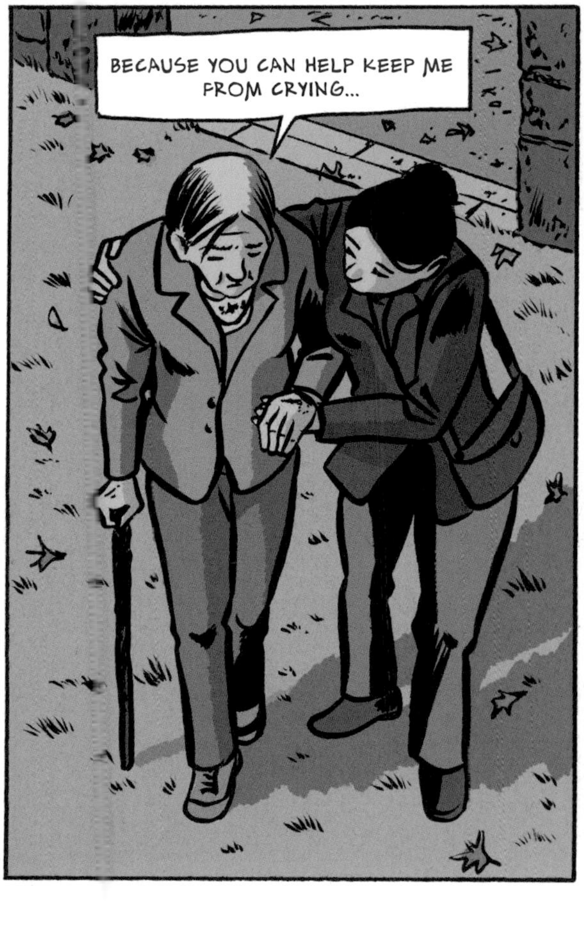
BECAUSE YOU CAN HELP KEEP ME FROM CRYING...

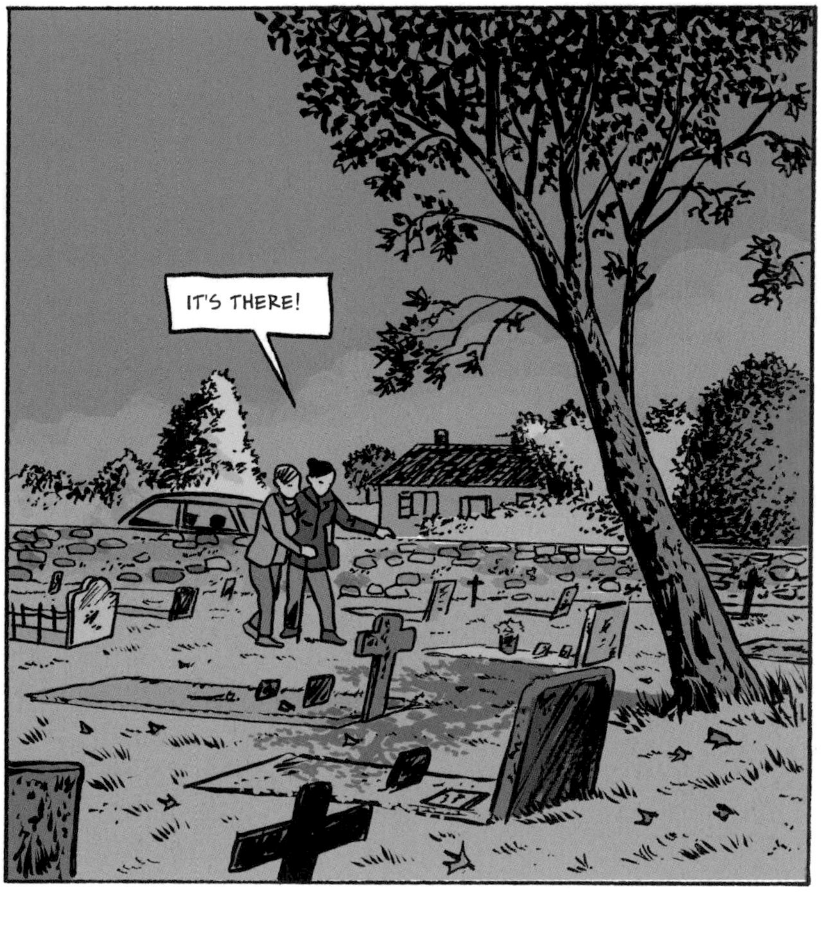
IT'S THERE!

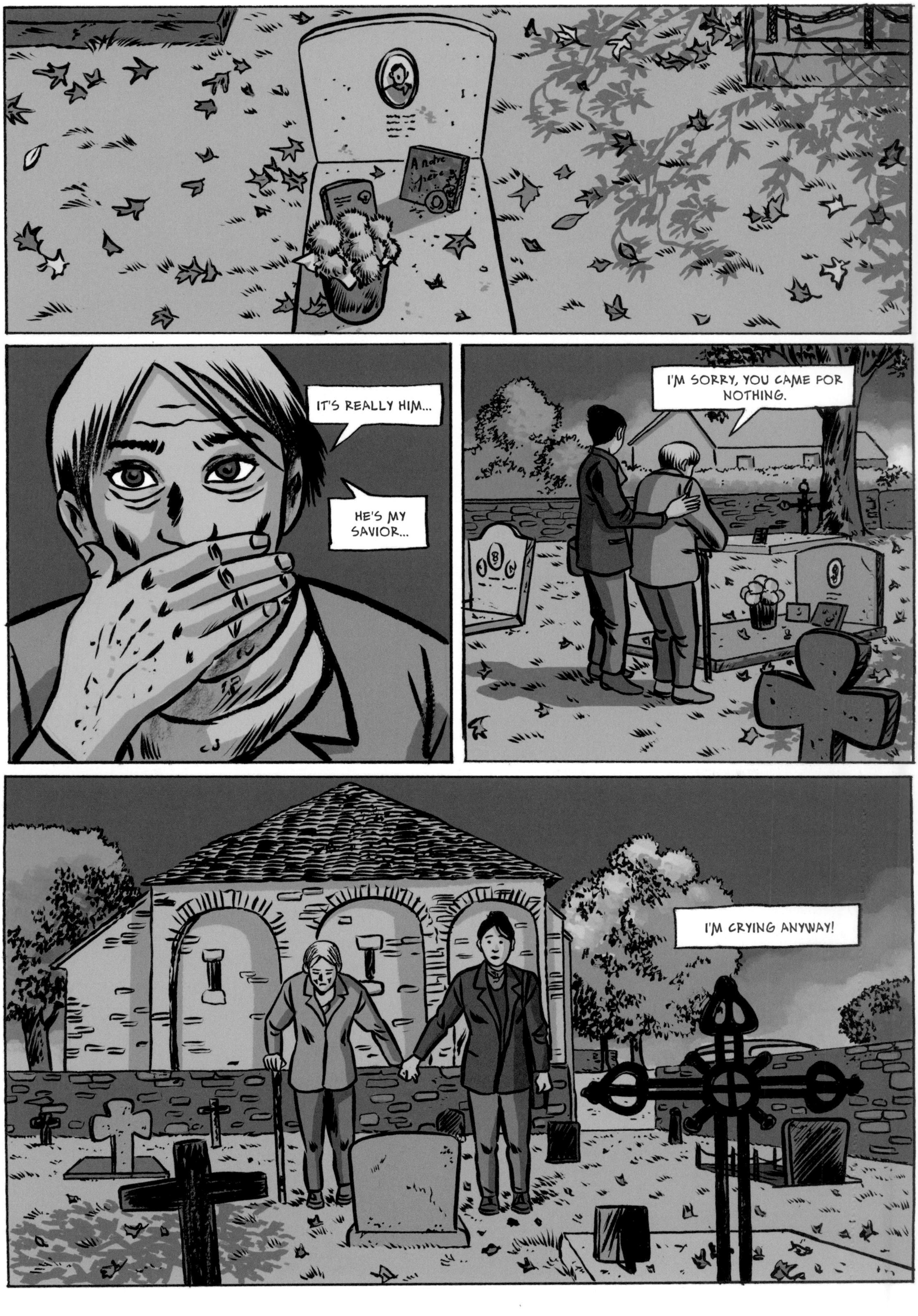
IT'S REALLY HIM...
HE'S MY SAVIOR...
I'M SORRY, YOU CAME FOR NOTHING.
I'M CRYING ANYWAY!

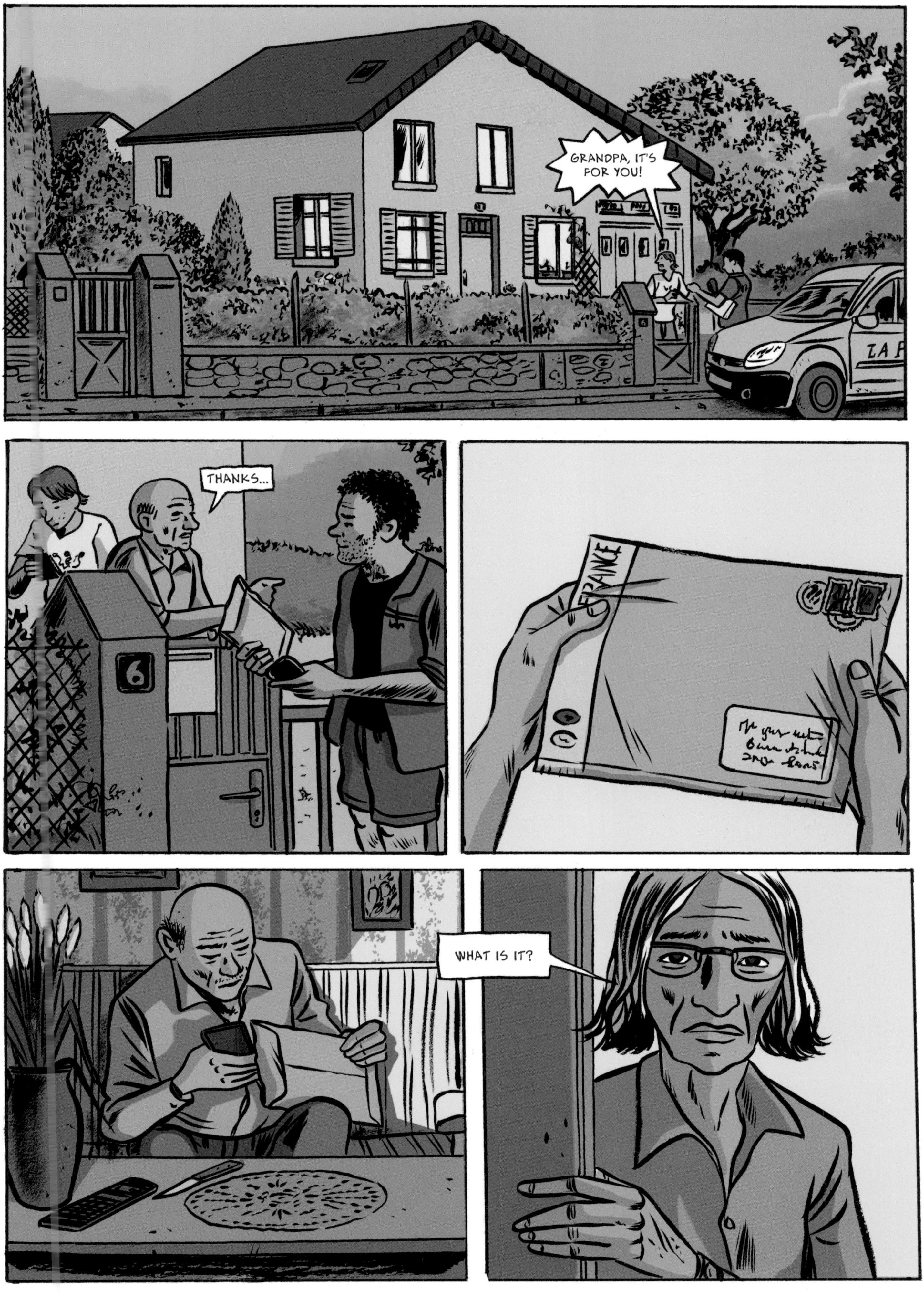
GRANDPA, IT'S FOR YOU!
THANKS...
FRANCE
WHAT IS IT?

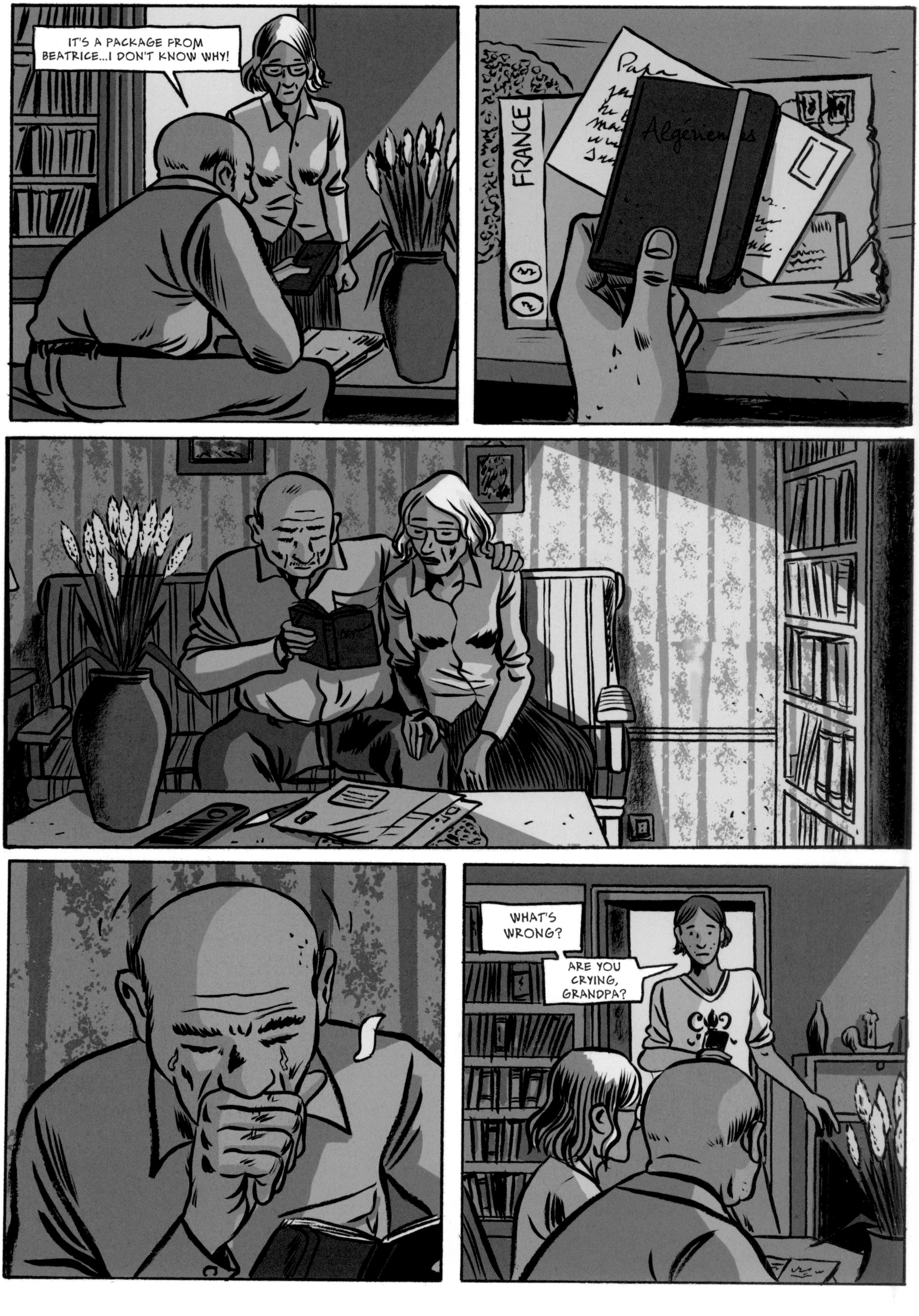
IT'S A PACKAGE FROM BEATRICE...I DON'T KNOW WHY!
Papa
FRANCE
WHAT'S WRONG?
ARE YOU CRYING, GRANDPA?

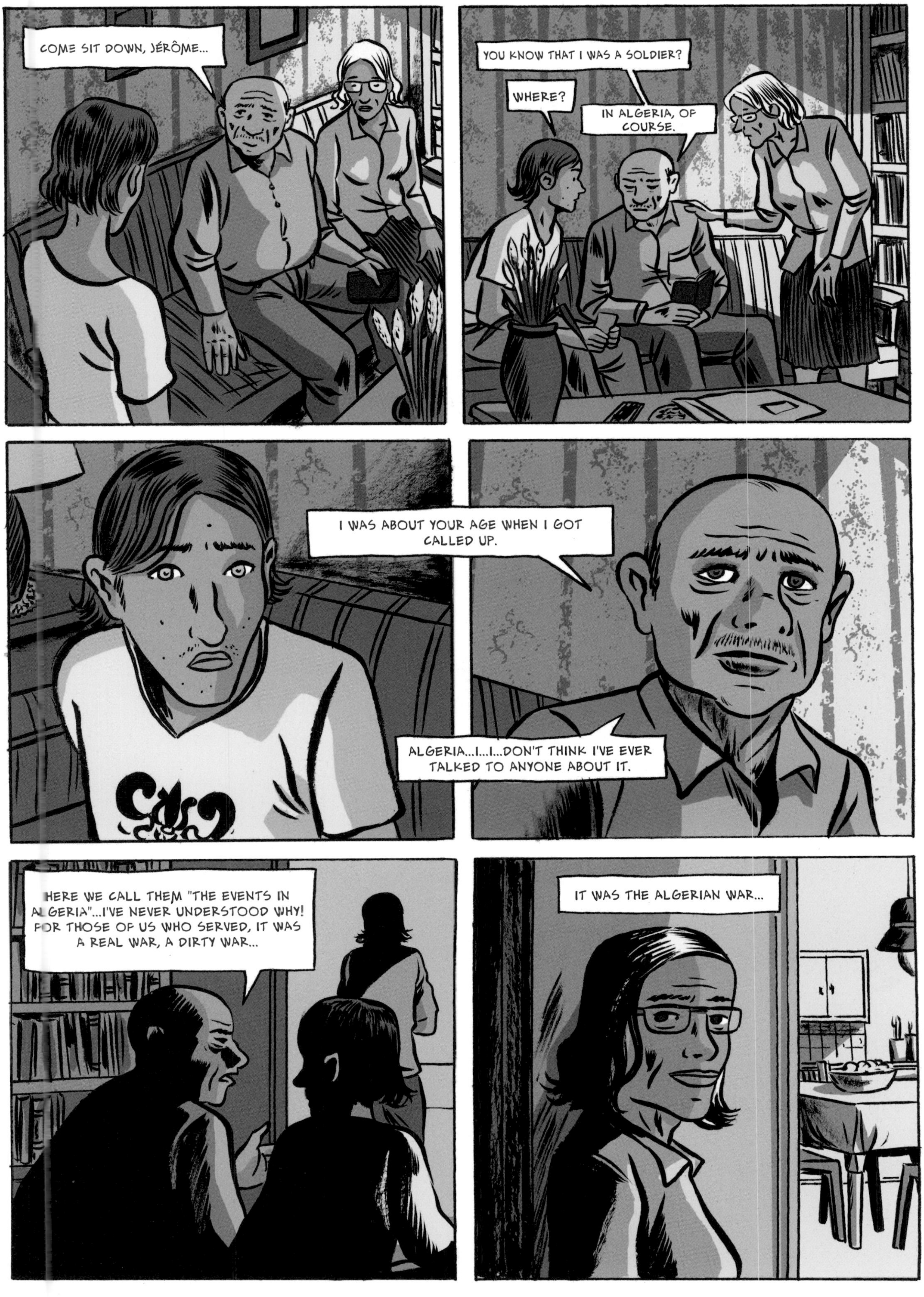
COME SIT DOWN, JÉRÔME...
YOU KNOW THAT I WAS A SOLDIER?
WHERE?
IN ALGERIA, OF COURSE.
I WAS ABOUT YOUR AGE WHEN I GOT CALLED UP.
ALGERIA...I...I...DON'T THINK I'VE EVER TALKED TO ANYONE ABOUT IT.
HERE WE CALL THEM "THE EVENTS IN ALGERIA"...I'VE NEVER UNDERSTOOD WHY! FOR THOSE OF US WHO SERVED, IT WAS A REAL WAR, A DIRTY WAR...
IT WAS THE ALGERIAN WAR...

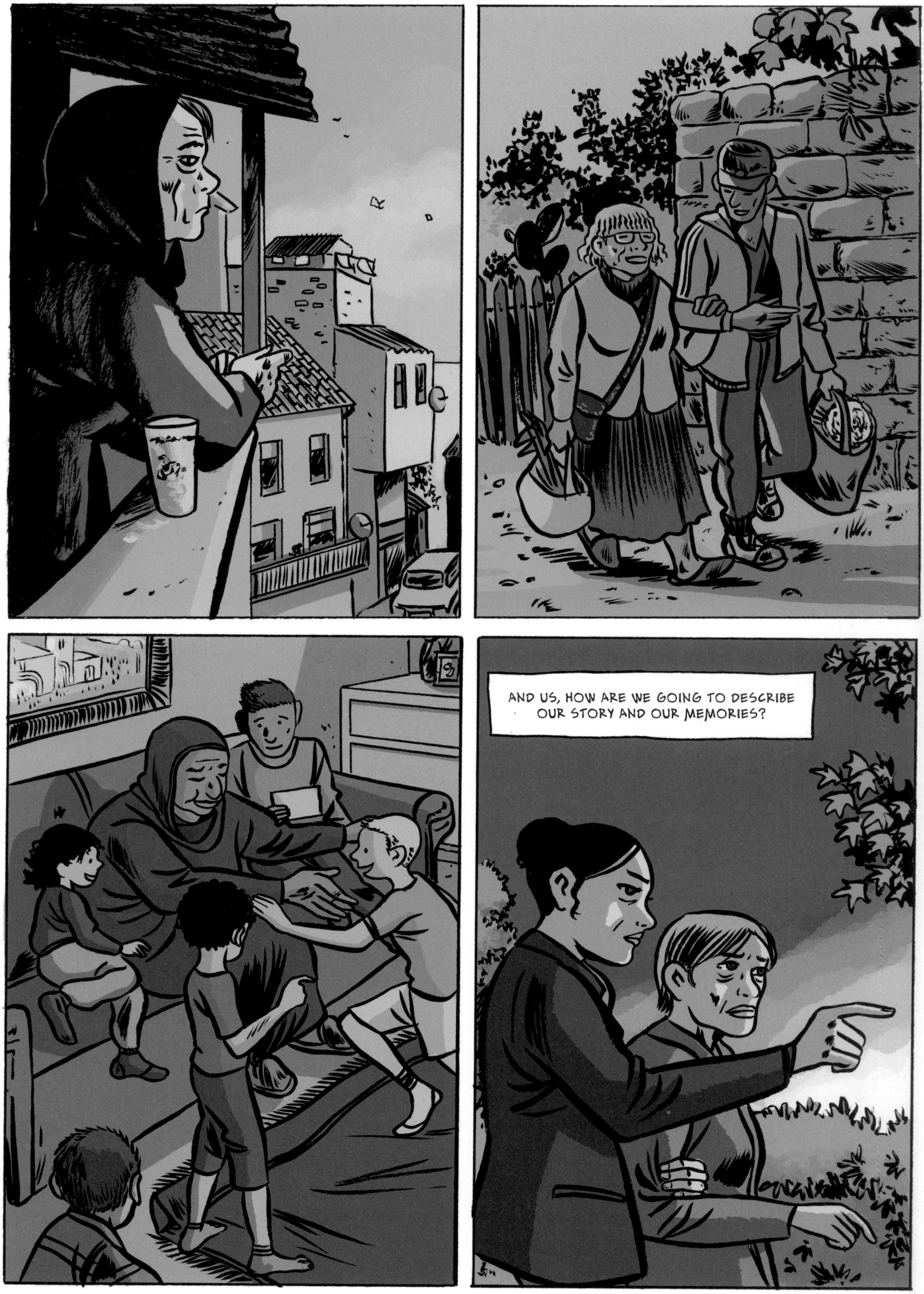
AND US, HOW ARE WE GOING TO DESCRIBE OUR STORY AND OUR MEMORIES?

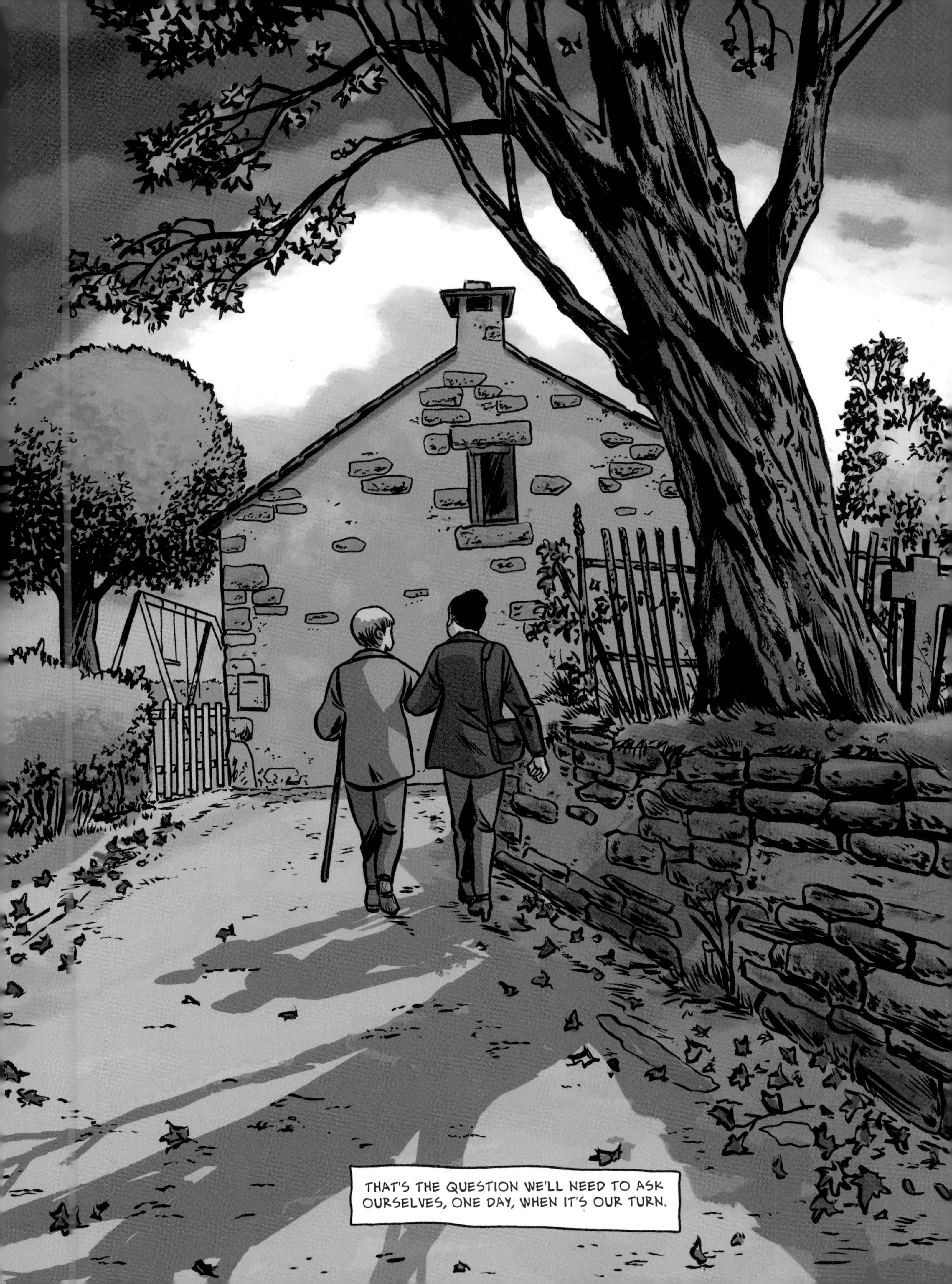
THAT'S THE QUESTION WE'LL NEED TO ASK OURSELVES, ONE DAY, WHEN IT'S OUR TURN.

The authors would like to thank Claude Latta and Cathy for reviewing this work for historical accuracy, and Marc and Anne-Marie Bonnet and Malika, their impromptu guide, in Algiers.

Deloupy would like to thank Marco, in particular, for the photo that served as inspiration for the first panel on page 70.

Swann MERALLI was born in 1985 in Lyon. After graduating from engineering school, he divided his time between urban planning and artistic collaborations. He worked on short films, directing a dozen, including *Chroniques de banlieue* (2015) and *Persona* (2017), and he also often collaborated with comics artists and children's book illustrators: *L'Homme*, with Ulric Stahl, was published by Éditions Jarjille; the series Petits livres qui disent, with Carole Crouzet, was published by P'tit Glénat; and his *Fermons les yeux*, with Laura Deo, was published by Alice Éditions.

DELOUPY was born in 1968 in Saint-Étienne. He has a degree in comics from the Angoulême School of Beaux-Arts. He works as a freelance illustrator in advertising and, since 2002, has been publishing children's books. With Alep and Alain Brechbuhl, he co-founded Éditions Jarjille, where he published a three-volume autobiographical work, *Journal approximatif*, as well as, with Alep, *Collisions, Comixland*, and the trilogy *Une aventure de la librairie l'Introuvable*. In 2016 Delcourt published his *Love story à l'iranienne* with Jane Deuxard, which has received a number of awards, including the prestigious Prix France Info in 2017 and BD Zoom 2017 (Switzerland). He contributed to the collection *Correspondances*, which collects the work of French and Quebecois comics artists (Lyon Comics Festival 2016). In 2018 Delcourt published his *Pour la peau*, co-written with Sandrine Saint-Marc.

GRAPHIC
MEDICINE

Susan Merrill Squier and Ian Williams, *General Editors*

Editorial Collective

MK Czerwiec (GraphicMedicine.org)

Michael J. Green (Penn State College of Medicine)

Kimberly R. Myers (Penn State College of Medicine)

Scott T. Smith (Penn State University)

Books in the Graphic Medicine series are inspired by a growing awareness of the value of comics as an important resource for communicating about a range of issues broadly termed "medical." For healthcare practitioners, patients, families, and caregivers dealing with illness and disability, graphic narrative enlightens complicated or difficult experience. For scholars in literary, cultural, and comics studies, the genre articulates a complex and powerful analysis of illness, medicine, and disability and a rethinking of the boundaries of "health." The series includes original comics from artists and non-artists alike, such as self-reflective "graphic pathographies" or comics used in medical training and education, as well as monographic studies and edited collections from scholars, practitioners, and medical educators.

Other titles in the series:

MK Czerwiec, Ian Williams, Susan Merrill Squier, Michael J. Green, Kimberly R. Myers, and Scott T. Smith, *Graphic Medicine Manifesto*

Ian Williams, *The Bad Doctor: The Troubled Life and Times of Dr. Iwan James*

Peter Dunlap-Shohl, *My Degeneration: A Journey Through Parkinson's*

Aneurin Wright, *Things to Do in a Retirement Home Trailer Park: . . . When You're 29 and Unemployed*

Dana Walrath, *Aliceheimers: Alzheimer's Through the Looking Glass*

Lorenzo Servitje and Sherryl Vint, eds., *The Walking Med: Zombies and the Medical Image*

Henny Beaumont, *Hole in the Heart: Bringing Up Beth*

MK Czerwiec, *Taking Turns: Stories from HIV/AIDS Care Unit 371*

Paula Knight, *The Facts of Life*

Gareth Brookes, *A Thousand Coloured Castles*

Jenell Johnson, ed., *Graphic Reproduction: A Comics Anthology*

Olivier Kugler, *Escaping Wars and Waves: Encounters with Syrian Refugees*

Judith Margolis, *Life Support: Invitation to Prayer*

Ian Williams, *The Lady Doctor*

Sarah Lightman, *The Book of Sarah*

Benjamin Dix and Lindsay Pollock, *Vanni: A Family's Struggle through the Sri Lankan Conflict*

Ephameron, *Us Two Together*

Scott T. Smith and José Alaniz, eds., *Uncanny Bodies: Superhero Comics and Disability*

MK Czerwiec, ed., *Menopause: A Comic Treatment*

Susan Merrill Squier and Irmela Marei Krüger-Fürhoff, eds., *PathoGraphics: Narrative, Aesthetics, Contention, Community*

Aurélien Ducoudray and Jeff Pourquié, *The Third Population*